With The Lost Legion in New Zealand

G. Hamilton-Browne

With the Lost Legion in New Zealand

The War Against the Maoris 1866-71

G. Hamilton-Browne
(Maori Browne)

With the Lost Legion in New Zealand
The War Against the Maoris 1866-71
by G. Hamilton-Browne
(Maori Browne)

First published under the title
With The Lost Legion in New Zealand

Leonaur is an imprint of Oakpast Ltd

Copyright in this form © 2012 Oakpast Ltd

ISBN: 978-0-85706-856-9 (hardcover)
ISBN: 978-0-85706-857-6 (softcover)

http://www.leonaur.com

Publisher's Notes

The views expressed in this book are not necessarily those of the publisher.

Contents

Preface	9

Part 1

Why I Joined the Lost Legion	11
The War On the East Coast—The Hau Haus	17
I Start to Join the Lost Legion	26
I Join the Lost Legion	44
My Baptism of Fire - Otapawa	57
A Frolic With the Kupapas	71
Bushwhacking	80
"And We Die, and None Can Tell Them Where We Died." —Kipling	94
I Join the Troopers	108
How Maoris Should Be Fought	121
Sport à la Lost Legion	130
The Year of the Lamb	143
Te Ngutu-O-Te-Manu	157
Moturoa	168

Part 2

War on the East Coast of New Zealand—Yarn of the Gate Pah	175

Te Kooti	191
Ngatapa	198
Back To the West Coast	210
The Uriwera Campaign	222
The Taupo Campaign	235
The Taupo Campaign—Continued	245
Hide-and-Seek With Te Kooti	258
The End of New Zealand Wars	264

This Work is
Dedicated By the Author
To the Memory of
The Officers and Men of the Lost Legion
Whose Bones Lie Buried in Forgotten Graves
On the Wild Fern Ranges and in the
Dense Bush of New Zealand
Where They Fell Fighting For
Queen and Flag

> I've had my share of pastime, and I've done my share of toil,
> And life is short—the longest life a span;
> I care not now to tarry for the corn or for the oil,
> Or for the wine that maketh glad the heart of man.
> For good undone and gifts misspent and resolutions vain,
> 'Tis somewhat late to trouble. This I know—
> I should live the same life over, if I had to live again;
> And the chances are I go where most men go.
>
> A. Lindsay Gordon.

The Lost Legion

> There's a Legion that never was 'listed,
> That carries no colours or crest
> But split in a thousand detachments
> Is breaking the road for the rest.
>
> We preach in advance of the army.,
> We skirmish ahead of the Church,
> With never a gunboat to help us,
> When we're scuppered and left in the lurch.
> But we know as the cartridges finish.
> And we're piled on our last little shelves.
> That the Legion that never was 'listed
> Will send us as good as ourselves.
>
> Rudyard Kipling.

Preface

Every Johnny not a professional novelist has, I suppose, some reason besides making money when he sits down to write a book, for, as far as I can see, there is deuced little pleasure to be gained by the author while occupied in doing so, especially if, like myself, he should have passed some forty years of his life on the frontiers of the Empire, and, with the exception of writing an occasional letter, has never, during that time, taken a pen in his hand. My reason is that during the last three or four years, since broken health and bad luck drove me back to civilisation, such as it is in England, I have frequently been knocked end-ways by the woeful ignorance of all classes of Englishmen, not only of the history of the various colonies that form the Empire, but also of the struggles of the men in acquiring and holding the same. Again I have noticed no one ever gives the colonial irregular troops the least credit of having fought and suffered in the Imperial cause, nor does anyone in this country seem to be aware of the debt the Empire owes to the men of the Lost Legion.

Not long ago I dined at the same table with a big city pot, who after dinner gassed inordinately about OUR Empire, laying a great stress on the "our," as if he had been a prime mover in the settlement of every country contained in it. New Zealand was the country under discussion, and amongst other twaddle he discoursed on the wonderful progress WE (a very big "we") had made in those islands. During a pause in the conversation I humbly asked him: "How did England acquire this fruitful country?" With a disdainful smile he condescended to inform me Captain Cook found it and gave it to England.

"But," said I, "surely in my young days I remember a lot of fighting going on there."

"Oh yes," he replied, "there was some trouble out there, but WE" (a big "we" again) "sent out our soldiers, who soon put a stop to that, and then WE" (a huge "we" this time) "developed the country until it is one of the gardens of the world." Still with due humility I asked if he were a New Zealand colonist, and was not astonished when he replied: "Good gracious me, no; I have never been in the country, and except to occasionally visit the Continent, I never leave England."

This and many other instances determined me to jump into the breach, and try if a yarn, even written by such a duffer as myself, can educate some few of my countrymen, and let them know what sort of a life the men of the Lost Legion led during the wars that took place in New Zealand from 1866 to 1871, which wars eventually pacified the North Island, and were fought without the assistance of a single Imperial soldier.

Moreover thousands of novels have been written with plots founded on the splendid achievements of our gallant army and navy, then why should not one be penned about the deeds of the Lost Legion, the men who have not only rolled out the map of the Empire, as the deft hand of a cook rolls out a lump of dough, but who have also held that ground until properly settled by their own country-men.

Innumerable and unknown are the graves of the Lost Legionaries, slain as they have been by the bullet, *tomahawk* and *assagai* of their savage opponents, or cut down by hunger, thirst and the malarial fevers of the lands into which they have penetrated.

And now if I need any further excuse for inflicting this badly written (for I claim no pretensions to literary skill) yarn upon you, let me inform you that in the main the facts are all strictly true, and that the men I have tried to depict lived, starved, fought and died in the very manner described in this volume.

So now that we are inspanned let's trek.

PART 1

CHAPTER 1

Why I Joined the Lost Legion

I, Richard Burke, at least so I am told, for although present myself I cannot claim a vivid recollection of the fact, was born shortly before the middle of the last century. My father was a major in H.M. army, having the reputation of being a very smart soldier, and was also looked upon as being one of the best sportsmen in the service, as he was justly famous, not only in the saddle, but also as a shot, a fisherman and a general good all-round man. This, together with being descended from a very ancient Irish family, made him popular both in the service and in society. My mother was a member of an old Lancashire county family, most of whose menfolk had for generations worn the Queen's scarlet, so that from both sword and distaff side I inherited the longing to be a soldier. My paternal grandfather, who had been a distinguished cavalry officer during the Peninsular War, was a big county magnate, and on his death left two large estates, my father inheriting the old family demesne and mansion situated in the north of Ireland; and now I think I have told you quite enough about my family belongings.

I was the fourth son, and from my earliest youth was looked upon as the unlucky member of the family, being always in hot water. At a very tender age I took a delight in watching my father's regiment at drill, and the first licking I ever got was for a breach of military discipline, the crime being that while under lawful control of my nurse I had committed mutiny by direct disobedience of orders, and had aggravated that crime by conduct unbecoming a soldier, insomuch as by crawling through a drain I had broken away from my escort, who, being portly, not to say fat, was quite unable to follow me, and in direct defiance of her repeated orders had betaken myself to the barracks, where I was subsequently discovered and arrested while playing at soldiers with the barrack children.

Keep me out of the barracks they could not, and when I was seven years old I am certain that had I possessed sufficient strength I could have gone through the drill as well as the regimental fugleman. It was therefore, at the age of seven, I was sent to a private school in Derbyshire, kept by a dear old rector, the squire of the parish being an old service friend of my father.

This worthy old gentleman was also a great sportsman, and took charge of my education in all branches of field sports. Young as I was, I was most anxious to acquire strength, so that I became a devotee to all gymnastic exercises, especially boxing; consequently when I reached the age of thirteen I was a good horseman, shot and swimmer, while, being naturally a robust boy, I had acquired the muscle and strength of a lad at least four years older than I really was. At this time a maternal uncle who had served many years in the H.E.I.C.S. cavalry returned home and took up his quarters with us in Ireland. He was a noted swordsman and *shikaree*, who, having distinguished himself greatly during the Indian Mutiny, had retired as colonel when the company's service was merged into the Imperial.

Although an Englishman, he was a great respecter of, and authority on, the ancient pastime of duelling, and he quickly instructed us boys in the strict etiquette of the duello. It was now quite time for me to choose a profession, and after a long confab it was decided I should go into the artillery, so I was despatched to a public school that has been very famous for passing young fellows into the service, especially into the scientific branches. There I remained over four years, gaining far more laurels in the playing fields than in the lecture-rooms, for although I worked hard in a desultory way, still my best efforts were given to the play-ground and the gymnasium.

This being the case my father determined to send me to Lausanne, so as to perfect myself in French, science and mathematics, an idea my uncle fully approved of, as there resided at that place a most noted *maître d'armes*, who he thought would be the very man to put a polish on my swordsmanship. At Lausanne I stayed for some months, working hard by fits and starts and enjoying myself thoroughly, and here I was joined by my eldest brother, Jack, a gay and giddy subaltern in a crack cavalry regiment. Together we started on a trip through northern Italy, and while at Milan I had the opportunity of putting into practice the precepts my uncle and the celebrated *maître d'armes* had taught me.

It happened in this way. I was called out by an Italian nobleman of sorts, who objected to some small attentions I had paid to a Tyrolese *chantress* in a *café*. Him I easily defeated, wearing him out by my better training and then administering a pin-prick on his forearm, whereon he insisted upon embracing me and we became great friends. Towards the end of the trip, however, I had a misunderstanding with a French artillery cadet at Strasbourg, who, as I was too self-confident, ran me through the arm. He also embraced me and we became good friends.

After the completion of our trip I returned to London, where I really worked hard, and I had no doubt I should have passed into Woolwich all right, when on the eve of going in for my last paper I was poisoned by a fiend of a woman, whom I was perfectly innocent of harming, and so, not having qualified for the requisite number of subjects, I was spun.

In a fit of disgust I enlisted in the R.H.A. as a driver, and for a few months soldiered in the ranks at Aldershot, but, just when I had had enough of it, I was discovered by my father's cousin, who had assumed command of the camp, and who promptly had me discharged. Saying goodbye to my comrades necessitated my imbibing too much beer, so I reached my father's town house full of beans and benevolence, where, with my usual bad luck, I ran foul of two very big military swells, who in my exuberance of spirits I astonished and quite unintentionally insulted. Next afternoon, by my father's orders, I attempted to apologise to the mighty potentates, and should have most likely been forgiven had not my infernal bad luck still stuck to me, for just at the moment that the *tomahawk* was being buried, I handed my father a vile squib cigar which I had placed in my case for the benefit of my eldest brother, who I considered had been too handy with his toe while assisting me to bed the previous night, and which I had completely for-gotten. The debacle that ensued was too much for my nerves, and I fled from the house.

In my agony of mind I remembered an appointment with my brother and made for his club, a very fast one, where I told my pitiful story. He and his wild friends were delighted with the yarn, and a council was promptly held to discuss what was to become of me. At this council one of them, a Roman Catholic of very high rank, suggested I should join the Papal Zouaves, at the same time offering me letters of introduction to the big-wigs at the Vatican. These I gratefully accepted, and in less than a fortnight became a *sous-lieut.* in that cosmopolitan corps, in which I thoroughly enjoyed myself. However, it was not for long, as at the end of five months I was summoned home to present myself at the examination for a direct commission.

On my return to England I took up my residence with my uncle at Brighton, and while there came in contact with the celebrated Gipsy Lee, who told my fortune, and that so truthfully I think I may be forgiven should I repeat her prognostications.

It fell out in this way. One day I chanced to meet an old schoolfellow, and together we walked out to the Devil's Dyke, and while lolling on the grass were accosted by Gipsy Lee, then a handsome middle-aged woman, who insisted on telling me my fortune. In a chaffing spirit I replied to her solicitations: "Ah, mother, I know my fortune. I am going up to be examined for the army and shall then go to India, but come along, you shall tell me if I am to pass high up on the list." Putting my hand carelessly into my pocket, meaning to give her a small piece of silver, I accidentally drew out a sovereign, which I handed her, then, seeing my mistake, said, with a rather rueful laugh: "Keep it, mother, you're in luck's way today." She shook her head and looked at my hand for some time, then gravely said:

> An open-handed, free giver you are, and as it was born in the blood, so will you remain till your death. That is as it should be, but you are and always will be reckless, never learning the value of money, although you will often suffer for the want of it. You will pass your examination high up on the list, but will never enter the army. You will wander over the world, through lands I have never heard of, but you will never go to India. You have already been a soldier; there is blood on your hand, and there will be much more, for, although you will never join the army, you will take part in many wars and light in many battles. You will suffer much, you will experience hunger, thirst, cold and poverty. You will pass through many dangers, from fire, from water, from savage men and beasts.
>
> You will lose many friends through war and sickness, but though often hurt you will live a long life of disappointment. Others will make fortunes round you, but you will remain poor. Women will be your best friends and your worst enemies, and you will be robbed of your birthright by your own brother. Many times you will have grasped the cup of good fortune, only to have it dashed from your hand. Yet you will meet every disaster

with a laugh, and will learn nothing. Still keep up your heart, for, although you will live a rough, hard life, you will live a long one. The end is hidden from me, but remember there is often a burst of sunshine at the end of a cloudy day.

Had I been superstitious, this prophecy might have upset me, but, although an Irishman, I merely laughed at it, and in due course of time went up to London and passed my exam. There I was joined by my brother, who was on long leave, and accompanied him to Spa, so as to put in the three months previous to joining the regiment I should be gazetted to. Among my brother's friends was a Belgian nobleman, who, being a great patron of the turf, owned a string of racehorses and was very pleased to obtain my services as a gentleman rider for that year's Spa and Liège races.

While waiting in Spa to oblige him I got into serious trouble. Among the gang of blacklegs and *chevaliers d'industrie* who in those days hung about the Continental gambling resorts was a man called Baron Touchais, who with his wife clung to the fringe of the fast society that frequented the tables and took part in the gaieties of the very gay little town. I was quickly introduced to these people, and very foolishly allowed myself to be drawn into a flirtation with the lady, who was a pretty, vivacious little Frenchwoman. The man was a well-dressed, plausible fellow, a past master at all games of chance, who, not having yet been discovered cheating, was still a member of the clubs, and tolerated by the fast set. I, however, very soon got sick of the whole business, and strove all I could to break loose, but it eventually ended in a scene, evidently prearranged for the purpose of blackmailing. The lady, with her hair down, weeping and hanging on to my shoulder, is discovered by the bold, bad baron, who rushes in with a sword-cane, but, getting knocked end over end by a straight left between the eyes, reclines on the floor drumming with his heels and vomiting blue blasphemy.

The infernal row he made brought everybody in the hotel into the room, and the publicity of the affair forced him, very much against his will, to call me out, as it was cash he wanted, not blood, as of course had he not done so he would have been kicked out of society. Naturally I was obliged to go out with him, although I did so much against my will, especially as H.R.H. had just promulgated an order that any officer taking part in a duel would be at once cashiered, and although I had not yet been gazetted I knew full well that if a duel got bruited about I should not be permitted to serve in H.M. army. Notwithstanding this I had to go out, two of my Belgian friends kindly volunteering to act as my seconds. It was arranged that the duel was to be fought with pistols *à la barrière*, and I received instructions from Baron Le Noble, my principal second, that unless my opponent advanced to the mark I was to allow him to fire two shots, delivering my own in such a manner that all the seconds could see that I missed intentionally.

These orders I carried out, receiving my enemy's fire and then knocking up the turf three or four feet from him. The duel should now have terminated, but my opponent claimed a third shot. This for some time my seconds refused to allow, but at last gave way, and Le Noble, as he handed me my pistol, said to me: "You have done all that honour demands, now fire at him." Again I obeyed instructions, for on the word being given Touchais strode up to the barrier, and was taking deliberate aim at me, when I dropped him. As the wound was considered mortal, my seconds hurried me out of the country, and I crossed over to England.

The duel made some stir, although Touchais made rapid progress to convalescence, but as there was no hope of being allowed to join the service, by the advice of my uncle and one or two very senior officers I determined to go out to New Zealand, where plenty of fighting was going on. This I did, and in a very few days, with plenty of money in my pocket, and a bundle of letters of introduction, I bade farewell to my uncle and brother, and, accompanied by my servant, set sail for the antipodes.

CHAPTER 2

The War On the East Coast—The Hau Haus

Before I begin my yarn of the New Zealand wars it may be as well to tell you about the ferocious fanatics I assisted in exterminating, and you will find I always speak about them as Hau Haus. This is not the name of any tribe of Maoris, but was the designation given to all the natives who joined the extraordinary faith which I am now in this chapter attempting to explain, and to do so I must dip into New Zealand history.

Christianity was first introduced into New Zealand in 1814 by Marsden, who started the first Church of England Mission. The Wesleyan missionaries arrived in 1822 and the Roman Catholics in 1838; other denominations quickly followed. Up to the year 1830 very few converts had been made, but in 1838 more than one-fourth of the natives had been baptised, and the numbers increased rapidly. In 1838 the New Testament, published in the Maori language, was in the hands of the converts, and the complete Bible was finished in 1853. Very many of the natives had learned to read, and the Sacred Writings were read with avidity.

Now the Maoris were puzzled, like many others, by the different dogmas set forth by the various denominations, each claiming they were right and that the others were wrong, yet all asserting they drew their inferences from the same Book. Among the tribes existed bitter rivalry, hatred and jealousy, so they gloried in belonging to different sects, and consequently added religious rancour to their tribal hatred. Missionaries, however, travelled through the country with impunity, not one receiving any harm until 1865. There was, however, a very great desire on the part of a vast number of the natives to find out which was the real and true faith, so that many of them joined one sect after another, as if to discover which fancy brand of religion suited his own constitution best, and being highly intellectual and keen reasoners they came to the conclusion that each sect was only formed from the interpretation by the devotees of the Book itself, and that therefore they (the Maoris) had a perfect right to interpret the Sacred Writings in any way they saw fit.

Just previous to the promulgation of the Pai Marire faith the Maoris had elected a king. Why, therefore, should they not have a new religion? Hence the growth of the Hau Haus. The Hau Haus first came into collision with the white men in April 1864. For although this extraordinary religion was known to exist previous to this date, the majority of the settlers and the authorities only looked upon it as a farce, and never for a moment thought that the natives, most of whom professed Christianity, could tolerate such an absurd, fantastic and fanatical creed of murderous tendencies as that denominated the Pai Marire or Hau Hau religion. The origin of this fanatical creed is obscure, as well it might be, for the author, Te Ua, had up to the date of his inspiration been considered a harmless lunatic, and had been tolerated by his tribe as such. (The Maoris, like all other wild races, never interfere with and are always kind to the demented.)

Previous to the teaching of Te Ua the majority of the tribes had for a short time combined together for mutual support against the white men, and had chosen a king (the head chief of the Waikato tribe). This coalition did not last long, as the intense jealousy between the various tribes caused many of them to abandon it, some of them remaining neutral, while others joined the Government and fought with the greatest gallantry on our side. This alliance was strengthened by the acts of the apostles of Te Ua, the disciples of whom spared neither white man nor Maori refusing to join them or their absurd faith.

Te Ua, although a man of weak intellect, was of a peaceful disposition, and more friendlily disposed towards the white settlers than he was toward the king, so much so that when the ship *Lord Worsley* was wrecked on the Taranaki coast he attempted to persuade his tribe not to plunder the ship nor passengers. In this he was unsuccessful, as the sight of so much loot was too tempting to the nature of the Maoris. He was much upset by his failure, and solaced himself by long-continued prayers to his *atua* (god or spirit), Pai Marire.

Just about this time he assaulted a woman, whose husband seized him, and, after tying him up, left him in a *whare* (hut) to meditate and repent. Had Te Ua been in his right mind the man would have killed him. It was during this punishment that his *atua* stood by him and rendered him the assistance that made him famous and all-powerful among the superstitious tribes. His yarn was this, and, absurd as it may seem to us white men, yet it was swallowed and implicitly believed by the majority of the natives, most of whom were so-called Christians. Te Ua asserted that the archangel Michael, the angel Gabriel, and a host of minor spirits landed from the wrecked ship. *Lord Worsley*, and came to him. Gabriel, who took the lead in everything, ordered him to break his bonds, which he did easily, whereupon the woman's husband, finding him loose, tied him up again, this time using a chain.

Again at the angel's command Te Ua burst the chain in fragments, and afterwards was considered by the superstitious natives to be a man under the direct protection of God. After this Gabriel visited Te Ua frequently, and between them they concocted a wonderful religion. The angel instructed Te Ua to plant a pole a certain height in the ground, to be called *Niu*, around which all true believers were to worship, and those found worthy were to be granted the gift of tongues and also to be rendered invulnerable to the bullets of the white man.

The symbol of their faith was Pai Marire, which may be interpreted, if each word is taken separately, as good, peaceful, but the words must have had a very different meaning to the worshippers if we may judge by their actions, where very little that is good or peaceful can be found. The meanings of the words *Hau Hau* also received from the angel are very obscure, as they simply mean wind, wind, but probably referred to the wind which was supposed to bring the angels to the worshippers round the pole, as the spirits were always spoken of as *Hau Anihera* (wind angels). No matter what meaning the words conveyed to the Maoris, they were convinced that the utterance of them, at the same time raising the hand with the palm turned towards their enemies, would render the true believer invulnerable, causing the hostile bullets to deflect and fly high.

These words, after the first fight, became their charging cry; pronounced short they sounded like the bark of a dog, and the hostile tribes, no matter what their proper tribal designation was, were soon only recognised by the name of Hau Haus.

Up to April 1864 Te Ua and his disciples lived in a peaceful manner, and the religion had not been looked on as a factor in the war, but now he was unable to control his zealous followers, for a furious, fanatical and murderous spirit was soon shown, which took a form of hostility not only against the white man, but also against all the natives who refused to adopt the Hau Hau faith, and this turned the North Island of New Zealand into a pandemonium of cold-blooded murder and savage warfare. The Maori wars which began in 1860 had up to 1864 been carried on by the natives in a manner that had earned them the respect of our men. Their splendid courage, combined with their wild chivalry, made them an enemy worthy of the highest praise, and very many men, such as Sir George Grey and Bishop Selwyn, looked on them with esteem and affection. This now was all to be changed, and the subsequent wars, which lasted till 1871, were wars of savage murder, treachery and torture on the one side, and bitter reprisals on the other, until the remaining Hau Haus, unable to face us any longer, fled for refuge to the King Country and remained quiet.

On the 6th of April 1864 a party of the 57th Regiment and a few military settlers, in all about one hundred strong, under the command of Captains Page and Lloyd, were destroying crops in the Taranaki district. They had piled their arms while at work, when they were surprised and rushed by a large band of natives. Captain Lloyd and six men were killed, twelve more were wounded and hid in the fern, the remainder falling back in something like a stampede to the Potuka redoubt and the town of Taranaki. Reinforcements were quickly on the ground, and found the bodies of the slain shamefully mutilated, the heads having been carried away. This brutality was quite a new feature in Maori warfare, and was the intimation of the barbarities that were to follow.

The 57th regimental call was sounded, when the wounded and a few fugitives crept out of the fern. They informed their comrades that the natives had rushed upon them, barking like dogs, and seemingly quite regardless of their own lives. Our men were much astonished at this conduct, as little was known of the new faith at this time, but it was soon discovered that it was the result of the fanatical belief of the Maoris in their invulnerability. Now it is a strange thing, but none of the four men whom the Maoris had lost in the above skirmish had joined the Pai Marire faith, and this fact added to the natives' belief in its virtue. The heads of Captain Lloyd and his men were carried round the district as a proof of this victory, and were buried, but Gabriel ordered Te Ua to exhume and preserve the Captain's head, and to use it as a medium through which the angel could communicate with himself and his disciples.

There was no delay or ambiguity in Gabriel's orders through this oracle, for the head spoke at once to Te Ua, saying, "You are the chief prophet of Pai Marire. Matene and Hepanaia will be your apostles." Te Ua was also informed that all his followers should be called Pai Marire, that the head should be carried peacefully round all the tribes, and, that having been done, Gabriel with legions of angels would assist the Maoris in their general rising, help them to slaughter all the white men, and then bestow upon the faithful a complete knowledge of all the languages, arts and sciences in the world.

These supposed instructions were admirably conceived, and reflect great credit on Te Ua, who, it must be remembered, was a man of weak intellect; for had the head been carried by its escort of fanatics peacefully through the country, and had these fanatics abstained from hostility towards the tribes who professed friendship to the white man, there is but little doubt that all the tribes would have been converted and that when the general rising took place it would have been most disastrous to the Europeans even if Gabriel and his promised hosts had not rendered the looked-for active assistance.

It must be remembered and thoroughly understood that the magnificent service afterwards rendered by the friendly Maoris was not prompted by their love for the white man, but by the hatred and jealousy they entertained against the hostile tribes, in very many cases their bitter enemies in old-time wars. It was indeed fortunate for us that Te Ua's subalterns, Hepanaia, Matene, Kereopa and Patara, allowed their diplomacy to be outrun by their ferocious desire for blood, and the savage murders perpetrated not only on inoffensive white men but also on friendly natives roused such desires for revenge in the hearts of the latter's tribes that caused them to be just as anxious as the white man to stamp out the fiendish brutality of the Pai Marire faith and allowed us to retain our hold on the North Island, which we should have undoubtedly lost, at least for a time, had they joined the Hau Haus.

The first among Te Ua's apostles to make a stir was Hepanaia. For some time Pai Marire had been preached through the Taranaki district, and there were hundreds of zealous warriors waiting a prophet to lead them. This want was soon filled by Hepanaia, a very brave warrior, but one lacking in discretion, for he promised the natives, if they would attack the fort on Sentry Hill (the strongest post in the district), not only victory but absolute immunity from injury or death; also that with the assistance of Gabriel the soldiers should be turned into stone.

The fort stood on a steep hill, the sides of which had been scarped, and was held by Major Short and fifty men of the 57th Regiment. Hepanaia sent two hundred men to the rear of the fort to make a false attack, but these men, not liking the look of the place, and perhaps being new converts and so not strong in the faith, wisely went home, leaving the prophet with three hundred men to do the work himself. There was no attempt made to surprise the place, for previous to the assault at daybreak on the 1st of May 1864 the fanatics danced a war-dance (a very noisy ceremony) and went through their incantations. These finished, they advanced in close formation to the attack.

Hepanaia must have been very strong in the faith, for he led the charge in person, accompanied by some distinguished chiefs. One of them, Titokowaru, was afterwards to become our bitterest enemy on the west coast, and one who, on two occasions, defeated us.

The natives, three hundred strong, advanced in broad daylight in close column, shouting "*Hau Hau*" and confident of gaining a bloodless victory. Something, however, must have gone wrong with their incantations, for the angel Gabriel was not on deck on this occasion to deflect the bullets, nor even to turn the Tommies into stone.

The latter lay quiet behind the parapet until the *taua* (war party) reached the peg that marked the three hundred yards' range from the fort, then, jumping up, poured a steady volley into the head of the advancing column, and also opened fire with two Cohorn mortars. The immediate slaughter took the natives by surprise, but they were Maori warriors, as brave as any men on earth, and they charged home, attempting to escalade the steep, scarped sides of the hill, a feat of impossibility without scaling ladders, only to be swept back by the steady fire of the Diehards, and at last they had to turn and bolt, as strong reinforcements of the troops advanced.

In this defeat Hepanaia and most of the principal chiefs were killed, Titokowaru losing an eye. Anyone would think that a disaster of this sort would make the natives pause in accepting and believing in their wild faith. It did nothing of the sort, as Te Ua quickly persuaded them that the men who had been killed must have broken one of the numerous directions given by Gabriel through the medium of the head, and thereby caused the jealous angel to bring about the catastrophe. So the crazy superstitions spread and flourished until the whole of the west coast and the interior of the island reeked with murder and violence.

Te Ua's second apostle, Matene, had been despatched to the tribes on the Upper Wanganui River. These readily received the new faith, but their relations on the lower part of the river refused to do so, or else there is no doubt that the rising township of Wanganui would have been wiped out. Not only did they refuse to join the Hau Haus, but they informed them that if they attempted to descend the river that attempt would be resisted, and wound up by offering to fight them on the island of Mutoa.

It is not for a moment to be thought that the Lower River natives were prompted to act in this way by their love for the white man—not a bit of it—they only acted as they did to assert their ownership to the right-of-way on the river. This sporting challenge was accepted, the numbers and date agreed on—the fight to take place on the aforementioned island—date fixed, 14th May 1864; numbers, on hundred a side. These arrangements being amicably settled a tremendous fight took place, fortune varying during it, both sides fighting hand-to-hand with the greatest ferocity, but in the end the Lower River natives won the day, killing seventy and wounding twenty of the Hau Haus, the remainder being driven into the river and forced to swim for it. Matene was among the latter, but he was soon recognised and followed by Te Moro, who killed him with his *mere* (short battleaxe) when he reached the bank, notwithstanding the incantations used by the misguided prophet.

Te Ua had thus lost his two factotums in their first fights, and this ought to have been a set-back to the new religion; but it was not so, as he asserted, and with justice, that they had both disobeyed the orders of the angel, who had directed that the head should be carried through the country peacefully and without bloodshed, so that Hepanaia and Matene were to blame for bringing disaster and death to the faithful through their disobedience.

Accordingly he despatched two more apostles, Kereopa and Patara, who were to take Captain Lloyd's head, together with two white men prisoners or deserters (for strangely enough several men deserted from her Majesty's forces and joined the rebels), and preach the Pai Marire faith to the east coast and Taupo tribes, so that there could be no mistake this time.

Te Ua gave them the following written orders:—

> While on your journey be careful not to interfere with those whom you may meet; do not quarrel with the *pakeha* (white man). When you reach Taupo, go on to Whakatane, thence to Opotiki, from thence to Waiapu, and finally to Tauranganui,

where your journey will end. If this piece of paper should get torn or dirty, ask another piece from your white friends and rewrite it, that it may arrive clean and in good condition to Hirini Te Kani at Tauranganui. Give him also this flag and the man's head.

The apostles, far from obeying these orders, at once began to pillage and murder. To start with, on their reaching Taupo, Patara began by breaking into the house of the Rev. Mr Grace, who at the time was absent, and, appropriating the reverend gentleman's goods, sold them to the Christian flock, who at once became converts to Pai Marire. This was playing a low-down game on the absent missionary, but much worse was to follow.

Having converted Taupo, Kereopa and Patara again disobeyed orders, for instead of proceeding direct to Whakatane they altered their route to the Uriwera country and held a meeting that for crazy devilry would be hard to beat. Forming some two or three hundred of the Uriwera warriors into double rank, facing inwards, they then proceeded down them, carrying the head, forcing each man to look into the dead eyes, at the same time working them up to a pitch of mad fanaticism by their wild prayers and incantations which drove their hearers into a raving frenzy. Then calling for the widows of the warriors slain at Orakau to come forward, Kereopa directed them to vent their revenge on the head and the two wretched white men.

The women, mad with excitement, pretended to eat the head, but it was eventually taken from them; the fate of the white men, however, had better be left to the imagination of the reader.

The apostles, having converted the Uriwera, departed and left for Whakatane, where all the people at once joined them, and proceeded to Opotiki, a flourishing mission belonging to the Church of England, under the charge of the Rev. C. S. Volkner, who had resided there several years. This gentleman by his admirable conduct had justly earned the respect of both settlers and natives, the latter especially (his own flock) professing much love for him. Yet on the advent of the apostles they at once joined the Pai Marire faith, their Christianity falling from them like a garment.

Mr Volkner was absent in Auckland when Kereopa and Patara reached Opotiki, and the latter, before proceeding on a short journey, wrote him a letter telling him not to return. Mr Volkner, however, accompanied by Mr Grace, was on his way, and reached Opotiki on the

1st of March 1865, in the schooner *Eclipse*, which was immediately boarded and seized by his late parishioners. All the passengers and crew were made prisoners (with the exception of Captain Levy, who, being a Hebrew, was considered a Hau Hau of sorts), and marched up to the Roman Catholic Church, inside which Kereopa was holding a council to try Mr Volkner on the most absurd charges. The council was adjourned, the prisoners being confined in a tumbledown hut, but again met that night, when, with the exception of two or three, all of the tribe voted for their minister's death.

Next day at two p.m. Mr Volkner was led out and murdered in a most brutal manner, being hung, Kereopa firing a shot into him at the same time. The body was then carried into the church, where this fiend ordered it to be decapitated, and directed his new converts to drink and smear themselves with their victim's blood, which they all did, Kereopa giving them a lead by gouging out the eyes and swallowing them. The first to participate in this horrible act was Volkner's own woman-servant, who from a child had been brought up and educated by the Church Mission. Patara returned the same night and was bitterly angry with Kereopa on account of this foul murder, although he had annexed and sold all Mr Volkner's belongings previous to his departure on his short journey.

A few days afterwards the cutter *Kate* put into Whakatane and was immediately boarded by the Hau Haus. Her crew and passenger, Mr Fulloon (a Government agent), were soon brutally murdered. Kereopa, followed by Patara, reached Poverty Bay.

At once the Christians joined them, and Bishop Williams of Waiapu was only saved from being murdered, together with his whole family, by two or three chiefs who remained loyal to him, and these would have failed had not the Bishop just escaped in the nick of time on board a steamer.

The Hau Haus built a *pah* at Waerenga-a-Hika (the Bishop's residence), where they were subsequently attacked and defeated by the colonial troops in November 1865, who killed over one hundred of them and forced over three hundred of them to surrender. The prisoners were brought to Tauranganui, where two hundred of them were transported to the Chatham Islands, the remainder being allowed to return home. Small bands of the most fanatical of the natives, who had escaped, still wandered about the district.

Just before the last of these events I had set sail for New Zealand.

CHAPTER 3

I Start to Join the Lost Legion

It was on the 14th September 1865 the ship *Queen Bee* was towed down the river and dropped anchor at Gravesend, so as to allow the crew to sober up, and the captain to join. In the mean-time my servant and myself arranged and made comfortable my state-room, stowing away and making fast everything in its place. I may also, while we are at anchor, take the opportunity of bringing to your notice my man, Tim Egan. He had not been with me very long, but as the circumstances under which I met him, and subsequently engaged him, were unique, and as he not only faithfully served me, but stood by me, as a gallant comrade and a true, if humble, friend for many years, until a *Kaffir* bullet put an end to his life, I may be pardoned should I digress and relate them.

It happened some months previously, when I was staying at Brighton, I had been asked to play in a cricket match against a crack light infantry regiment, and on the evening previous to the first day's play had proceeded to the town at which they were quartered. On my arrival I was sitting at a window of the principal inn when my attention was attracted to a couple of soldiers coming along the road, one of whom was very drunk indeed, while his comrade, a fine, slashing-looking young fellow, was trying to convoy him home to barracks, which was a difficult job, as the drunken man was not only a big, heavy fellow, but also hung back and resisted.

These two warriors were followed by a crowd of jeering roughs and hobbledehoys, who annoyed them, and seemed inclined to obstruct their journey. The drunken man resented this conduct, wishing to stop and fight, but the sober one took no notice of the gang and only tried to get his comrade along, until they came just opposite to where I was sitting, when a big rough jostled the votary of Bacchus, evidently trying to trip him up and upset them. It would have been better for him had he left them alone, for, placing his helpless comrade against the wall, the Tommy turned on his aggressor, who, encouraged by the rabble, was about to renew his attempt, exclaiming in a voice that at once denoted he belonged to my own country: "Arrah, ye blaggard, ye want it, do ye? Thin begorra ye shall have it," and with that he lashed out with his left, landing his opponent flat on his back in the middle of the road. Then stepping back, he stood in front of his mate, hitting out right and left at the gang of roughs, who now tried to rush him. I was running out to assist him when six or seven policemen came up, who without the least inquiry proceeded to arrest the two soldiers.

But this piece of brutal Saxon injustice to Ould Ireland was more than my countryman, whose fighting blood was now up, could stand, for no sooner had a bobby placed his hand on him than he knocked him down, and as the others rushed in he served them the same way, until the footpath was strewn with recumbent Peelers, and I believe he would have come out top dog had not a rough legged him, when he was brought to the ground, sat upon and captured. I had never seen a more gallant resistance, and my heart warmed to the victim, so that I immediately proceeded to the barracks, called on the adjutant and gave him full particulars of the row, offering, at the same time, to bear witness of the correct conduct of his man.

This in due course of time I did, when my evidence saved the poor fellow from imprisonment. Now it had always been a family custom that whenever one of us joined the service he should take with him, as servant, some young man or other reared on the estate, and as I should shortly want a servant, and had taken a fancy to this man, I asked to see him. When I did so he warmly expressed his gratitude for my volunteering evidence on his behalf.

"But sure," said he, "ave a Burke of Clonkil wouldn't stand by a poor boy from his own county, who wud?"

"Oh, so you are a countyman of mine?" I asked.

"Deed I am, yer honour, and mind ye and your brothers well. Bright boys ye were, an' full of divilment."

"Well," said I, "I am joining the service soon, and want a servant. If I buy your discharge, would you like to come to me? Of course you will have to enlist in any regiment I may have to join."

"Is it come to you and sarve ye I'd like? Troth I'd give an arum for the chance. An' do ye mane it, Mr Dick? Do you mane it, sor? Be the holy cross of Clonkil, I'll sarve ye as long as life blood rins, and me four bones hang together."

So then and there the compact was made. I lodged the money and directed Tim to report himself to my uncle at Brighton, so soon as he should receive his discharge. All this had taken place and Tim, accompanying my uncle up to town, had joined me, when I explained to him my change of plans, at the same time offering to take him with me, provided he saw fit to follow my very uncertain fortunes. "Is it go to New Zaland wid ye, Mr Dick?" quoth he. "Sure it's to hell I'd go wid ye, and maybe that's farther. An' it's fighting ye say there is in thim outlandish parts. Well, an' why not, sure it's our trade it is, an' maybe there's some loot to be picked up, an' some purty gurls to colougue wid, an' it's thankful I'll be to visit forin' parts, for sure so many young women have been so kind to me that it's bothered I am, for it's Mormon I must turn, to satisfy them all, God bless 'em."

Both my uncle and Jack considered it was right for me to be accompanied in my exile by a faithful follower who could be depended on to stand by me, so that when the good ship *Queen Bee* sailed from London port she carried the two of us to seek our fate in the antipodes. Tim Egan was indeed a man any young fellow might be proud to have at his call. Standing five feet eleven in height, he was a picture of a *beau-ideal* Irish soldier, square in the chest, broad in the shoulders, narrow in the flanks and well set up, every bit of him looked made for strength and activity, while his handsome, clean-cut face, that usually carried a pleasant smile, and his dark blue, merry eye made him one that must attract the notice of a girl be she white, black or brown. Such was Tim Egan, and I may say here that a truer, braver comrade, friend and soldier, never took the Queen's shilling.

As soon as the tide suited, and the crew had slept off the thick of their drink, all hands were roused out, the anchor weighed, and the tug, getting hold of our hawser, towed us, during the early hours of the morning, out to sea, casting us loose as we opened the Channel, when with a fair wind we hoisted topsails and topgallant sails, to the good old-time chanty of "*Renzo, boys, Renzo,*" and with our main royal set we bore away on our course to the other side of the world.

Going to sea in the sixties was a very different matter from going to sea nowadays, (as at time of first publication). At present you step on board a huge floating hotel, with all the comforts and most of the luxuries of the best London establishments, finding innumerable well-dressed stewards to attend to every want, while your comfortable though small cabin is provided with everything necessary. Then again the cold storage chamber furnishes the table with fresh meat, game, poultry, fish and ice for every meal. While in those days you were accommodated with an empty square cell lighted by a dim port hole, this chamber being called a state-room, and you could furnish it to your fancy at your own expense. Then as regards the commissariat, here there was a great difference—no ice, no cooling drinks, no well-filled menu—true a number of sheep, pigs and poultry were carried, but these rarely lasted out the voyage, and in our case a heavy gale we ran up against in the North Atlantic deprived us of most of ours, and I have frequently seen the steward and cabin boy washed into the lee scuppers, together with the dinner they were conveying aft to the cuddy, from the galley that was located abaft the foremast.

Again at the present time, (as at time of first publication), you know to the day, even to the hour, when you will reach your destination, while then you did not even know, to the month, when you would get there. Still I loved the old wind-jamming days, and can look back to many a jolly hour lazed away on the breezy decks of the old *Queen Bee*. Our saloon passengers consisted of an old major, going out to take up a grant of land and settle in New Zealand; three or four young subs, just off the barrack square, *en route* to join their regiments; and eight young fellows who, as the old song runs: "Had played in the eleven, or pulled five or six or seven in the 'Varsity or else their college boat," who were going out to learn sheep farming; at least, poor lads, they thought so.

In the 'tween decks were one hundred and twenty single women sent out under the *segis* and, I believe, at the expense of Miss Burdett-Coutts, and in the fore part of the ship were some forty Tommies and twenty male emigrants, so she had the makings of a very gay ship. I am not, however, going to write a history of that voyage, as a good many of the incidents that took place on board would not bear telling, as they were very gay, and as regards the passage itself nothing very startling took place. We met two very severe gales, but weathered them safely, only losing one boat and two topsails, blown to rags, and we also passed close to a large raft, but as there was nothing on it we did not stop to examine it, so after a passage of one hundred and eighteen days we dropped anchor in the beautiful harbour of Wellington on the 10th January 1866, and were very glad to get our feet on dry land once more.

New Zealand in 1866, the year I landed, was in a very bad way indeed. The war in the North Island, begun in 1860, showed still no signs of terminating, and blazed up wherever the white settler came in contact with the native. For although General Sir Duncan Cameron had, with overwhelming numbers, forced his way into the interior of the country, and had built chains of forts with which to hold it, yet no white man's life was safe out of rifle range of these works, and the settlers, especially on the west coast, had all to abandon their farms, and send their women and children to the South Island for safety, while they themselves had to take up arms and form themselves into defence forces.

A year or so before there had been a great impulse given to the trouble by the invention of the new religion, called Pai Marire, that had turned the Maoris, both Christian and pagan, from chivalrous, if savage, enemies into howling, bloodthirsty fanatics who murdered in cold blood, with every vile atrocity, man, woman and child not only of the white race but even also of the Maoris who refused to join their crazy faith. It is not my purpose, however, to write a history of New Zealand and its troubles, but of how I came to join for good the Lost Legion, the men who live and die on the frontiers of the Empire, and who, reckless of life, health and everything else that makes existence endurable to the carpet soldier, have gradually rolled out the limits of Old England's possessions as the deft hand of a cook rolls out the lump of dough on a pastry board.

Directly we landed I made inquiries as to the whereabouts of Sir Duncan Cameron, but was quickly informed he had resigned the command of the forces to Sir Trevor Chute, and that the latter was at present on the west coast, but that it was impossible to say where. This was a disappointment, but as I had more than one string to my bow I bent my way to the Mount Cook Barracks, as, among others, I had a strong letter of introduction to the colonel commanding the regiment stationed there. I was most hospitably received, asked to dine, and, after a few minutes' chat about mutual friends in the old country, I asked the best way how to get to the front and take a hand in the fighting.

The colonel looked surprised, but said, "Well, look here, Mr Burke, if you really want to see what they call fighting in this country" (he had served through the Crimea and Mutiny and like all the rest of the regular officers was sick and disgusted with the long-drawn-out war), "the best thing for you to do would be to join one of the colonial defence forces. We get news very slowly here but the day for regular troops in this country is past, and before another twelve months is over there will be but few left in the island. The only way to put an end to the war will be for small bands of irregulars to follow the Hau Haus into the bush, live, or rather starve, in the bush, and keep in pursuit of the enemy until they are worn down and killed off. Now I will, if you like, at the club this evening, introduce you to some of the colonial leaders and you can discuss the matter with them, but you will find it a hard, brutal life without any chance of gaining honour or distinction."

After a pleasant dinner he took me down to the club, and there I met several leaders on their way from the east coast to the west, for, as the enemy held the whole of the interior of the island and there were no roads, all communications between the two coasts had to be sea-borne. I was also introduced to several members of the Colonial House of Parliament who were at that time in the capital, and, among others, to the Defence Minister, to whom I mentioned my desire of taking service. He was evidently amused at the idea of a man travelling over fifteen thousand miles to run the chance of getting killed and turned into long pig but assured me there were plenty of openings in the country for a man desirous of seeing hard, rough fighting, and asked me to call at his office next morning.

Well pleased with my evening I said goodbye to my host and returned to my hotel, where I found my shipmates full of beer and excitement, drinking in company with some half-dozen tough, weather-beaten, fine-looking young fellows dressed in blue jumpers, Bedford cord riding breeches and smasher hats, who on being introduced to me I discovered to be troopers in the Colonial Field Force. They were all men who belonged to the class that go to public schools and Varsities, and in a very short time I discovered that most of them had come out to learn sheep farming, but finding the cadet business to be a swindle had thrown it up and joined the irregular forces. Their tales of the wild life they led quickly captivated my companions, who one and all declared they would join the irregulars and let the sheep farming go swing.

Other men trooped in, and seeing every likelihood of a very wet night I slipped off to bed and managed to get some hours of sleep, notwithstanding the rough choruses that were howled out for some hours as the troopers, taking the only chance they had, after months of hard work, and knowing they were on the threshold of another campaign, were determined not to let that chance slip but employ it so as to knock down their cheques and blue all the hard-earned pay they had in their pouches.

Next morning at breakfast, which was partaken of by all the guests at a sort of *table d'hôte*, there were many troopers present and I got into conversation with one of them. Up to the present I had been rather surprised to see the principal hotel of the New Zealand capital thronged with men serving in the ranks, but my eyes were quickly opened by my new acquaintance, who told me that the corps to which he himself and most of the men present belonged was the Wanganui Defence Force, and that as every able-bodied man in that district was forced to serve, most of them at table with us were well-to-do men, holding good positions in the country but, having been forced to abandon their farms and businesses, had been enrolled into a corps; that they had been serving on the east coast, and had been recalled to the west coast; that the day previous their transport had put into Wellington, where it was going to remain three days, so that they were taking advantage of the stoppage to enjoy a few days' life of civilisation between the two campaigns.

They seemed to be all very keen about the new campaign, as they considered the new general to be a far better man, for the work, than the one who had lately resigned, whose method of conducting the last five years' operations they criticised in the most unmerciful manner, while their open comments on the inutility of the regulars, both officers and men, made me wince with astonished indignation, so that it was with the greatest difficulty I could restrain myself from starting a row.

The man I was sitting next to evidently noticed my vexation, for he said: "If you have finished breakfast let's go out on the back verandah and have a smoke, and, if you have nothing better to do, a chat for an hour or two."

As he seemed a very good fellow, and I was most anxious to gain knowledge, I gave him my card, telling him I had only landed the day previous. "Yes," said he, "I can see you are a new chum, and I saw you were getting riled at the talk of the boys inside, but you must remember that the majority of those men have been ruined by the pig-headed procrastination of the general, who with twenty thousand men at his disposal has not been able, after five years' warfare, to gain any permanent advantage over savages who have never at any one time exceeded two thousand fighting men. Now," he went on, "my name is West. I own a large farm on the west coast. I have been out in this country seventeen years. and, having sunk my capital in land and stock, had put in twelve years' hard work in clearing ground, fencing farm and improving stock.

"Five years ago I was well off, with every prospect of becoming a rich man, having a comfortable house, a wife and two children, good horses, valuable cattle and sheep, and was contemplating a trip home for twelve months. The war broke out. I just saved the wife and kids; my house is burned, my stock and horses driven away and looted, my fences destroyed and my farm a wilderness, so that when this wretched business terminates I shall have to begin again. I am just completing three years' service in this force, and as far as I can see we are no nearer to the end than what we were the day we began."

"But why blame the general and troops?" I asked. "Surely you have out here thousands of officers and men whose splendid conduct and courage during the Crimea and Mutiny will live in history as long as the old flag flies? "

"Mr Burke," he answered, "you do not understand. The man who speaks a word against the courage and devotion of H.M. troops lies in the throat, but nevertheless, from the general downwards, they are simply useless for this sort of work. If you have the patience, and," with a laugh, "promise not to go for me, I will try and explain. The facts are these. The general and a vast majority of the senior officers are hidebound in the old traditions and customs of the British army, so much so that they are quite incapable of adapting a new style of warfare to novel circumstances, while the training of the men itself renders them unfit for bush warfare. I read, as a boy at school, how General Braddock, refusing to take the advice of his colonial officers, was cut up in an American forest.

"It is the same here, and it has only been our overwhelming strength that has saved similar disasters in this country. Look here, let me give you a few examples of what has happened in the past five years. You have, you say, been educated for a soldier, and have come to this country to lend us a hand; it will therefore do you no harm to hear and ponder over some of the absurdities that have been perpetrated, remembering that I am speaking with no ill-will against the general or troops but only just telling you how Maoris should not be fought. In 1860, when the war broke out in the Taranaki district, and we settlers saw our life's work go up in smoke, although the Europeans outnumbered the natives ten to one, it seemed that nothing could be done.

"The Maoris built *pahs* at the edge of the bush, often on deserted farms. General Pratt, then in command there, would besiege these, as if they were Sebastopols, and when with a vast amount of hard work he had sapped up to them he would find them deserted, the natives having with-drawn into the bush, where the general refused to follow them. The Maoris therefore used to plant their potatoes in perfect security, then, while their crops were growing, would announce the shooting season to be open, and invite their friends to come and pot white men, making raids into our country right up to musket range of the forts, killing and looting everyone and anything they came across.

"Occasionally the general (the Maoris called him the rat, from his burrowing and sapping propensities) would ginger up and try to make what he called a combined movement, and even to venture into the bush, but always to come to grief. *Par exemple*, at one of the very first fights, the attack on the *pah* at Waireka, Colonel Murray with two hundred regulars and one hundred and twenty Colonials were detached to take it, the latter being ordered to make a detour through some very rough country and take up a position in rear of the place, while the regulars were to rush it from the front.

"The Colonials after a sharp skirmish took up the position assigned to them and held it all day, but the attack was never made, and at nightfall the regulars drew off and returned to the town, leaving the Colonials planted there with their retreat cut off and ammunition nearly all expended. They were in a tight fix, and it would have gone hard with them had not Captain Cracroft, R.N., who with a party of sixty blue-jackets had just landed from H.M.S. *Niger*, heard of their predicament. He at once took action, got hold of three young fellows to guide him, and started off with his jacks to do their best to help their stranded countrymen. Captain Cracroft wasted no time over formulating complicated plans or strategy but made straight for the *pah*; it was pitch dark and when he reached the vicinity of it his party fell across a mob of the enemy.

"One volley the blue-jackets fired, then out cutlass and revolver and charged the astonished natives, who fled for the protection of their works with the sailors in close pursuit. The stockade is reached, but that does not check the shell-backs, who, giving one another a leg up, enter the place, and gut it as clean as a red herring. The Maoris, who had bailed up the Colonials, hearing the row ran to see what was up, and the latter, taking advantage of their absence, retired in safety. So far so good, but the conduct of the soldiers' O.C. in botching the show caused heaps of ill-feeling.

"Subsequently, after an immense amount of talk and preparations, a field force goes out to attack Puketakauere, more combined movements and high-falutin strategy, all of which, when it comes to the point, proved unworkable in the bush, and we have to clear out after losing sixty soldiers, shot down like sheep. Again, look at the game Cameron has played in the Waikato. With an overwhelming force he attacks Rangiriri. Mind he is fully cognisant that the natives have neither food nor water in the *pah*. He surrounds the place, and instead of waiting for them to be starved out he assaults the *pah* three times, getting beaten back with the loss of over one hundred and thirty men.

"Next day the *pah* surrendered, as its defenders are dying of thirst. The following year at Orakau he played the same silly game. He knew the enemy had neither food nor water, yet he tries five times to rush the place, loses heaps of men, and the Maoris, unable any longer to endure the pangs of thirst, sally out, break through the surrounding troops, and many of them escape.

"During the same month comes the Gate *pah*. Again over one hundred men are lost, through folly, blind stupidity, nothing else. The general has learnt nothing, is incapable of learning. True, the Tommies caught the same fellows within two months at Te Ranga, and pretty well wiped them out with the bayonet. Then the war breaks out again on the west coast. What is done? General Cameron starts to march up the coast to Taranaki with two thousand men.

"I was with the mounted portion of the force, and the first day out the column had marched fifteen miles when it was halted, early in the afternoon, to pitch camp. The adjutant-general, Johnston, had picked out a site at Nukumaru. My O.C, an old hand, who knew the country well (I was acting as his orderly) rode up to the staff. 'General,' said he, 'don't you think we are rather too near the bush, especially as that long *Toe-toe* grass grows right up to the tents, and we are only five miles distant from the Weraroa *pah*, the principal stronghold of the enemy. 'Pooh, pooh. Major,' answered the general, 'do you imagine, sir, for one moment, that any body of natives would dare to attack two thousand of H.M. troops?' 'Yes, sir,' said the major, 'fifty Maoris are quite capable of doing so.' But it was no good talking, so we rode away to our lines. 'Keep your horses saddled, boys,' said the major, 'we may be wanted any moment,' and we did so.

"Well, sir, the troops had just finished pitching the tents when rip comes a volley from the *Toe-toe* grass. Over rolled Adjutant-General Johnston and sixteen men dead, and there was hell to pay: men rush-

Colonel McDonnell.

ing to the piles of arms, bugles blowing and officers shouting contradictory orders, while the natives continued blazing into the camp, some of them even rushing in with their *tomahawks*, one of them being killed within twenty yards of the General's own tent.

"At the first shot our O.C. had yelled out 'Mount,' and as we were standing to our horses we were on them in a moment. 'Charge,' sings out the O.C, and we charged through the long grass right into the middle of the Hau Haus, there not being more than fifty of them all told. Maoris won't stand mounted men, so we swept them back to the bush, killing a good lot. On our return to camp we found all the soldiers standing in rows, looking very pretty, and the general very angry, declaring it was not warfare for fifty savages to attack two thousand British troops.

"Now the general ought to have learned something from that lesson, but he didn't, for next night, a gale of wind blowing, the column was halted to bivouac in long dry fern. Fine beds for tired men long dry fern makes, provided there is not a gale of wind blowing and the Hau Haus are not hostile, but on this occasion such was the case, and we were roused out by shots and bugle calls to see a wall of fire, twenty feet high, charging us faster than a horse can gallop. Gad, sir, it was a case of *sauve qui peut*, and we all bolted for the sand-hills like redshanks, the Maoris *tomahawking* five of the 18th R.I. picket and a lot of others. This last affair so disgusted the general that he refused to leave the beach, and, without making another attempt of any sort, consumed fifty-seven days to march fifty-four miles, while the Maoris, only a handful in number, used to chaff us and called the general the lame seagull.

"I'll give you one more instance of incapacity, or call it what you like. Sir George Grey asked the general to attack Weraroa *pah*. The general insisted it was impregnable to the force he had at his disposal, and that he should require at least six thousand men to do so. After a lot of blarney he sanctioned an attack to be made by Sir George, who, with less than five hundred Colonials and friendly Maoris, took the place.

"Now look here, we settlers are sick of the war, and want to get back to our farms and businesses. We are paying the British Government forty pounds sterling *per annum* for every regular, and when it takes an army fifty-seven days to march along an open beach fifty-four miles we don't think we are getting our money's worth. Besides we can tackle the natives better ourselves. We men you see here are on our way back from the east coast, where, without the help of a single regular, we have smashed the Hau Haus, taking their *pah* Waerenga-a-Hika, and, with only twenty-three casualties, have killed one hundred and fifty of the enemy, and forced four hundred more of them to surrender, two hundred of whom have been transported to the Chatham Islands, so that they are out of the way.

"Now the reason I have told you all this is, you say you have come out here to see fighting. That being so, my straight tip to you is to join a colonial corps; all the fighting during the coming campaign will be done by them. Don't bother about a commission; join the ranks under Von Tempsky or McDonnell and learn your work; then, after you have done that, you may take a commission if you like, and your men will think all the more of you. Now then I'm dry with talking, come and have a drink, and I'll walk with you as far as the Defence Minister's; he is an old pal of mine. What, you don't drink? Well so much the better for you, so let's get."

With my new friend discoursing on things in general we strolled along to the Government Buildings, where we had not to wait many minutes before we were shown into the minister's office. This is a funny country, I thought, where a trooper in uniform, if such a garb can be called uniform, can call unasked on an important minister; but new countries, new customs, so I made no remark but accompanied my companion into the presence of the big man, who greeted him with much cordiality.

Presently, turning to me, he said, "Mr Burke, you are fortunate in making the acquaintance of my old friend West, and you will be wise in taking any advice on colonial matters he may offer you. I have been thinking over your case. Now this is how it appears to me. Although you have been educated and trained as a soldier, still you have had no experience in bush fighting, and without that are of no use to us. I should therefore recommend you to join a colonial corps as a private, and you will quickly gain promotion, when you have gone through the mill and gained the required knowledge. Pay, I believe, is of small consequence to you; the hardships and dangers of the campaign, which are very great, must be borne equally by officers and men alike. Good birth and education are desirable, but it is the best men we want, and the best man gets ahead in this country. You have travelled fifteen thousand miles to see fighting, and therefore don't want to serve as a town guard, so I will give you a letter to Colonel McDonnell, one of our most experienced officers, and can promise you that you will see enough savage warfare and experience every phase of irregular fighting. What do you say, West?"

"You have given him the same advice as I have already done, so that if you will scribble a chit to McDonnell and give Burke a pass up in the *St Kilda* I will look after him and see him through."

The advice was sound and I determined to profit by it, so, thankfully receiving the letter and pass, the latter including the name of Tim, we shook hands with the minister and backed out.

No sooner were we clear of the Government Buildings than West said: "Let's go down to Prosser's; we are sure to find some of McDonnell's men there, and you can make acquaintance with them. You will find them a warm lot, but all right in the field, and perfect devils to fight."

Prosser's, at that time, was the great sporting headquarters of the up-country man, and was much frequented by the driver and stockrider class, every one of whom is more or less a sportsman and lover of horseflesh. An odd prize-fighter or rowing man might be found there occasionally, while diggers on their way to and from the goldfields used it largely. It was, however, a well-run establishment, owned by a very good fellow. On our entrance we found the place swarming with men of a type I had not as yet met, but although I have used the word "type," and anyone could see they were men who followed the same occupation and had much in common, yet in nationality, birth, education and manners they differed greatly, and this difference was far more marked than had been the case among my old comrades in the Papal Zouaves.

Here, carelessly lounging against the wall, you saw a man whose clean-cut features, correct mannerism, cultivated voice and easy abandon proclaimed him unmistakably to have been a former denizen of the club and drawing-room. Yet he is talking and drinking with a huge, burly fellow whose sunburnt face, open jumper, tattooed arms and shoulder-of-mutton fist branded him as a shell-back from before the stick. Yes, they were all there, the ex-public schoolboy, the ex-army man, the ex-sailor, stock-rider, bushman, gold-digger, professional man, ay, and, had you looked carefully, you would no doubt have found the unfrocked parson.

The great majority of them are British, but among them is a sprinkling of vivacious Frenchmen, stolid Germans, hang-dog-looking Dagos, and even a few half-caste Maoris and South Sea Islanders. No matter what nationality they belonged to, they all had the same indescribable air of reckless good-nature, combined with determination and latent ferocity, which fully convinced an observer that although they might be a dangerous and godless crew, yet they were a fearless one, and that he could plank down his bottom dollar on the assertion that they would stick to a leader of their own choice to the last gasp.

West knew some of them, and, having spotted the man he wanted to get hold of, we elbowed our way through the crowd towards him, refusing many invitations to drink *en route*. My appearance seemed to cause considerable excitement among them, and I was nearly deafened with the number of chaffing questions put to me. "Hullo, mate," quoth one, "what's the last news from the big smoke?" "How's Kate and Rose thriving, and is the old market as naughty as ever?" "Have a drink, pal, and tell us what you were lagged for," bellows another. "Good old collars and cuffs, who's the best girl in London nowadays?" While one big fellow raised a laugh by roaring out: "Come and have a wet, new chum. Don't you tumble, boys, to it? Why, he must be the new little general who's been sent out to teach us how to lick the Hau Haus."

Taking no notice of these embarrassing but good-natured remarks, I pushed on after my leader, till we reached the man he was making for, who was a tall, good-looking, bearded fellow whom I at once saw to be a man in every sense of the word. "Hutton," quoth West, "come out of this. I want you to come over and *tiffin*, also to introduce you to a new chum friend of mine. Mr Burke, Mr Hutton. Now you know each other, come along."

We shoved our way outside and soon reached the comparatively quieter hotel, where under the back verandah we sat down to chat. "See here, Hutton," said West, as soon as we had been served with long drinks, "I want you to give our young friend a hand. He is going up with us in the *St Kilda*, taking a letter from the Defence Minister to McDonnell, whom he is going to join as a Ranger. Now we were both of us new chums once, and you can do him plenty of good turns, as I do not expect to go myself farther than Wanganui."

Hutton looked me over for a minute, and said:

I don't want to be inquisitive, Mr Burke, but I think I know a good deal about you. I used to know London well years ago, and have still an old pal in the Guards who writes to me. I expect you are the Dick Burke who made himself rather notorious by fighting duels, blowing up your ancestors and joined the Papal Zouaves. Well, if such is the case I think you will do for a Ranger, provided you can stand the work and hardships. We are chiefly composed of individuals who have run awful muckers, the balance being men from the gold-diggin's, together with the sea-drift of the Pacific slope and the South Seas. But why on earth should you plunge into the pit? Remember a man who once joins *Les Enfants Perdus* is lost forever, not one man in a hundred ever returning to civilised society. Look here, Burke—we have no misters in the Rangers—I was once the same as you are now. Good old family, public school, crack regiment, best society in London, and all the rest.

What am I now? A knock-about adventurer, stock-rider, prospector, digger, all those I've been and plenty more. I ran a mucker, never mind how, but do you think I never regret the past? My God!" and his face became suffused with blood and his eyes glared, "you see me and hundreds of others like me. You see us drink, hear us laugh and shout, and think what a jovial, high-spirited crowd we are. Jovial, forsooth, yes, with the joy of hell in our hearts and the high spirits born of rum in our laughter; and do you think there is no thought or longings for the old life and the sweet women whose companionship our folly has cut us off from forever? Yes, by God, as the man dying of thirst in the desert longs for water, so we long for the past life we shall never live again.

"Yes, yes, old chap," said West soothingly; "but remember the honours you have gained."

"Honours!" almost shouted Hutton. "Do you think that one of our fellows, in a corps like ours, whose name will be forgotten in this country six months after we are disbanded, and will never be even heard of in England, count honours for anything, when even if we won them we could not share them with those who are never, save when we are drunk, out of our minds? No, West, my dear fellow, you fight for your home, for your wife and kids, and for the country of your adoption, but what have we to fight for? New Zealand to us is only a wayside station passed on our journey through life. Yes, by the Lord Harry, I may well ask you what we do fight for. It's not for our six bob a day, for any man can make his pound a shift at the diggin's for half the fatigue and none of the exposure; no, nor is it for the offal served out to us called rations; nor for the gilt and glory of war, for there is none here.

"So I ask you again. West, what is it that makes a man like me, another like Ginger Dick the blackbird catcher, or Holy Joe, the drunken, unfrocked parson, fight like we do and suffer the hardships we have to undergo? Why is it, answer me that?"

West said not a word, but pointed at the flag that floated at the peak of a ship of war, removed his hat and whistled a bar or two of "God Save the Queen."

In a moment Hutton was on his feet. "Yes, by Satan, you've struck it!" he shouted. "It's the Queen and flag, God bless them, that claims us, and gives every one of us skallywags and ne'er-do-wells a chance and right, no matter what we have done in the past, to at all events die like gentlemen in their service. But look here, you fellows, I must apologise, must have gone a bit dotty. It's Burke's fault. Why the deuce do you come among us with your London-built coat and your Bond Street rig-out, to make a poor devil remember? Never mind, care killed the cat. There goes the *tiffin* gong. Let's make the most of our remaining chances at the fleshpots of Egypt, for in a short time, Burke, you will have to exist on rations that you only eat to keep body and soul together, so sling ahead and let's russle our hash."

After lunch I informed the horrified Tim that we were to join the Forest Rangers as privates, that for a time the difference between master and man must be forgotten, and that in future we must be comrades on the same plane.

The worthy man took some time to absorb the information, and when he had fully grasped the idea blurted out: "Well, begorra, we won't. Fancy the likes of me being chummy with the likes of you, Mr Dick. Av course, sor, av you join as private, I join too, but I'm your man, sor, still, and be this an' be that, I'll be so."

Later on, under the guidance of Hutton, I purchased my own and Tim's outfit. Riding breeches and boots, also good flannel shirts, in those days called Crimean shirts, we had already, but after Hutton had picked out two blue jumpers he selected with great care two strong and warm but light woollen shawls.

"What on earth are these for?" I asked, as we had plenty of rugs.

"Oh," he replied, "when we enter the bush we discard breeches and trousers and wear shawls round our waists like kilts."

"And what for am I to be turned into a Hielander, sor?" quoth Tim.

"Why," replied our mentor, "you see we have often to use a creek or river-bed as a road, either to wade up it or keep on crossing it, and it's deadly work having to march in wet trouser-legs, but with a shawl you can raise it out of the water, and continue your route with ease, also make an extra blanket of it, and, my word, you need it. Remember you will have to act as your own pack horse here; every man has to hump his own swag—that is, you will have to carry on your own backs everything you take out with you on a foot patrol."

Orders were given out that night that every man must muster at noon next day, so the reckless boys set to work to blue their remaining money, and Wellington was painted scarlet. As for me, I persuaded Hutton, West and some others to dine with me. All the rest of my shipmates had joined various corps, and we not only had a first-rate dinner but a jolly good spree after it. Tim had packed up, all our goods had been warehoused, so next morning I had nothing to do but pay my bill and walk down to the *St Kilda* that was to sail at two p.m. for Wanganui.

CHAPTER 4

I Join the Lost Legion

It was on a lovely afternoon that the old tub *St Kilda*, crowded with men and looking far from safe, steamed slowly out of the harbour and made for Wanganui. Fortunately the weather was very fine and calm, so next morning we were off the heads at the mouth of the river, where we received orders to proceed farther up the coast to the Patea River, close to the mouth of which the camp at Patea was situated. This was very fortunate for me, as I now should be landed right at the front, where General Chute was himself in command, and Colonel McDonnell was also present. The bar across the mouth of the Patea River is a very bad one, only to be negotiated by boats or small steamers at high tides, and during calm weather.

We were, however, lucky, and crossed it in safety, anchoring shortly afterwards in front of the settlement and camp, where I, as I was still my own master, at once went on shore, landing in the midst of turmoil and bustle that made it very difficult to gain any information. It was evident to me that some expedition on a large scale was contemplated, as strings of pack horses, soldiers, Rangers and a good few Maoris jostled, shouted and worked.

At last I managed to get hold of a sergeant of the 57th, who, as he had evidently been lately wounded in the arm, was willing to converse, and asked him to direct me to the general's quarters. He informed me that the general had gone on to a new camp farther up the coast, with a strong party of the 14th Regiment, Colonials and friendly Maoris; that there had been some sharp fighting lately, and that his own O.C., Lieutenant-Colonel Butler, was in camp, but leaving with a strong detachment of his regiment some time during the next twenty-four hours.

As I had a letter of introduction to this officer I determined to call on him and try to get some definite information, so proceeded to his camp, where I was fortunate enough to find the gallant lieutenant-colonel for the moment disengaged. He received me very kindly, and told me Colonel McDonnell was in camp, having been wounded by a ball in the foot at Putahi a few days previously, but that, far from lying up, he insisted on accompanying the field force that was to operate north of the Patea River. He also informed me that if I wished to join it, no time was to be lost, as within the next twenty-four hours the whole of the men to complete the general's column would leave the base camp, and he very kindly offered to guide me over to McDonnell's lines and introduce me.

This offer was, of course, too good to refuse, and in a few minutes I found myself face to face with the man who had done perhaps more Maori fighting than any other in the country, and who was in the future to be the chief factor in eventually putting a stop to the war.

Colonel McDonnell was a big, powerful man, who sported a heavy moustache, with large, bushy whiskers and eyebrows; from under the latter looked out a pair of glaring eyes, while the expression of his face was that of stern determination, almost pitiless, and you could see, when in motion, every movement denoted strength and activity. I had heard many yarns about him during the last few days, and they all bore witness to his wonderful knowledge of the natives, his courage and endurance, while he was accredited with having killed, in single hand-to-hand fights, ten Maoris. He had been wounded a few days before, but had no intention of going on the sick list, and when we were announced was engaged in earnest conversation with several Maoris. Still, on hearing Colonel Butler's name, he ordered us to be at once admitted.

In a few words the colonel stated our business, and I presented the Defence Minister's letter, which he hurriedly read, glancing occasionally at me over the paper. Then he laughed and said something to the natives in Maori which seemed to amuse them. Then, turning to me, he remarked: "Well, Mr Burke, you wish to join me and see some fighting. Very good, you are just in time. We start at two a.m. tomorrow morning. I will put you in the way of gratifying your desires. The first thing to be done is for you to sign your attestation paper, etc. Orderly, go and bring Mr Roach here."

In a few moments a tall, powerful man, some thirty years old, entered, who looked as hard as nails.

"Oh, Roach," said the colonel, "this is Mr Burke, who has come from England to see some fighting, and wishes to join us. Be good enough to attest him and his companion, attach them to your own company and let them go with us tomorrow. And now, Colonel Butler, I have put your friend in the way of seeing some fighting, whether he will enjoy the road that leads to it remains to be proved."

With a good-natured nod to me, and a "So-long, Colonel," to my companion, the interview terminated, and we left the tent. After I had thanked Colonel Butler for his kindness we also parted, and I accompanied my new officer-to-be to the office tent of the corps, where in ten minutes myself and Tim had signed away our liberty for three months, or six if required, in the Forest Rangers, and had been served out with carbines, belts and pouches. We drew nothing else from store as we preferred to use our own revolvers, and, thanks to the advice of Hutton and West, I had purchased all the other articles necessary, of better quality, in Wellington.

After a few words of instruction and advice from Mr Roach we were handed over to the sergeant-major, who took us to the lines, and we were told off to a tent and mess, when I was glad to find the man in charge of the former to be Hutton.

I have already described, *en bloc*, the men composing the Rangers, but I think my tent companions deserve a word or two individually, especially as you are already acquainted with myself, Egan and Hutton.

Now the most important man in a mess is the cook. Of course in an irregular corps everyone has to bear a hand and take his turn, the consequence being that the food you have to eat is neither tempting nor palatable, but occasionally one man shines out, pre-eminently superior to the rest, when he is at once handed over the big iron ladle and enthroned cook. A cook must be born, not made, and when in a mess a man is discovered who has a knack of making a good meal out of nothing he is indeed a treasure. Such a one we possessed, for no sooner had myself and Tim conveyed our scanty belongings from the St *Kilda* to the tent than the dinner call went, and I was glad to hear it, albeit doubtful of being able to procure the wherewithal to satisfy a remarkably sharp appetite.

"Come on, Burke," shouted Hutton; "just in time. Squat down on your blankets and buckle to." And no sooner had I taken my seat than two men entered bearing a steaming pot and a bucket full of tea.

In a moment these were placed on the ground, each man dipping his tin pannikin into the bucket and securing his allowance of sweetened though milkless black liquid, on the top of which floated innumerable small sticks, which caused the said liquid to be called, through the forces, post and rail tea. In the meantime the piece of plank that served as a lid had been removed from the pot, when at once a goodly odour filled the tent, and on being handed a deep tin plateful, I found the taste to more than justify the scent.

But the cook himself! He was a big, raw-boned Frenchman from the south of France, bearded like a *pard*, his open and tattered jumper revealing a huge crucifix tattooed on his chest, while his long hairy arms and huge hands were also covered with red and blue figures. The only other garment he wore was a greasy, ragged shawl, worn very short, and fastened round his waist by a belt in which was thrust a murderous-looking knife. Head, feet and legs were bare, the former being covered with a thatch of long, thick black hair, and the latter with a skin nearly burnt black by exposure to sun and weather.

No sooner had he served out his delicious ragout, with a big iron ladle, than he squatted down alongside his companion and fed with him out of the pot, the two combined making a picture that if painted would have been received in any art gallery as a study of gnomes feeding. For his mate, the man who had brought in the tea bucket, was, as far as dress and appearance went, his exact duplicate, though not of the same nationality, as he was a Levantine Greek who, although a tall, wiry man, was by no means as big or powerful as his French partner.

These two beauties were presented to me as Pierre De Feugeron and George Kantuarius, and were as extraordinary a half section as I have ever tumbled across. Each man, in his youth, had been a sailor, Pierre having originally started as a French naval man, George probably as a pirate, to which latter profession, at the time I met them, if one could judge by appearances, they both seemed fully qualified, notwithstanding the fact that Pierre, especially after his tongue had been loosened with a tot or two, always asserted that he had, at one time, been *chef de cuisine* to the French Admiral commanding the Mediterranean Fleet, and had on more than one occasion cooked dinner for the emperor himself. Certainly he was the most wonderful cook, though how he came to abandon that profession was always a mystery he would never divulge. He and George had been mates for years, having met in Central America, where they had served together under Walker and Garibaldi. They had drifted over to New Zealand with a cargo of mules, had joined the Rangers, and were here. I shall relate more of them later on.

The man who squatted opposite to me was also a man to be noticed. He likewise had evidently been a sailor, belonging to that class that is now extinct, and looking at him as he swallowed his food my thoughts at once flew back to Drake, Morgan and the Buccaneers, and I easily pictured to myself my new comrade serving on some old-time ship that hoisted the Jolly Roger. He was about five feet ten inches in height, but of enormous breadth of shoulder and chest; the latter, like his face and immensely long and muscular arms, burnt mahogany colour, were covered with cicatrices of ancient knife and bullet wounds, while with an enormous hand grasping an iron spoon, which it almost hid, he shovelled his food into his capacious jaws with an enjoyment and sound that reminded me of a half-starved hound gulping at a trough.

Still, when he all of a sudden paused and looked at me I saw he had the wide-open blue eye, the frank, fearless look, and the determined mien that stamped him as a chip of the old English block grown in Devon, that county that has bred so many gallant hearts, gentle and simple, who have done so much for the honour of our glorious old flag.

Yes, Jack Williams was a Devonshire man who, having been born within sound of the sea, had taken to it, and followed it all his life, most of which had been passed on the South Seas. Jack had put in many and very wicked years among the Islands, upon the Pacific slope, and even as far north as China. He had been a sandalwood trader, an opium smuggler, with more than likely a turn of piracy added, a blockade runner, a blackbird catcher, and had shipped in every desperate and bloody adventure that had been perpetrated on the coast, and in Central America, till at last he had drifted over to New Zealand and brought up in the Forest Rangers.

Of the other two members of the mess, one, named Buck, was a typical digger, who had followed the gold for years, and was now putting in a few months with the Rangers on the chance of striking something good in the hitherto un-prospected country over which he might be called on to scout or fight during his service. He was a quiet, reserved man, but a good comrade, who seldom went on the bust, and was not rowdy when he did so. He had been brought up as a gamekeeper in Sussex, and had emigrated to Australia during the great gold rush to that country in 1856.

The remaining man was one of the many mysteries in that polygenous corps. He called himself Smith. That he had once occupied a very different position in life was evident, and must have, at one time, made a considerable reputation at one of the Varsities. What he had been we never learned, but he possessed the most varied education, not only being conversant with ancient literature, but having a marvellous knowledge of mediaeval and modern writers, and I have never met a man who could spout so readily any ancient or modern prose or poetry. He also possessed an unquenchable thirst, and would go to any extreme to obtain liquor, drinking any spirits he could get by the pannikinful until he became overcome, ranting the whole time passages from Shakespeare, Racine, Homer or Horace with equal facility. When sober he was of a saturnine disposition, rarely speaking to anyone, but was the very devil in action, and could stand any amount of hardship.

Well, this queer crowd sat round the tent devouring Pierre's excellent ragout with iron spoons, the said spoons, together with iron three-pronged forks, our sheath knives and our tin plates, comprising all our table equipments. Very few remarks were made during the repast, but when it had concluded and George had cleansed with sand the greasy utensils, Hutton drew out, from his roll of blankets, a bottle of rum and a bundle of cheroots, which he placed by the pole of the tent.

"Here you are, boys," said he. "I brought these up from the canteen so as to welcome the new chums. You will find both the cheroots and men all right, so sling round the pannikins, Pierre, and let's drink them luck." This was promptly done, and after the bottle had gone round conversation became general.

I began by congratulating Pierre on the wonderful dish he had given us, and told him it reminded me of a *plat* I had partaken of in Marseilles.

In a moment he was off. "Oh, the beautiful Marseilles, and does *Monsieur* know Marseilles, perhaps *Monsieur* also speaks French?"

This I allowed was correct, and in a moment he burst out with a volubility that none but his own countrymen can equal, and was going ahead nineteen to the dozen when Jack brought him to with a growl like an enraged lion.

"'Ere stash it, yer darned frog-eater. This 'ere's an English ship an' yer don't jabber yer *dago* lingos aboard us."

Pierre answered with the snarl of a wild cat, but the row was fortunately cut short by a bugle blowing the assembly, which necessitated us all falling in.

It was not for a long parade, however, we were required, but only to warn fifty of us, whose names were read out, to hold ourselves in readiness to parade at one a.m. next morning for field duty, and that ten men, who were to act as scouts, were to fall in at sunset.

Among the latter I was rather surprised to hear the names of Pierre and George called, but was delighted, when my own and Tim's, together with the rest of our mates, were included in those composing the main body.

No sooner was the parade dismissed than we set about making preparations for the march, and it may be as well here to give you some idea of our armament and outfit.

The Rangers were, at this time, armed with a breech-loading carbine of the most primitive pattern. It was loaded with a cartridge the powder of which was contained in a thin skin bag at the base of the bullet, and when loading in a hurry it was quite on the cards you burst the skin and spilt the powder. Then you had to fit on a cap, and after you had the weapon loaded you were more likely to miss a church two hundred yards distant than hit it. Heavy muzzle-loading revolvers, tomahawks and sheath knives completed our outfit of lethal weapons, and every man had to carry one hundred carbine cartridges and thirty revolver ones.

Besides this, a man had to hump his swag (carry his pack), the amount and weight of each swag depending entirely on the strength and ability of the humper and the country over which it had to be humped. We had no transport of any kind nor knapsacks, so whatever we carried was wrapped up in our blankets, which were rolled, drum-shape, and suspended up and down our backs by straps over the shoulders, but not worn across the chest, this method giving free play to the arms; but it required a man to be square-shouldered and not shaped like a soda-water bottle.

It must not be imagined there was any hard-and-fast rule or uniformity required as to how the Rangers carried their packs, or even if they carried any at all; in fact the only uniformity required was the blue jumper and carbine, all the rest was left to the man himself, who could go as he darned well pleased. Boots were not considered essential, nor was the pattern of shirt or shawl taken into consideration, very many men, like Pierre and George, never wearing boots nor carrying blankets during the summer months.

It will therefore be thoroughly understood that the Rangers were not for show, and that the gilt and gorgeous panoply of war was as absent from their ranks as hymn-books.

In accordance with Hutton's advice we at once started making our preparations, which were as follows:—Our English clothes were stripped off, and everything we had that we did not intend to take with us was packed in a canvas kit-bag and stored. The expedition was to be made on foot, so discarding our trousers we donned the shawls and were instructed how to wear them. Flannel shirts, our blue jumpers, smasher hats, strong laced boots and worsted socks completed our garbs.

Then the blankets were packed. Pierre had drawn four days' rations for each man, and proceeded to distribute them; mine consisted of four pounds of cooked salt pork, four pounds of biscuits, a small tin of tea and sugar mixed, and a smaller tin of pepper and salt mixed. A spare shirt, a pair of socks and a few odds and ends completed my outfit. All these, with the exception of the pork and one day's biscuit, which went into the haversack, were rolled up tightly in the blanket, and the *pekau* straps (shoulder straps) carefully adjusted; then after we had had some food and tea we lay down to get what rest we could before the fall-in went.

It was some time before I dropped off to sleep, but I seemed only to have slept a moment when I was aroused up by Tim, and it took me a minute or more to pull myself together. I found the other fellows sitting up, each with a pannikin of steaming cocoa in his fist, and, sleepy as I still was, I soon joined them.

Presently bugles began to sound all over the camp, and Hutton growled out, "There they go. That's the way the Maoris are informed of our movements."

Pierre and George had disappeared, and Hutton informed me they, being the best scouts in the corps, had left camp at dark, and that by this time they would be miles away along the road we were to travel.

We soon finished our cocoa, pannikins were slung on the belts, swags and belts were buckled on, carbines picked up, and we were ready for the word to fall in.

At two p.m. sharp the word was given, and we fell in without any bugle blowing or noise of any sort; every man knew his place in the ranks, so there was no roll-call, numbering off, or proving the company. Mr Roach silently walked along the line, then at a whispered word of command we formed fours and moved out of camp as silent as a lot of ghosts. Heavily loaded as we were, we pushed on fast along the rough trail, which in places led us through deep sand, very fatiguing to march over, no conversation or smoking being allowed, and as it was very dark we stumbled frequently.

Unaccustomed as I was to carrying a pack, I soon began to feel the discomfort of it, but of course said nothing. I must break myself into it, and till then must grin and bear it. Another thing that added to my discomfort was, I had only landed a few days previously from a long voyage, so was not in good fettle for foot slogging, and I was very glad when at daybreak a halt was called and we were given a quarter of an hour's spell.

The moment we halted Tim was alongside me. "Is it getting on all right ye are, Mr Dick?" quoth he. "Sure ye'll be finding the pack and pouches bothersome at first, but glory be to God ye'll soon get the hang of thim, and, Mr Dick, dear, yer feet are not blistered, are they? For sure it's the heels of yer socks I rubbed well with fat, I did, and a quartermaster's tot of rum I soaked into yer boots, I did, so plase God your feet will harden widout blistering, they will, and I filled both the flasks wid the crater, I did, so if it's a nip you are wanting, sor, sure it's convanient at all times, thank the Lord."

I had barely time to assure the good fellow I was all right when the word was again given to march, and we started at a slinging pace to complete the remainder of the journey to the new camp at Kumikumiti, where the general and the advanced party, destined to make the expedition, were.

As the daylight increased we were able to get a look at the country we were marching through. On our left lay the sea, the road running through sand-hills covered with stunted *manuka* bushes, fern and rough wiry grass, and on our right lay a chain of hills covered with bush, but the eyes only glanced over these, for in a moment they centred on the glorious mountain in front of us, that, rising in its lonely grandeur, formed a picture none who have ever seen are likely ever to forget. Of course I allude to Mount Egmont, the glory of the west coast, and very beautiful indeed it looked that morning, with the rising sun shining on its splendid peak, while its densely bushed slopes fell gracefully away from it, fold on fold in masses of light and dark green. But mark time, Dick, you can no more do justice to that lovely spectacle than you can fly.

"Pretty picture, Burke," said a voice alongside of me, and turning I saw Mr Roach was marching on my outer flank.

"Yes, sir," I answered; "a very lovely picture, and what a magnificent mountain!"

"Yes," he replied. "We shall know more of that mountain before we have finished with it, and perhaps many of us will remain on its shoulders and foot-hills forever, as they are going to be the battleground for a year or more, and many a weary day and night's march we'll have over them, untrodden as yet by foot of white man. Mr Burke, I want to give you a tip or two about bush lighting, and if that's your comrade alongside of you, it's as well that he should also listen. Well, the first thing you have to remember in bush fighting is, that you must learn to work independently, as every man has more or less to act on his own initiative, and as it is absolutely imperative to work in extended order you very often lose sight of the men on either flank of you and fancy you are left alone.

"This feeling in men untrained to this special sort of fighting has often caused a catastrophe, as it is the nature of Englishmen to close in and fight shoulder to shoulder, therefore men finding themselves, as they fancy, alone, close in, and if they do so they are easily surrounded and may be shot down like sheep in a pen by invisible enemies. I therefore want to impress on you fellows that, no matter what happens in the bush, remain in extended order, and wait for the bugle to close. I expect we shall be in action in a day or so, and we have one or two tough nuts to crack. Sir Trevor Chute has already shown himself to be far more enterprising than the late general, and the hostile natives have gathered great strength through the new religion."

He remained beside me, chatting in the free-and-easy colonial way, for some time, during which I gathered much information about the country and war, and was surprised to discover how utterly ignorant people in England were of all things colonial. He also told me he had come out to the country as an infant and had served all through the war. During that march I took a great fancy to my new officer, and we started a friendship that has lasted over forty years.

Well, mile after mile, through the ankle-deep sand we toiled on, at least I did, for the rest of the men, hardened as they were to marching and accustomed by constant practice to humping their swags, made light of the road and swung along as if they had nothing on their backs at all, while I could only grit my teeth and determine I would hang on to the last, but was very glad when an opening in the *manuka* bushes showed us a river on the other side of which stood a large, well-ordered camp. This river was the Manawapou, which we easily forded, and, pushing on through the camp, bivouacked in a clump of *manuka* just in rear of the outlying picket. Oh, but I was glad, very glad, when the order was given to form bivouac and I could slip off my pack and belts even for a minute, for, as soon as we had had a stretch, the latter had to be replaced and continually worn, day and night, nor were our carbines ever allowed to be out of reach of our hands.

Mr Roach picked the camp ground and pointed out the places where each four men were to make down their *mi-mis* (beds). This was done so that in case of an alarm a man had only to turn on his face, as each man slept with his carbine under his blanket, and be ready to repel an attack. It was wonderful to see the rapidity with which the bivouac was formed and the *mi-mis* made down.

"Here, Egan," quoth Hutton, "take this water-bag and fill it. Jack, you get the fern. Burke, out *tomahawk* and help me to clear the ground." In a moment we were all at work, Hutton and myself chopping down the tough *manuka* bushes and tearing up the roots so as to make a soft lying-down place.

Tim soon returned with the water and then helped Jack to bring in huge armfuls of dry fern, which they deposited on the ground we had by this time cleared, while the fire we had already lighted had burned down to red embers, in which we quickly placed our pannikins filled with water. These did not take long to boil, and when they did so, tea and sugar mixed, according to taste, were added, our haversacks opened and we piped to dinner.

"Gord," growled Jack, "I'd give some'ut for a tot this morning, but s'pose it's not to be come by."

"Don't be so sure of that," I chipped in, handing him my silver flask. "Here you are, drink hearty."

He took the flask in his huge discoloured hand, it lay in his palm like a new half-crown on a fire shovel, although it held a pint, and turned it over and over as if he had never seen such a thing before, then handed it back and growled out: "Yer don't think I'm agoin' to take yer last sup, and you a ruddy new chum and a blankity blank soft swell, do yer? 'Tain't likely, is it, mates?"

But I pacified the grousing old buccaneer and persuaded him there was enough to go all round, and as Smith and Buck had completed their mi-mi next to ours and joined us, we all had a wet, and I had won a corner in the ancient pirate's rugged old heart for ever.

Directly the meal was over, which, primitive as it was, I had thoroughly enjoyed, old Jack fetched more fern and made the *mi-mi* down scientifically. Tim brought another bagful of water and then insisted on taking my boots off, examined my feet carefully, and made me put on a dry pair of clean socks as a preventive to blisters, then, as the bed was finished, and, if properly prepared, there is no more comfortable bed in the world than New Zealand fern, we all lay down, booted and belted, to get some sleep, for, as old Jack truthfully remarked, it was as well to rest when we got the chance, as no man in the Rangers ever knew when the watches on deck might be doubled, and the watch below be a forgotten luxury.

When I woke up it was evening, and the first thing my eye rested upon was Pierre squatting in front of the fire, on which was a big pot and a bucket, while alongside of him squatted his fellow-gnome, sharpening a knife, the very sight of which was enough to make a man shudder. Now I was not surprised to see either Pierre or George, but where the deuce did the pot and bucket come from? The advent of these utensils puzzled me, so I strolled up to Pierre and wished him good-evening, at the same time remarking: "You are indeed fortunate to have found such a beautiful pot."

"But, *Monsieur*," he replied, "I have not found this pot. It is the same pot and bucket out of which *Monsieur* has already once dined."

"But, Pierre," I said, "I know you and George to be the most intrepid scouts, how therefore can you manage to carry your pot and bucket through the bush?"

"*Monsieur*," he replied with dignity, "a *Cordon bleu* should never part with his *batterie de cuisine*. True my hands are occupied while in the bush scouting, so I wear this magnificent pot as a helmet; my friend George likewise wears the bucket, so that, having no use for hats or caps, we have always the wherewithal to cook the dinner, and it affords much pleasure to cook dinners for gentlemen of taste such as *Monsieur* and Monsieur Hutton. As for the other savages, ah, bah!"

This I found on inquiry to be the truth. These men, hardened by incessant exposure, during the summer months carried no blankets, packs nor rations, neither did they wear boots nor hats, but lived on what they could find, and when they halted just threw themselves on the ground and slept like animals. This unnatural training had rendered them capable of covering immense distances, and going for marvellous long intervals without food, sleep or rest. Yet they were born marauders, could and did steal everything and anything that came in their way, and as it was Pierre's chief idiosyncrasy to cook dinners our mess lived well when other messes were mumbling tough, bad rations.

That night there was no need to use our homely rations, for Pierre's helmet contained a wonderful stew, and I noticed everyone abstained from asking any questions as to how or where he had obtained the ingredients. Pierre and his pard were scouts and they had chances which they never neglected to profit by.

At sunset we fell in for orders and guard mounting, and were told that we were to march before daylight next morning to attack a very strong *pah*, named Otapawa, which had been scouted that afternoon by Ensign McDonnell, the colonel's brother. The scouts had been discovered and had had to make a running fight of it, but, although heavily fired on, had escaped scathless. Colonel McDonnell, together with Colonel Butler and a strong party of the 57th Regiment, had also reached camp, and Major Von Tempsky with his Forest Rangers was also close by, so it was pretty certain we should have a warm day. As none of my party were wanted that night for duty, we over-hauled our arms carefully, lay down and slept the sleep of the just.

Chapter 5

My Baptism of Fire - Otapawa

We were roused from our slumbers at one a.m., but alas there was no cocoa for us, and the pannikin of tea served out in lieu did not supply an adequate substitute, but we had to make the best of it, and as we were ordered to leave our packs behind us I for one did not grumble. Our scouts had gone on two hours before, and when we had fallen in Colonel McDonnell approached and gave Mr Roach his instructions. The latter was standing in front of me, so close that I could not help overhearing the conversation.

"See here. Roach," said the colonel, "the general has determined to rush the *pah* with the bayonet, and I know the Maoris will stand. You will advance along the road in line till you reach the bush, but as both of your flanks are protected and the scouts are in front, you need only take ordinary precautions. When you reach the bush extend your men along the edge of it, your centre resting on the road, take cover and wait for further orders, but on no account try and precipitate an action. Von Tempsky will be on your left and will operate on the right of the *pah*, and the *Kupapas*" (friendly natives) "are working round to your right to hold the left and rear of the *pah* so as to prevent the Hau Haus' escape."

Then sinking his voice he murmured: "By gad, Roach, the general is inclined to rush things a bit too fast today. I fear he has not allowed the *Kupapas* time enough to get round, and if they don't the majority of the Hau Haus will escape. Now, time is up, move off your men, good luck to you."

I was centre man of the company that day, and as we moved in line I had the advantage of marching in the middle of the road, which was fairly smooth. The trail led inland and was well defined as it had originally been a road leading to a fine farm, but the farm had been burnt and a *pah* built there instead.

We marched steadily as we had only a short distance to go, and of course no smoking or talking was allowed, and also halted frequently, so that none of us were in any way fatigued.

Just as the daylight had begun to light up the top of Mount Egmont, and we had covered about five miles, a long wall of dense blackness appeared in front of us which we knew to be the bush, and we reached it when it was light enough to see a man thirty yards from us.

Previous to this we had received the whispered order: "From your centre, five paces extend." So we were advancing in skirmishing order, and when we were still some twenty yards away a whisper of "'Ware scout" ran along the line as a dim figure stepped from behind a tree and came towards us. This turned out to be George, who with the tea-bucket on his head looked, in the dim light, a blood-curdling apparition. As we had extended from the centre the road made a gap between the two half companies, and being centre man I was next the road on the right-hand side of it. Mr Roach's position while the company was in skirmishing order was also in rear of the centre, so that he was alongside me when George met us.

"Well, George," said he, "what have you got to tell me, and where is Pierre?"

It is no good my endeavouring to try and write what George called English. Talleyrand, I think it was, who said, "Speech was given us to conceal our thoughts with." Certainly Providence never expected George to convey his in the English tongue, so I will transpose his jargon so far as I understood him.

"The bush," said George, "is not a mile through, and is fairly an open one. The *pah* stands in a clearing about two hundred yards from the edge of the bush on this side, but not so far on the other. On this side, for more than one hundred yards the trees are cut down after you get out of the bush, but the stumps are left, though the trunks and the branches are all cleared away, as is also the brush-wood. The stumps, however, will give good cover. For a distance of eighty yards round the *pah* all the stumps are pulled out, and there is no cover for a rabbit. Over one hundred Maoris have come out of the *pah* and are waiting in skirmishing order in the bush half-a-mile in front of us. Pierre is still watching them."

Just as George had finished. Colonel McDonnell, riding on a pony, reached us, and having heard the report, said:

Roach, the general has determined to attack as soon as he arrives, although I am sure the *Kupapas* will not have had time to come up. I am going to prolong your line of skirmishers to the right with Northcroft's party, who will try and overlap the left of the *pah*. The Maoris who are in front of you will not offer a strenuous opposition, it's their dart to try and draw you on to attack the *pah*. You will therefore drive them back across the ground on which George says the tree-stumps are still standing. When you reach the far edge of it take cover and try to smother the Maoris' fire from the trench.

The 14th and 57th are to rush the place. When the storming party has passed through your skirmishers sit tight until you are sure they have entered the works. If you see they have done so with a good chance of success, double your men, as fast as you can, round the left of the *pah* to the rear of it, so as to try and cut off the enemy's escape. Should the attack fail, hold your ground till the last gasp and cover the stormers' retreat. I shall have the Rangers call blown and the advance when I wish you to move. Here comes the column. What a row they make!

He was turning to ride away when his eye caught mine as I lay at the foot of a tree. With a nod he said: "Well, Burke, so you are already going to see some fighting. By Jove, if we could all get our desires granted so easily, what a jolly world it would be!" and with a pleasant laugh and another nod he rode back to the head of the approaching column that was advancing with a jingle and row you could hear a mile off.

The gallant Tommies were supplied with abundance of mess-kit, which they carried loose in their haversacks, instead of the single pannikin we carried on our belts, and this kit made a big rattle, besides which there was the rumble and thump of the Armstrong guns.

I was meditating on this noise when our corps call, followed by the advance, rang out, and in a moment we were in motion. Faith, it is an anxious—I was almost writing a solemn—feeling that comes over a man when, for the first time, he advances through a silent bush, knowing full well that every step he takes brings him nearer to possible wounds or death.

It is not like an advance in the open, where as one of a mass of men marching shoulder to shoulder the numbers and continuity of comrades gives one a sense of security and companionship, nor is it like sitting on a good horse waiting for the trumpet call to charge, for then also you have fellowship of the very best. But to skirmish through a bush, even a fairly open one like this one was, is quite enough to give a new chum a fit of the jumps, for a sense of loneliness comes over a man, and the inclination to close in becomes intense. This, however, was not to be thought of, and I found myself boiling with excitement, keeping my line easily as I worked alongside the road, and instinctively moving forward with the others.

Occasionally I could see Tim, who was next me on my right, and sometimes three or four others as we moved rapidly from tree to tree; but still the dim light of the bush, its intense silence and the ghostly, gliding figures were conducive to serious thoughts, while once the bell-like note of the Tui bird made my heart jump into my throat.

Nearer and nearer we glided towards where, we knew, the line of savages was awaiting us, and Mr Roach had just taken up his position by me as I crouched forward to my next cover and knelt down on a mass of dry fern that lay against the root of the tree.

Holy Moses! I nearly jumped out of my skin, and could scarcely smother a yell of consternation as I felt the fern heave under me, and heard a voice whisper: "If *Monsieur* will have the goodness to remove his knee from off my back I will get up."

I at once rolled over, when Pierre wriggled, like a snake, backwards from under his cover, at the same time placing his finger on his lip and extracting from its hiding-place his cherished *batterie de cuisine*, which he placed carefully on his head.

"Not more than fifty paces in front," he hissed to Mr Roach, who nodded, and I slid on to the next tree, then to another.

I peered into the bush in front but could see nothing. Mr Roach again joined me and again nodded, and once more I crawled forward. I was under a low *punga* (tree fern), making for a big rata-tree some twelve feet farther on, when a rush of flame and smoke darted out of the bushes not twenty yards in front of me, and I heard the fern leaves just over my head torn to ribbons, while the howl of the slugs through the air and the crash of the volley sounded simultaneously.

One spring took me to the *rata*-tree, round the root of which I peered, but saw no meat to fire at. I glanced to my right. Tim was on his face taking aim, and I could hear the crack, crack of individual carbines answering the volley, which in another second was repeated.

A few moments before the bush had been as silent as a grave, but now it was an inferno; fire darted from the roots and from the sides of the tree-trunks in front of us, while yell after yell tore the disturbed air; and the smoke from the black powder either lay low on the ground or curled in spiral wreaths up through the trees.

Nor were our own men silent, as cheer after cheer answered our opponents' yells, and carbine shots rang out all along the line.

Up to this I had not fired a shot, as I had seen no one to fire at, and an intense longing to advance came over me, so spotting a tree some six or seven yards farther on I ran, crouched up and bending low to it, throwing myself down on my face at the foot of it just as a piece of bark the size of my hand was torn from its bole and the deflected bullet passed me with an angry whir that sounded extremely unhealthy.

My idea of advancing must have come to many others simultaneously, for I saw several men rush forward to fresh cover, and we were now in the enemy's smoke, that hung close to the ground, and had to breathe the saltpetre befouled atmosphere.

Another advance and we were already on the position the Maoris had originally occupied; it was therefore quite evident they were giving ground, besides which the distance between us had increased, as we could tell by the sound of the reports of their firelocks, for they still continued to fire heavily although only an occasional shot was fired by our men in reply.

"Forward!" shouted Mr Roach, and the word was echoed along the line, and we shoved ahead, although we still took cover.

Soon the trees grew thinner, and we increased our pace, until it became a running fight which rapidly turned into a pursuit, and as we cleared the bush we saw a long line of Maoris making off as fast as they could towards the *pah*.

At these we fired a volley and pressed on loading, in doing which I experienced much difficulty in getting hold of a cap and placing it on the nipple of my carbine. The clearing was, as George had described it first of all, some hundred and fifty yards of ground with the stumps still standing in it, and then perhaps sixty or seventy yards of ground scraped as bare as the palm of your hand.

Firing ceased entirely as we crouched and crawled from stump to stump, and we took advantage of this to correct our intervals and the dressing of the line, while word was passed from both ends of it that with the exception of a few chips being knocked off no one was hurt.

Presently we came to the end of the stumps, where, in accordance with orders, each man lay down behind the most suitable cover he could select and waited for what was to eventuate. And now while we are waiting there, let me try and give you an idea of the *pah*.

Less than eighty yards in front of us, and for about one hundred and twenty yards in length, stretched a fence, flanked at both ends with well-formed bastions that looked, from where we lay, flimsy to a degree, it being composed of straight sticks of unequal length, say from fourteen to twenty feet long, and about the thickness of an ordinary broomstick. These were not placed touching one another, nor stuck into the ground, but lashed two or three inches apart to stout cross-pieces and suspended a few inches above the ground, the cross-pieces in their turn being lashed to trunks of trees or stout posts sunk deep into the earth at intervals of from twenty to thirty feet. This fence, as I said, looked flimsy, but it was not, as the sticks it was composed of were *manuka* saplings, a wonderfully tough, hard wood, quite unbreakable, while should artillery be brought to bear on it, a shell would only break one stick and the fence be still impassable. Just in rear of this fence is a trench, dug deep enough for the defenders to stand in and fire under the fence along the level of the ground in front of it, and behind this trench is the earthwork and the heavy palisadings of the *pah* itself.

The inside of the *pah* is connected with the trench by underground passages, so that the defenders may take refuge inside, should the *pekerangi* (outer fence) be carried by assault, but the natives regard it as their principal bulwark, and usually try and bolt if it be destroyed.

It had been in assaulting the *pekerangi* at Rangiriri and Orakau that the British troops had suffered so heavily in the past, and it remained to be proved today whether the *pekerangi* at Otapawa was to be the scene of success or disaster to its gallant assailants.

"Burke," said Mr Roach, "look at the foot of that post to your right front; you will see the head of a beggar peeping over the edge of the trench. Try and put him out of mess."

Looking at the post indicated I could just see half a Maori's head peeping out, evidently trying to spot what was going on, so as directed I took a steady aim and fired.

"Good shot," ejaculated Mr Roach, "but I don't think you got him, for he ducked at the flash like a coot; anyhow you have given him a strong hint to lie low, as you knocked a splinter off the post just where his head had been. By Jove, here the column comes."

I looked back and saw the head of the column debouching from the

Major Kemp.
Meiha Kepa Te Rangi-Hiwinui.

bush, and when four companies had reached the open they wheeled left and right and left the road clear.

"Wonder what they are doing that for?" soliloquised Mr Roach, but he was soon answered, as over our heads shrieked an Armstrong shell, which passed over the palisading and plumped right into the middle of the *pah*, where it burst and kicked up any amount of row, smoke, dust and bobbery. This surprise packet was quickly followed by several others, and a burst of flame told us that some of the huts inside had caught fire. Still not a shell had touched the defences, and as all the defenders would be in the trenches it was not likely any of them would be hurt. Subsequently it was discovered that only one man had had his head blown off, which went to prove the inutility of bombarding Maori *pahs*.

Suddenly Mr Roach shouted out: "Look out, men, the stormers are advancing. Keep your eyes on the foot of the *pekerangi*, take good aim and make the Hau Haus keep their heads down."

Glancing round I saw the troops formed in two columns, and heard the advance blown, but then had to concentrate all my attention on our own business, which was to prevent the Maoris from raising their heads out of the trench so as to take aim at the stormers. This we did, as the moment an over-inquisitive Maori bobbed his head up to take a look or get a shot three or four bullets would splash around it as a hint to him to tuck in his twopenny.

Presently from the rear I heard the measured tramp of advancing columns, and soon the order was given for the leading companies to deploy, previous to making the rush. We were now very busy, as the heads were popping up a dozen at a time, but as yet not a shot had been fired nor a sound uttered from the *pah*.

The Maori individually is a vile shot and quite in-capable of hitting anything he aims at, at fifty yards from him, but when he flies a volley from a trench with the muzzle of his firelock only an inch or two from the ground that volley is a very deadly one indeed, especially as the object is never more than fifty or sixty yards away from him, sometimes closer. Again, most of them were armed with double-barrelled guns, so that they could pour in a second volley at a storming party more or less disorganised by the first discharge. A Maori moreover is a cool, brave warrior, who is brought up to regard courage in war as not only essential but also as the only quality by which he will be remembered and his name honoured by his descendants.

I was lying behind my stump, with my eye fixed on the foot of the *pekerangi*, when the trampling feet came up to me, and Colonel Butler, with his sword drawn, passed within a yard of me. Behind him came a party of pioneers carrying axes, while a few of them had charge of a long stout pole to the centre of which was attached a long chain. Close up behind these marched, in line, a company of the 57th, the old Diehards, whose fathers had fought at Albuera as these men had fought at Inkermann and through the Mutiny. Oh, but my heart did beat fast at the sight of their gallant Irish faces, for at that time hardly an Englishman was in the regiment, as they swung through our skirmishing line and advanced to the grim and silent *pah*. On their left marched another company in line, led by another field officer, Colonel Hassard, and in rear came two more companies in support.

My work was now over, as the moment the attacking party had passed me they masked the *pah* from my fore, though my comrades at the extreme flanks were still firing as fast as they could load so as to cover the advance of the forlorn hope.

Ye gods, how excited I was, an excitement equally shared by Tim, who howled out: "Oh, begorra, Mr Dick, mayn't we go wid thim, sor? Say the word, sor, and let's go."

But it would not do. Discipline in action above all things, and we had to remain spectators. The rear rank of the company had not cleared me more than five yards when a tremendous yell rose from the *pah* and the simultaneous roar of at least three hundred rifles and guns, while sheets of lead crashed into the advancing companies, or went whistling over our heads, which in a second strewed the ground with dead or wounded men writhing in their agony.

For a moment the advance was checked and the line wavered. Good God! surely these old Crimean warriors are not going to flinch! Not much. For like a trumpet-call out rang Colonel Butler's voice: "Steady, Diehards, go back, or come on. I am going on. Charge!"

Did those grizzled old veterans hesitate? Not for a breathing space. Their much-loved countryman and commander was in front of them, so was the enemy, and with a yell wilder even than the Maori warcries every man able to move rushed forward. At the double, howling for blood, the supporting companies rush past, a rush that the second smashing volley of the Maoris, although it sadly thinned their ranks, could not check, and in a few moments the whole storming party had launched itself against the *pekerangi*. Would they succeed, or was it to be another Rangiriri? Half mad, I jumped on to the stump that had sheltered me and glued my eyes on the proceedings. Mr Roach and all my comrades had done the same, and though the dense smoke hid most of the conflict from us, still we could hear the ferocious yells of the natives, the cheers and savage imprecations of our struggling men, while occasionally the ring of the axe-blades on the fence reached us, although deadened, as they well might be, by the continuous firing.

All of a sudden I saw the long pole that the pioneers had carried launched over the fence, and my mind pictured the line of men swaying on the chain. What's that? as a triumphant shout is raised, and with a rip, crash, down comes some fathoms of fence. Yell on yell goes up, the shots lessen, the bayonets flash, the smoke blows away, and we can see the wild Irish, cheering like mad, pour through the breach and into the trench.

Did we cheer? You bet we did, and many a smasher hat was slung skyward and many a laudatory cuss was cussed. "Who dare say a word agin the Quane's reglers now?" howled Tim. "God bless the boys from Ould Ireland. Wud to God I was wid thim."

But the *pah* is not taken yet, the earthworks and permanent fence still remain to be negotiated, and we see the Tommies swarm up the parapet, every inch of which we know to be flanked, and rush at the palisades, giving one another backs to surmount them.

With his sword hanging to his wrist by the sword-knot, a young officer is the first man up. He is on the top, grasps his weapon, steadies himself for a moment, preparatory to leaping in, but throws up his arms and falls backwards, dead. Now there are two men up, their rifles hanging to their right shoulders by the slings, one falls back but the other, regaining the hold of his rifle, jumps in. Before he can have reached the ground three or four more are over, then a dozen, then a swarm, and then, as Tim remarks, "they are lepping over like crickets," and the dust, smoke and yells float up to the bright blue sky.

But we are called to order, for Mr Roach shouts, "By the Lord, they've taken it. On your right, close. Double!" and we rush to our right, forming into a column of fours as we close in.

Small time is given to the men on the extreme left to join up, for in less than a minute our O.C. gives the word: "Come on, boys, double!" and we run as hard as we can round the left flank of the *pah*, and make for the rear of it, taking no notice of the shots fired at us.

As we come round to the rear we catch sight of a long line of natives evacuating the place and making for the bush, that on this side was less than one hundred and fifty yards from the work, and we race to try and cut them off. Many of them however are women and children, so we do not fire, but our attention is speedily distracted by a sharp fire opened on us from the bush.

Like a gate we swing round. "Extend and charge!" shouts Mr Roach, and we rush at the bush full pace, reaching it two men short, and at once take cover.

Here we have a pretty little skirmish, the natives falling back while we press on for over half-a-mile, when a loud yelling proclaimed they had been joined by another party. "By Jove, they are going to charge us. Form groups!" shouted Mr Roach, and on this order Hutton, Jack and Tim race up to me, Mr Roach also joining our group, all of whom have good cover.

"'Ord blast this carbine," growled Jack as a fresh yell rose from the natives. "'Eyer's this blankity blank powder-skin busted, and the ruddy bullet's jammed. 'Ord rot ye," he howled, throwing his useless weapon down and drawing his knife and revolver. "Come on, yer blankity blank swine, and let's get to handgrips with yer."

"Dick, see your pistol's clear for drawing; they are going to rush us," whispered Hutton, and we all stood wound up ready for anything.

All at once a dead silence fell that lasted for a few minutes.

"By God," growled Jack, "I believe the rotten swine have cleared," and he picked up his carbine, withdrew the cleaning rod and proceeded to knock out the jammed bullet. "Just like our ruddy luck, to be sold when yer think ye're in for a bit of sport," and the bad words rumbled out of the old buccaneer like the grumblings of a distant thunderstorm.

Jack was right in his surmises, for the cunning natives had pretended to charge us so as to gain time to retreat. We were still chewing the rag over our disappointment when from the rear our corps call sounded, followed by the retire, so Mr Roach, after ascertaining we were all present, reluctantly gave the orders to fall back on the main body, and my first fight in New Zealand was over.

We fell back slowly, as, although no one was badly wounded, still some of the boys had corners chipped off, and we parted with our friends the enemy with regret. We made for the *pah*, retiring over the same ground we had previously crossed, passing a strong picket of the 14th, who, with advanced sentries, outheld the edge of the bush. Our two men who had fallen in the open during our advance had already been picked up, and we were soon back at the bloodstained *pah* itself. I should have very much liked to have gone inside, but was unable to do so, as no sooner had we reached it than we received orders to return to camp and get ready for the next day.

We therefore marched round the flank of it, getting a sight of the breach in the *pekerangi*, and also passed a long line of our dead comrades, whose remains we saluted with shouldered arms; then passed the wounded, among whom the doctors, with rolled-up sleeves, saws and knives were busy; and then, striking the road, slung along it at a topping pace.

Missing Pierre and George I remarked the fact to Hutton.

"Oh, don't you worry yourself about them, Dick," quoth he; "and don't you fill yourself with mouldy biscuit. Pierre and George may not have been the first men into the *pah*, but I'll bet they got a start when the looting began, and I'll wager we shall have a good dinner tonight. As scouts, you see, they have a fairly free hand, come and go as they please."

Hutton prophesied truly, for when we reached camp there the two giddy marauders were, squatting over their pot like two disreputable he-witches, and as soon as we had cleansed our arms, refilled our pouches and washed ourselves, Pierre slung us up a dinner fit for a duke.

An issue of grog that night loosened our tongues, and the fight was fought over again many times, most asserting that if the general had waited for the *Kupapas* not one of the enemy would have escaped; the others, among whom were the most experienced men, declaring that had the Hau Haus not been aware their retreat was open they would not have stood, and we should only have captured an empty *pah*; but all hands expressed their confidence in the general, their admiration for the Tommies, and agreed that the capture of Otapawa had been a well-fought action.

Yes, the capture of Otapawa had been a gallantly fought action, though the escape of the bulk of the Hau Haus rendered the success almost, if not quite, nugatory, and we had lost heavily. Colonel Hassard had fallen, sword in hand. Lieutenant Swanson of the 14th was badly hurt, while the long lists of dead and wounded nearly equalled the number of dead Maoris found in the *pah*.

Again the natives were still in force in the bush, so the victory would not enable one settler to return to his homestead, nor would it permit any cessation of the campaign, for the Maoris had many *pahs* and only regarded these places as a suitable battle-ground, the loss of one of them not affecting their morale in the slightest degree.

I have stated that Colonel Hassard fell while leading on his men.

Well, the same night a yarn was started, how, or by whom, the Lord only knows, but it ran like wildfire through the camp, and was implicitly believed, that the man who picked him off was Kimball Bent, an infamous deserter from the 57th.

This yarn, like many another lie, such as the "Up Guards and at them" of the Iron Duke, the sinking of the *Revenge*, and numberless other picket-line stories, crept into history and is believed by the masses, but in this case the fact remains that the tribe who harboured K. Bent, Esq., were not present in the action at all, and it is therefore most improbable that the aforesaid scoundrel had any hand in the gallant officer's death.

Incredible as it may appear to home-staying people, there were soldiers capable not only of breaking their oaths and deserting their colours but also of joining the enemy, even when such an enemy should be bloodthirsty, fanatic savages reeking with the blood of slaughtered white women and children. Yet such was the case, and several of H.M. soldiers did so; among others this villain, Kimball Bent.

This man was an Irish American who had enlisted in the grand old Diehards, in which corps he worked in the armourer's shop, being, moreover, one of the best shots in the regiment. Having committed a crime he was tried by court-martial. Colonel Hassard being president, convicted and punished, whereupon he deserted and joined the Hau Haus.

Well the yarn went round that he had shot Colonel Hassard, and had he fallen into the hands of his countrymen his end would have been a very rough one, for anyhow he had fought against his own regiment, a crime never forgiven by a British Tommy; so it would have mattered but little whether he had shot Colonel Hassard or not. He was never taken prisoner, but for all that came to a bad end, as Nemesis was on his track, and his punishment was heavier even than it would have been had he fallen into the clutches of his enraged comrades.

On his desertion he had joined the Ngatiruanui tribe, whose fighting chief, Titokowaru, a fanatic and bloodthirsty Hau Hau, was the white man's bitterest enemy on the west coast, and who on more than one occasion defeated us. As Bent was an armourer, and very useful to the natives, he was at first well treated, and there is no doubt he fought against his flag and late comrades with such savage courage as to make a great reputation among the natives as a high-toned fighting man. But he must have always been in mortal dread of his ferocious protector, as he continually wrote letters, which he contrived to leave about so that they should fall into our hands, bewailing his fate and begging for mercy.

At last reports, circulated by some settlers among some friendly natives, that Bent had offered to shoot Titokowaru, provided he received pardon, came to that chief's ears, who at once decided to make away with him, especially as he had another deserter whom he employed converting hymn-books, prayer-books, and goody-goody literature into cartridges. He therefore gave orders for Bent to be killed, but the latter's suspicions had for a long time been aroused, and he never moved without his arms, while his great reputation as a fighting man also prevented a big rush of applicants for the job of executioner.

However, no man can keep awake forever, and although the miserable wretch knew men were ever on the watch to take him at a disadvantage, he at last fell asleep in his *whare* (hut). The man who spotted him crept into the hut and tried to *tomahawk* him, but through nervousness only wounded him.

At once the intrepid scoundrel grappled with his assailant, overthrew him, and would have killed him had not a number of others rushed up, who cut him to pieces, his remains being then used as *porkaroa* (long pig), a fit ending for a traitor to Queen and flag.

All the other deserters met the same or, in some instances, a far worse fate, and the one or two of them who escaped and gave themselves up were only too thankful to accept any punishment they received.

I must sue for pardon for this digression, but I have recounted it as one of the thousand of facts that took place in the New Zealand wars of which the good people in England are blissfully ignorant.

That night when orders were read out we were warned to hold ourselves in readiness to march at daybreak for the Waingangora River, and on being dismissed we hurriedly sought our *mi-mis*, so as to get as much sleep as possible, for we saw the days were approaching when, as old Jack remarked, it would be double watch on deck and no watch below.

CHAPTER 6

A Frolic With the Kupapas

The late general had not deemed it expedient for the regular troops to enter the bush—that is to say, to follow the Maoris into the trackless mountains that, covered with enormous forests, constituted the interior of the North Island and surrounded Mount Egmont, which a glance at the map will show the reader to be the centre of the big blunt promontory that juts out of the west coast of the North Island.

Sir Trevor Chute, however, saw the absolute necessity of carrying the war into the natives' own country and compelling them to sue for peace.

He had therefore determined to force his way due north through the bush to Taranaki and show the Hau Haus that the difficulties of their natural fortifications were not unsurmountable. By this march he would pass to the east of Mount Egmont and penetrate a country that had never previously, except on one occasion, by Father Pezant, been crossed by a European.

This was a big order, but I shall relate how it was carried through in due time. Suffice it for the present to say we left camp before daylight and saw the road all clear for the column, which joined us on the banks of the Waingangora during the afternoon.

Later on Mr Roach called me and said: "Burke, I have been ordered by Colonel McDonnell to accompany the chief, Te Kepa, who with one hundred and fifty *Kupapas*" (friendly natives) "leaves camp on a reconnoitring expedition. He has also instructed me to take four of my own company with me. Would you like to come? I will not disguise the fact that the work will be very hard and that we shall have a rough time, but we are sure to see some real Maori warfare, native against native."

Of course I jumped at the chance, and he despatched me to warn my three mates to draw four days' rations and be ready to start at sunset.

At the appointed time we joined our officer and proceeded over to the *Kupapas'* lines, where for the first time I saw the famous fighting chief, Te Kepa, who was even to rise to greater fame before the end of the war, and was undoubtedly one of the chief factors in terminating it.

Te Kepa was a Maori, able to grow a large beard, an appendage rare among natives. He was not above middle height, but had a tough, wiry look about him that denoted great strength and an ability to stand any amount of hardship. This chief was better known among the Europeans by the name of Major Kemp, and was highly respected by all ranks of society. His men were chiefly drawn from his own tribe, the Wanganui, and were about three hundred in number, big, brawny fellows, good fighting men, but an officer required the tact of Satan as well as an intimate knowledge of their manners and customs to handle them.

No sooner had we reached the *Kupapas* than night fell and Te Kepa indicated it was time to march, so we started along a rough track that led inland.

The object of the expedition was to reconnoitre a big *pah* called Ketemarae so as to ascertain if it were strongly held, as it was the intention of the general to move the column on there next day, and, in case we found it strongly occupied, Mr Roach was to find out the ways of approaching it.

Our scouts had gone on some time before we started, and we had hardly made a move when the heavens opened and it began to pour with rain, which it steadily continued to do all night long.

This made the march, which was over a bad bit of country, very miserable, as the track, if it could be called one, was intersected by many steep gullies, the sides of which were slippery to a degree, so that we were soon not only soaked through but became plastered with mud from top to toe.

We, however, must push on, and did so, arriving in the vicinity of Ketemarae just before dawn. Here we halted and shivered till the sun rose, when the clouds cleared away with every promise of a fine hot day; then as soon as we had made sure our firelocks would go off we extended and advanced towards the *pah*.

We had not moved more than a hundred yards when two of our scouts joined up, who reported that to the best of their belief the *pah* was unoccupied, which surmise Kepa very soon found out to be correct. It was a strong place, but we did not remain in it as Te Kepa deemed it better to take up a position in the bush. Here we rested, and I was glad of the spell, as it gave us the chance to dry our sopping clothes and get rid of some of the superfluous mud.

Mr Roach, Te Kepa and three or four chiefs now held a *runanga* (council), and I was much struck, although of course I could not understand a word uttered, by the elegant and forcible manner in which each chief gave his opinion, and how carefully and earnestly every man listened to the arguments of the others, notwithstanding, it was easily to be seen, there was a considerable difference in their ideas.

When each man had had his say Te Kepa gave his orders, to which they all acquiesced without demur.

As soon as the debate was over, Mr Roach kindly told me the purport of the meeting, which was to try and solve the problem why the *pah* had been abandoned without a show of resistance, as this was contrary to Maori war etiquette, which required at least one volley to be fired in honour of the *pah*, although it might not be deemed advisable to hold it to the bitter end.

The opinion therefore come to was that the *pah* was not abandoned, but that the Hau Haus, not expecting such unwonted activity on the general's part, had temporarily withdrawn for some purpose, probably to hold a *tangi* (wake) over the warriors killed at Otapawa, and were most likely to return that day to reoccupy the *pah*.

It was also decided that if they did so it would be as well to allow them to enter it, as then, our being on the spot, we could hive them, holding them inside till the arrival of the general, when not a man of them would escape. It was therefore Te Kepa's determination to lie dogo and try to entrap the Hau Haus in their own stockade.

The position we had taken up not being considered a satisfactory one to carry out this purpose, it was after much deliberation changed, and we made ourselves as comfortable as we could in the thick, damp bush, though as no fires were allowed, and the sun could not penetrate the dense foliage, the amount of comfort, thanks to the incessant drip from the trees, did not amount to a row of pins. Of course we had a patrol of scouts out on all sides of us, and on that day I began to take an interest and acquire a rudimentary knowledge of the fascinating, though highly dangerous, game.

The day dragged on and I was only able to get a few moments' broken sleep, as I was not yet sufficiently broken in to be able to sleep under such disadvantageous circumstances, and envied old Jack, who snored away on the soaked ground as if he had been on a feather bed. Nor can I truthfully say I enjoyed my dinner, composed as it was of sodden, rancid salt pork and a handful of wet mouldy biscuits.

As I said before, we had our scouts out, and we learned during the afternoon that the enemy had theirs out also, for one of our fellows came into camp with a gaping tomahawk wound in his shoulder, while his own weapon, and in fact his whole person, looked as if he had indulged in a bloodbath.

His yarn was short. He had met a Hau Hau scout face to face; neither of them could get away nor hide, so they turned to and had it out with *tomahawks*. Our man had the best of the argument, which he proved by producing not only the *tupara* (double-barrelled gun) and tomahawk of his opponent as a *spolia opima*, but also certain portions of the enemy himself, so that no doubt could exist in the most sceptical of his encounter or victory. He received great *kudos*, and submitted, without a tremor or complaint, to having the gap in his shoulder sewn up in the roughest possible manner. Nor did it seem to interfere with his appetite, as, noticing his eyes glued on my mass of putrid pork, I handed it to him, and he devoured it with a gusto I quite envied.

This little *contretemps* showed Te Kepa that the Hau Haus must be well aware of our presence, though perhaps not of our exact locality, and as he became extremely desirous of ascertaining theirs more scouts were detached for that purpose.

The trap was no longer to be thought of, as the enemy were far too astute to allow themselves to be shut in, especially as they must now be fully aware of the advance of the column, which in fact shortly arrived, heralded, as usual, by Pierre and George.

These two beauties we found out afterwards had smelt out our lurking-place early in the day, but, not being able to decide whether we were friends or enemies, had sat tight and waited for the main body to close up. They had, however, managed to get into the *pah* before the soldiers, where they discovered a hidden stock of potatoes, with which they joined us, so we had a feed of spuds that night.

As Colonel McDonnell still wished Mr Roach to remain with the *Kupapas* we camped with them. Te Kepa receiving orders to advance next morning and reconnoitre the country for another day's march ahead, his remaining men also joining us made up our party to over three hundred men.

We had now every prospect of a fight, as our scouts came in with information that large numbers of the Hau Haus were in our vicinity though they were so skilfully protected by their scouts it was impossible to locate them to a certainty, but still they were convinced they were mighty adjacent and hungry for a fight.

Te Kepa therefore took every precaution, each of which I noted carefully, Mr Roach being kind enough to explain their *raison d'être*. He also told the chief that I was not only a well-born *rangitera* (gentleman), the descendant of war chiefs, but was in my humble position so as to acquire the wisdom and knowledge of war, whereupon Te Kepa was good enough to take great interest in me, presented me to his principal warriors, and instructed his men to look after me as I was his guest.

This Mr Roach informed me with a laugh was better than taking out a life policy, as the natives hold themselves responsible for the safety of their guests, so they would take the greatest care of me, and that, even should I unhappily come to grief, my remains would be carried off at any cost, for to allow a guest to be turned into long pig would be the greatest disgrace that could befall the tribe.

Long before daylight next morning we were on the move, and it was simply wonderful how we slipped through the silent bush without a sound. I could no more have walked through that pitchy darkness under the trees and through the tangled shrubs by myself, much less have moved in a straight line, than I could have flown, but in accordance with Te Kepa's orders I was attended by four huge savages, one of whom led each of us, the one attending to me sometimes even placing my feet so as to prevent my tripping over obstacles I could not see.

After a sharp march which, for all I knew, we might have made alone, my attendant suddenly halted, pulling me down behind a big tree-root. What made him do so I knew not. I had not heard so much as a twig snap, not a whisper had passed along the line of invisible skirmishers, and why he had come to such a dead stop I could not divine, except it was some subtle instinct that warned him there was danger ahead, or that by some extraordinary system of transmission of thought his chief could convey his wishes to his men. Whatever the reason may have been, there we stuck until a dim twilight penetrated to our lurking-place, when I indistinctly saw we were close to the edge of the bush, which here ran out into an open glade some one hundred and fifty yards across, on the far side of which it began again.

All of a sudden, without a word of orders, my mentor rose, beckoning me to do the same, and we emerged from the bush simultaneously with the rest of the party, when in a moment the glade that had been deserted before was filled with a long line of men clothed in belts, pouches and a few feathers, devil a rag else, in extended order, looking, as Egan subsequently remarked, "like a regimint on bathing parade," but it showed how wonderfully the natives had kept their line and how exact pre-given orders or instinct had guided them.

That Te Kepa must have gained news as to the whereabouts of the Hau Haus is to me now evident, as, taking advantage of a slight ground mist, he moved us rapidly across the open, nor did anyone seem surprised when we were greeted by a tremendous volley which, strange enough to say, hurled over our heads without touching fur or feather.

Immediately our men let out a yell of derision, poured in their answering volley, and without a pause charged through the mist and smoke straight at their concealed enemies.

We reached the bush on the run and pressed forward, our men still being careful to take cover but yet advancing so rapidly that the enemy must needs give ground or stand up to a hand-to-hand fight, which, as we outnumbered them, was not to be thought of, so that after a short, sharp conflict, in which much powder was burned and an immense amount of breath expended in yelling, the Hau Haus retired at the run, leaving behind them three dead bodies, this in itself being an acknowledgement of defeat, as a Maori will run very great risks rather than allow a wounded or dead tribesman to fall into an opponent's hands. We had begun our day well but there was still plenty of work in front of us, and Te Kepa was not the man to waste time, so, dividing his men into two parties, he despatched one of them to try and cut off the retreating enemy, and with the other, among whom were our party, followed on the track of the flying Hau Haus.

They had not however, flown far, for before long we came to the remains of an old deserted *pah* in which they had taken post, and as we advanced opened on us with a heavy fire, at the same time yelling defiance, and challenging us to assault them.

To this our men replied with a step or two of the war-dance, a couple of volleys and a baldheaded rush that sent the rotten old palisading galley west, and into the ancient works we poured.

The Hau Haus fought well, but it was our boys' day out and they would not be denied but drove them helter-skelter out of the place, forcing them to abandon five more dead bodies.

Without a pause we followed on in full pursuit, but they had had enough of it, so broke and bolted all over the country. This, however, did not check Te Kepa, for, selecting the spoor of the biggest mob, we pushed on, but failed to bring them again to action.

During this pursuit our detached party joined up, who reported, producing evidence, that they had killed two more Hau Haus, and Te Kepa, after a short halt, decided to move on and attack, or at all events reconnoitre a large *pah* called Mawhitiwhiti.

This was decidedly a piece of presumption on our part, but the *Kupapas* were full of *wakahihi* (fighting spirit), profoundly believing it to be their lucky day. Up to now they had not a single man wounded, and at Te Kepa's orders would have attacked Old Nick himself.

Moving on, therefore, as jovial as a party of schoolboys out bird's-nesting, although not a precaution was relaxed, you bet Te Kepa watched that we came in sight of the place strong enough to make an army pause, and boldly advanced towards it, our men all game for a rush whenever they received the order. But it was not to be, for although the enemy fired volley after volley at us while we were at a long range, and yelled like blazes, yet the moment we started to close in and charge they evacuated the place and fell back to another position even stronger.

This was not playing the game, so our men got vexed, and we went after them hot-toe, attempting to surround the new *pah* in which they had taken post, so as to cut off their retreat should they be so inconsiderate as to try any more runaway tactics, but unfortunately we could only surround them on three sides.

The Hau Haus had also received strong reinforcements, so that both Mr Roach and Te Kepa deemed it advisable to send back to camp for assistance, which was done, but not wishing to waste time we set about the job ourselves, and that to some purpose, for, after both sides had fired and yelled as hard as they could for over ten minutes, word was passed that the Hau Haus were escaping down a steep, densely bushed gully on the side we had been unable to occupy.

Immediately a general rush was ordered and we charged the place at top speed, swarming over the defences like monkeys and driving out the last of the enemy, who fled precipitately, leaving behind them seven more bodies, together with a large number of fine fat pigs and an immense amount of potatoes. They had indeed left us their breakfasts, for the *hangis* (underground ovens) were full of deliciously cooked pork and potatoes, on which we regaled ourselves sumptuously.

The *Kupapas* now considered they had done enough work for

their day's pay and declined to follow on the flying enemy, but after a huge repast they indulged in a short war-dance and prepared to fall back on the camp.

First of all everything we could not take away with us was destroyed, and the dead bodies mutilated, in accordance with Maori customs, for although our men were not openly acknowledged cannibals, yet all the senior men had been, while the juniors were not a generation removed from the practice, so that mutilation of the dead and many other uncanny customs were still adhered to.

Then the *pah* itself was insulted and dismantled and everything inflammable burnt, after which we fell back, treating Mawhitiwhiti and the other places in the same way.

I was now to learn another lesson, for Te Kepa, notwithstanding our success, would not abate one jot of his precautions.

Our men were loaded with loot, they could please themselves whether they carried it or not, but they must do their duty, and it was well such was the case, for presently, when we were in thick bush, one of our rear scouts (yes, my would-be military reader, it is just as requisite in irregular warfare to scout to your rear as well as to your front, and don't you forget it) ran in with the information that the Hau Haus, furious and indignant with the treatment we had served out to them, were in full pursuit, determined to exact *utu* (payment or revenge) for our manifold misdeeds.

On hearing this news Te Kepa caused us to rapidly push on till we came to a long clearing in the bush, at the camp side of which he ordered two hundred of us to lie down and take cover, thus forming an ambuscade. The remaining men, after they had thrown down their plunder, he led back towards the advancing Hau Haus. These he quickly encountered and engaged, but after an exchange of shots he and his men, all at once simulating panic, turned tail and bolted, closely pursued by the now exulting enemy.

Away our men rushed in headlong flight, crossing the clearing and breaking through our hidden line like frightened deer, and after them rushed the triumphant Hau Haus, every man of whom was hungry for slaughter, and faith they got it, but not in the way they wished; for as they put on a spurt to cross the clearing they were met half way by a smashing volley, behind which came our charging line, which so astonished them that they turned about and sprinted all they knew to safer localities.

Te Kepa would not allow us to pursue, no doubt having good and sufficient reasons for not doing so. We therefore again humped each man his plunder—mine was a well-grown, succulent young pig—and continued our journey back to camp, where, loaded with good things, we white men rejoined our own company, who received us with open arms, while the *Kupapas* spent the evening in feasting, singing songs of triumph and dancing war-dances in honour of their own merit.

True, they had done well, for they had taken and burnt five *pahs*, killed a lot of the enemy, looted and destroyed large quantities of food, and done all this without having one single man wounded.

Individually, I was very satisfied. I was gathering lots of valuable information, could now hump my swag with but little discomfort, and had thoroughly satisfied myself that, no matter how rough and hard the life and work were going to be, I had go enough in me to tackle anything I might be called on to perform. So that I ate my dinner with gusto, sang a song when called upon to do so at the camp fire, and slept as soundly on my fern bed as an innocent child in its cradle.

CHAPTER 7

Bushwhacking

It was on the day following Te Kepa's successful reconnaissance that the troops destined to form the party for the general's projected march through the bush to Taranaki were warned to hold themselves in readiness to start the next morning, and I was delighted when Mr Roach informed us that our mess had been included in the party of forty Rangers that had been selected as one of the units of the column, which was to be composed of three companies of the 14th Regiment, eighty *Kupapas* and our forty Rangers.

There was a considerable diversity of opinion among our men as to the advisability of this movement, all the old hands being unanimous that it would be a bitter hard undertaking, especially as we were to be accompanied by a long string of pack-horses, without which it is impossible for regular troops to move. These would impede our progress and necessitate much arduous fatigue in the way of road-chopping and getting them across the deep gullies, creeks and watercourses that everyone knew ran from the mountain down between its shoulders and spurs, over which our route must lie.

Every yard of the journey ran through dense bush, and although Father Pezant had, with assistance of Maori guides, walked the distance in two days, yet that was a very different pair of shoes to conveying a long string of pack-horses, heavily laden, over the same ground.

Then again, would there be any fighting? Our sages thought not. The natives themselves rarely used the route. Father Pezant declared the country to be quite deserted, and the *Kupapas* also asserted that that part of the district had never been inhabited, although none of them were conversant with the locality.

We had therefore the pleasing prospect before us of slogging hard work without any fun to enliven it, and for the first time I heard colonial irregulars chew the rag (grumble).

Now there are two qualities of grumblers. One is the open grumbler who grouses because it is his nature to do so and he can't help himself, yet when it comes to the point does his duty and performs his work better, perhaps, than a more complacent man. Among such may be reckoned most old sailors and soldiers. The others are the stealthy grumbling dogs who incite young soldiers to mutiny, taking jolly good care to keep in the background, out of trouble, themselves. These are dangerous scoundrels who ought to be flogged and hung without mercy; no close season should be allowed for such vermin.

Of the first lot mentioned was old Jack, a typical grousing old shell-back whose whole existence, if you believed him, was a grievance. Still he was always one of the first to fall in for any extra work or hardship the corps might be called on to face, and would volunteer for any nasty job, grumbling while he performed it, as if he were a victim to bitter injustice, and had been forced against his will and out of his turn to undertake it. In fact, as Tim put it, "Sure ould Jack wud grumble if he got a first-class passage to heaven, wid free drinks at all the stoppin' places. But maybe he'd be right, seeing all his friends and acquaintances are in the other place, and maybe the ould boy wud fancy he'd been put in the wrong train agin his own inclinations."

Of the second class of grumblers was Mete Kingi Te Anaua, a chief of the highest rank among the *Kupapas*. It must be remembered that Te Kepa, although the head fighting chief, was by no means the paramount chief of his tribe, nor was he even, by birth, of first-class importance, for although of aristocratic descent he owed his position to election as the most highly intellectual fighting man among the Wanganui. Of this there was no doubt, and on the war-path his word was law, not to be quibbled at nor questioned, but in camp the men were very prone to be led away by the arguments emanating from such a high-born source as the Right *Dis*honourable Mete Kingi, who did everything in his power to render the utility of his tribe nugatory. Also it must not be supposed the *Kupapas* were fighting on our side on account of any love they bore the white man, far from it, the reason they fought being the intense hatred they entertained against the hostile tribes, their old-time enemies, who were in arms against us and also against the crazy, fanatical religion that had turned these tribes from being whitewashed Christians into howling bloodthirsty murderers.

Massa Mete Kingi hated the white man, and although self-preservation prevented him from open rebellion, still he wasted no opportunity of thwarting and hampering their movements.

This projected march of the general was of course far too good a chance for Mete to let slide, so he made his game accordingly, and played it for all he was worth.

Colonel McDonnell, however, had foreseen the probability of him raising trouble. He had been absent from camp for two days, but returned that night at twelve p.m., bringing with him Dr Featherstone, an old settler in whom the Maoris had great confidence.

These two gentlemen on their arrival went to the *Kupapas'* line, where they quickly ascertained that these Johnnies, prompted by Mete Kingi, had made up their minds not to start; in fact they announced their determination to at once return home.

A general *runanga* (meeting) was promptly assembled, to which Mr Roach, knowing my anxiety to hear and see everything appertaining to native customs, kindly called me.

It was indeed a weird sight, the Maoris squatting in a semicircle, with their chins on their knees, round three sides of the fire, the gap between the ends of their formation being occupied by the colonel, Dr Featherstone and Te Kepa, while a few of the principal chiefs squatted behind them.

On my arrival I at once took post in rear of the Colonel, and was immediately struck by the dogged, ugly look on the faces of the contumacious natives, whose eyes, lit up by the firelight, looked ferocious to the last degree, and I could scarcely believe that these were the same men who had joined so joyously in battle only two days before; but alas, it was so.

Colonel McDonnell and Dr Featherstone harangued them. It was useless; threats and entreaties were in vain. They squatted there, a sulky, ugly mob, one and all declaring they would not march, they would return home; let the white men go by themselves.

This refusal on their part was a very serious matter, as without their knowledge and bush-craft the expedition must end in a fiasco. Mete knew this and chortled in his joy. But Mete Kingi had on this occasion, as on many another, overlooked a very powerful factor, for among the crowd was a relative of his own and a much bigger pot, as, squatting quietly behind the colonel, was Hori Kingi Te Anaua, who was the head chief of the Wanganui.

This ancient-time warrior was a very old man, now long past war, but he had been a mighty fighting man before the Lord, and one who, not so many years back, had been regarded not only by his tribe but by all the surrounding tribes as quite the cock of the walk, while even now the glamour of his early deeds enveloped him with a halo, and he was looked upon by the Wanganui as more than human. This old nobleman was of such a great age that he rarely interfered with tribal business, and was occasionally overlooked by young and pushing upstarts such as Mete, but he was there, having accompanied the *Taua*, not in his official capacity but rather as a critic, so that he might form opinions of modern warfare and contrast them with old-time methods, also that he might once more steep his senses in the odour of battle.

He had moreover been a firm friend and protector of the white man from the early days, besides which he was a great personal friend of Dr Featherstone, who now drew him aside and besought his help.

At the moment they rejoined the meeting the *Kupapas* had again vociferated that they would go home, and there were indications of a rough house, but the instant the grand old warrior raised his still enormous bulk from the ground the silence of death fell on the crowd. For a minute he glared round on the squatting throng, every man of whom, fearing to meet his indignant eye, held his head down, then with a stamp of his foot he spake.

"Listen, ye men of the Wanganui, you who have refused to march with the *pakeha*" (white man). "It is well, go home; but I, Hori Kingi, will go with them, even though I go alone. It shall not be said that I deserted them; but I warn you all that if you desert me I will never again return to Wanganui. Henceforth the white men shall be my only friends, and my bones shall rest in Taranaki."

Such an awful threat had never been uttered before. Why, the very thought that their great hero's bones might be buried in the land of their hated enemies was dreadful. Not one of them dare even think of such a diabolical catastrophe. It was worse than blasphemy, and it took some minutes before the frightful idea could percolate into their understandings. There they squatted, open-mouthed and with goggling eyes, until the same thought seemed to flash simultaneously into their dazed brains, when they all raised their voices to let go the piteous howl: "We go, father, we go," and Mete Kingi was sold again.

Next morning the column moved out of camp, eighty picked *Kupapas* leading with an air of jollity about them as if the row of the previous night had been forgotten and forgiven, though I noticed that old Hori Kingi marched with Mr Roach as if he were still a little sore over his tribe's misbehaviour.

In rear of the *Kupapas* we marched; then a long line of pack-horses, while three companies of the 14th Regiment brought up the rear. The general having heard that Father Pezant had completed the journey in two days had reckoned on our getting through in three, and therefore three days' cooked rations had been issued to all hands.

The Maoris, however, the most improvident men in the world, especially as in this case they had not intended to come, had eaten most of theirs before we started, and then, in fear of Hori, had said nothing about it.

Anyway we were off. For the first few miles the track, although a very rough one, was well defined, and we pushed on, but just before noon we came to a very deep and narrow gully. The Maoris crossed this, so did we, but when it came to the pack-horses' turn the column came to a dead stop. They certainly could not get down, and, supposing they were chucked over the edge and survived, it was equally certain they could not get out at the other side, so it was a case of getting the picks and spades off them and making one slanting road down and another up. The Tommies tackled this job, but it was very slow work, and we lost a lot of time. At last all hands and the pack-horses were got across, and we proceeded, but had to camp, having covered a far shorter distance than the general had expected we should have done.

Next morning we again made an early start, but were brought up by more gullies, some of which we crossed as we had the first one, others we had to bridge in a way that I shall presently describe.

The Maoris up to now had been very useful, though they did not care for the work, still, thanks to Hori's presence, they had given no trouble, yet early in the day they had allowed the two Hau Hau prisoners we had as guides to escape.

These two fellows fled along the track, followed of course by a party of *Kupapas* who were at once put into good humour by the chance of spilling a little blood. The prisoners in their flight came across a party of seven Hau Haus, who, unaware of our proximity, were quietly enjoying their breakfast, and shouted to them to escape, but the Hau Haus, unable to realise that the white man had penetrated so far into their fastnesses, refused to budge and continued their meal. The fugitives, declining to tarry, escaped, but the *alfresco* repast was rudely interrupted by the *Kupapas*, who surprised the picnicking party, killing four men and capturing a girl.

This little interlude of blood somewhat cheered up the *Kupapas*, but the guides were gone, and the track that had been getting less distinct now entirely disappeared.

Other misfortunes now overtook us. The natives, having eaten most of their rations previous to starting, now demanded food, and caused trouble, still remaining sulky even when a day's rations were issued to them from the slender stock carried on the pack-horses, and then, to make us thoroughly cheerful, floods of water (you could not call it rain) began to fall, and continued to do so day and night without the slightest intermission.

We were in a hole. Guides gone, road lost, bush thick, a deluge falling, rations short, and many a man would have turned back, but the general, good man, was made of the right sort of stuff, and "go on" was the order.

"What," said he, "the road lost, is it? Then chop one," and our crowd, although they might grumble like hell, started in to give a lead.

The New Zealand bush is a stiff one to tackle, composed as it is of enormous trees growing close together and a dense undergrowth of evergreens and ferns. From the trees descend huge vines, some of them many inches in circumference, either hanging straight up and down, or draped in graceful festoons from tree to tree, both the trunks and branches of the latter being covered with patches of orchids and other parasites. Here and there amid the undergrowth springs up an elegant *punga* (tree fern), a broad leaf or a *koninonino* (fuchsia tree), while an occasional patch of lawyers, a thorny bush whose name is most appropriate, for if you once get into its clutches you can only get out pretty nearly naked, lies in wait for the unwary, these and many more being bound together into an impenetrable tangle by the ever-present souple jack and ground vine.

After reading the above very short and very imperfect description you will be able to understand that a New Zealand bush is not an easy one to cut a road through, even for pack-horses, especially when, as in this case, the line you wish to follow led you across the shoulders and spurs of a huge mountain which were furrowed by innumerable deep gullies, watercourses, and rivers.

The New Zealand bush is a very beautiful one, yet a very silent and lonely one; not a sound is to be heard in it, with the exception of the doleful dirge of the wind among the tree-tops, the coo of pigeons, the occasional *ka, ka* of the New Zealand parrot, or the rarer, bell-like note of the Tui bird.

However, such as it was, we had to chop our way, for over forty miles, through it, so with plenty of bad language, but heaps of determination, we buckled to and tackled the job.

Te Kepa took the lead with his men, *tomahawk* in hand, and chopped away the vines; our men followed closely after, who cut away the under-growth and cleared a road sufficiently wide enough for the pack-horses following behind us, these taking every opportunity of tumbling down, entangling themselves among the vines, rubbing off their loads and generally making themselves a darned nuisance. Of course we had to have the scouts out on all sides of us, and likewise strong covering parties, as it would have been far too good a chance for the Hau Hau to have missed, not to have taken advantage of us as we floundered along that miserable path. They did not do so; why, we never heard, but I fancy myself it was on account of the unceasing downpour of cold rain, which was certainly quite excuse enough to keep any self-respecting savage in his happy home.

All this work fell very heavy on us, as the regulars were of but little use in the bush, either as axemen or coverers, but we should have made light of that had it not been for the rain, that not only drenched us but turned the soft loamy bush soil into liquid mud, in which we sank nearly to the knee, and forced us to corduroy the path so as to enable the wretched pack-horses to get any footing, while men, horses, packs, arms and everything soon became plastered and caked with mud.

Presently we came to a gully with perpendicular rocky banks, in the bed of which, swollen by the rain, raged a torrent. Fortunately it was not a very wide one, not more than from thirty to thirty-five feet, but it was quite sixty feet in depth. It was impossible to make roads up and down this fellow; our old picks and spades, probably used by Wellington's men in the Peninsular War, were no use here, and we had neither drills nor explosives. No, it must be bridged; and I wondered how this was to be done. Now we had in our heterogeneous corps several old and skilled bushmen (men who live and work in the bush), the two boss men of whom were Nova Scotians, and what these two men. Brothers Jake and Vic M'Farlane, did not know about how to handle timber was not worth learning.

These two men now pushed in front and examined carefully the enormous trees that grew close to the edge of the ravine, out of which they selected two that grew close together, and then called for six men who they knew to be the most skilful axemen, to whom Jake gave instructions, turning at the same time a deaf ear to an Engineer officer who advanced to propound some learned theories, but who fell back, choked off by the good-humoured though scarcely respectful admonition: "Here, be a good boy, Johnny; now run away and play nicely by yourself," tendered him by the Blue-nose giant.

Then at the word, "Now get to it, boys!" the eight men sprang at the two trees like tigers.

It was simply marvellous to see these men work, every blow falling, notwithstanding the rain and slippery axe helves, just where it was aimed; while the men, although they put their whole souls into the job, did not waste an ounce of strength. First of all a large and deep scarf was opened in the trunks of the trees on the ravine side, two men working one opposite the other, each blow so timed to succeed the other as to make huge chips fly in all directions. At the same time the other two men were attacking the far side, though the depth of the wound on the creek side was kept well in advance of the other.

After some time both trees emitted deep groans, which drew a cheer from the bystanders though the axemen still continued to ply their weapons with unabated vigour; and the trees, as if in anguish, groaned and groaned again and again. Suddenly Jake yelled, "Spell-o," when every axe ceased, and after a few words with his brother he approached the general, who, with most of the officers, was watching the proceedings.

"Say, Boss," drawled the unsophisticated bush-man to the astonished old gentleman, "you and these 'ere galoots had better git, or I guess you'll be fouled by some of them darned monkey ropes, an' I kalkelate they'll bring down a heap of branches and dead wood."

"Ah," quoth the general, "I presume you think we may be in some danger in remaining here when the trees fall."

"You bet. Boss; you've struck it in once," replied the unabashed Blue-nose, who promptly returned to his mates.

"Your men," said the general, turning to Mr Roach, "do not seem to be very conversant with military etiquette."

"No, sir," replied Mr Roach; "some of them are a very rough lot, but I assure you, sir, no disrespect nor offence was meant."

"Quite so," returned the general, "and no offence is taken, but by gad we will take his advice and fall back a bit. That fellow knows his work."

"You bet. Boss," drawled one of the staff, and they all fell back, laughing.

Jake and his pard had gone back alone to their respective trees.

"Are you ready, Vic?" yelled Jake. "Let her go." And the two axes fell like one in a succession of lightning blows. "She is coming, mate," yells Jake.

"Mine too," gasps his brother, as rending cracks and portentous groans burst from the now shivering and swaying trees and rend the air.

"Stand clear, mate," yell both men as the now rocking trees make a half turn inwards on their bases, and then, bending gracefully over, as if bowing to their Creator, their sky-kissed tops sink lower and lower, until with a rending crash that echoes through the bush like thunder the two mighty monarchs of the forest fall side by side across the ravine, while ripping, tearing crashes announce the fact that the tough vines attached to them are tearing off huge limbs from other trees and, together with the concussion, bringing down a shower of dead wood.

How the two axemen escaped was to me a mystery. I dearly love a fine tree, and, although by no means a religious man, always seem to fancy they are the property of the Almighty and that it is an act of sacrilege to chop one down—this idea still sticking to me after years of bush life.

No such opinions, however, were entertained by the godless Bluenoses, who no sooner had the trees crashed down than they leapt on to table-topped stumps, jumped into the air, cracking their heels together, flapping their arms up and down and crowing like cocks.

Rude as was their ebullition of delight, their wonderful skill was manifest, for the two mighty trunks lay across the gully, side touching side, and the framework of the bridge was an accomplished fact.

"Guess you lobsters may be trusted to fill up that crack," remarked Jake to a disgusted-looking colour-sergeant of the regulars. "Come on, boys, let's lop and top t'other side," and he ran across the bole of one of the trees as if it had been a coach road.

There was plenty of hard work on the other side, so while the Tommies made a platform for the horses to cross by filling up the interval between the boles with brushwood, fern and mud, we set to to clear away the abatis of huge broken branches so as to allow them to get off the bridge when over.

Faith, I found it bitter hard work, it being my first attempt at manual labour, as it was also my first attempt to use axe or *tomahawk*, and it was heartbreaking to compare my clumsy efforts with those of my experienced comrades. Moreover, although blessed with great muscular strength, I quickly found out that without skill it was of but little use to me, as my hands became dreadfully blistered and very painful, though I still continued slogging away for all I was worth.

At last we were able to start getting the horses across, and a rotten job we had to manage the terrified animals, very many of whom had never seen a bridge in their lives before. Nevertheless by blindfolding them and making a staid, quiet old brute give them a lead we managed to get all over except four, who, plunging midway, fell off the rough structure, loads and all, into the now raging torrent, where they were at once swept away, and of course, as rations were scarce, all these loads were biscuits.

By the time we had got them over it was time to bivouac, so we set about the hopeless task of trying to make ourselves comfortable. Our mess, first of all, cut a lot of thick poles, which we placed side by side on the poached, sodden ground, then covered these with small branches of undergrowth and piled on the top a two-foot thickness of wet fern.

While we were doing this Pierre and George had lighted a fire. What, a fire in that pitiless down-pour? Yes, gentlemen, a fire. First of all Pierre sought out an old *miri* log, perhaps the hardest wood in the world, so hard it is almost impossible to cross-cut it, but it will split like matchwood and is as inflammable as pitch. Off this log Pierre split very many splinters and pieces, George in the meantime raising a platform of poles some half-foot above the mud. Under cover of his pot Pierre collected some of the inside bark of a tree, and, producing an oily piece of tow used for cleaning his carbine, under cover of George's bucket, held inverted like an umbrella, a fire is lit on the platform, fed steadily for a time with *miri* splinters, until it gains heat and power, when larger pieces are added, until eventually the fire gains sufficient heat to withstand the rain for the bucket to be boiled and tea made, for a pannikin of which we were very thankful.

As soon as our fire was in full swing others were lit from it, but the incessant rain at last got the best of them and they dwindled away, leaving the camp in inky darkness.

I was on guard that night and did my first sentry go, passing two hours crouching in the mud, peering into the black darkness, and listening to the rush of the rain and the chattering of my own teeth. I was but little better off when relieved, as all I could do was to throw myself down on a heap of soaked fern and cover myself with my drenched blanket.

Worn out by the unaccustomed labour, aching in every limb of my body and suffering great pain from my hands, I got but little sleep, yet felt thankful when the dim daylight announced another day. Not that it would bring us much comfort, for the moment our sopping blankets were rolled up and we had swallowed a mouthful of soaked mouldy biscuit and putrid pork, the word was given to turn to, and again we started the endless chopping.

My hands, however, were in such a state as to preclude my doing my work, and I was very nervous of being ragged by my comrades, as but little sympathy is ever shown in a corps such as ours to a man who is unable to do his share of work unless he is incapacitated by the steel or lead of the enemy, and I was quite prepared to hear myself sneered at as a kid-gloved new chum, or to be growled at as a waster who shirked his work and shoved his bit on his mates. In a crowd like ours men were not over-delicate in their satire, nor particularly considerate for the feelings of others.

We worked in relays, ten men chopping, ten men clearing away the cut brushwood, while the remaining twenty men held the workers' carbines and rested, two men out of each section of four working at a time.

Now I was in the second relief, Tim and myself having to replace Jack and Hutton, so that when spell-o was called we pushed forward, handing them their own and our carbines and taking from them the axes they had been using.

Stepping forward I approached Jack to hand him the carbines, when he noticed my hands, which were much swollen and quite raw.

"'Ere, look 'ere, mate," growled the old grumbler, "yer mud hooks ain't fit for this 'ere job, just you hold the ruddy carbines. Old Jack does your spell. Oh, clap a stopper over your jaw. You ain't no blankity blank shirker, and if any blooming swine guys yer they'll come athwart Jack's hawser, d—n 'em. Now you shove off." And all the day the old ruffian did my work for me, helped occasionally by Hutton, who reported my state to Mr Roach.

The latter took me to the surgeon of the 14th, who did what he could for me, but I was unable to do any more axe-work that trip.

It would be tedious for me to recapitulate that miserable march day by day; suffice it to say that every day the same work had to be done, gullies had to be bridged or roads cut down their banks, and these gullies and rivers grew more numerous as we reached our destination.

On the night of the fourth day the last of our rations was consumed, horseflesh being issued in lieu, but the downpour of rain, that never ceased for a moment, prevented any chance of cooking the raw sodden lumps of flesh served out to us. On the same night the colonel's brother. Ensign McDonnell, volunteered to push on and try to bring a relief party out to meet us.

He started next morning, reaching the frontier post the same night, and at once started back again, guiding a relief party of soldiers loaded with food. These met us on the evening of the sixth day, on the morning of which the general had sent on the Maoris. This supply of food, small as it was—my share consisted of one biscuit—was much appreciated, and on the morning of the seventh day we extricated ourselves from the infernal bush, and as we did so the rain suddenly ceased and the glorious sun shone out.

Never before, do I suppose, has such a gang of wretched-looking objects ever been mustered: drenched and sodden by five days and nights of unceasing rain, plastered from head to foot with mud, our clothes torn to rags by the bush, hung in dripping shreds, while our unshorn faces, filthy equipment and rusty weapons made a picture I shall never forget.

Our men took a speedy and practicable way of getting rid of our superfluous coating of filth, for on reaching a river we laid down our arms and belts and then marched deliberately into it, washing ourselves and rags at the same time, which, considering we had not a particle of soap in the whole outfit, was perhaps the most expeditious way of regaining that purity which is considered next to godliness, and was in fact the only virtue approaching it used in the ranks of the Rangers.

On the evening of the same day we limped into Mataitawa, where our weary pilgrimage ended, and we were the recipients of unbounded hospitality from the settlers.

A few days' spell with plenty of good food and new clothing made us forget past hardships, and we mustered gaily, when called upon to do so, for the return march along the coast.

There was much controversy for a long time as to whether this bush march had done good or not. It had certainly shown the Hau Haus that they could no longer rely on their forests as invincible protections, and had also taught the troops how utterly impracticable a string of pack-horses were in the bush, and that in future they must, like us Rangers, hump their own swags, as it does not pay to waste seven days over a march that should have been completed easily in three, to say nothing of the awful labour their presence entailed.

We started our return march expecting severe fighting, but were disappointed, as with the exception of a sharp brush at a large village named Waikoko, which the Rangers and *Kupapas* were ordered to rush, we met no opposition at all.

Here the *Kupapas* behaved badly, refusing to charge and drawing off to one side, this conduct being caused not through funk of the enemy, but because they entertained grave doubts as to the discriminating powers of the supporting regulars, who, they opined, might shoot them from behind as the Tommies had the unfortunate habit of loosing off at any Maori they spotted in front of them and then inquiring if he were an enemy or not.

True, they always apologised when in error, but our friendlies did not consider that that was a sufficient salve for their injured sterns, therefore no sooner had we deployed for the charge than they withdrew to one side, sat down and looked on.

The general thereupon threw forward a company of the 4th, who, game as pebbles, charged alongside of us, and notwithstanding a heavy fire we rushed pell-mell into the place, sweeping out the defenders, who fled, leaving behind them several dead bodies, our loss being one man killed and seven wounded, among whom was Tim, though I was delighted to find out not severely.

Two days after this pleasant little interlude we reached the camp on the Waingangora River, where the field force was broken up, ourselves being ordered to return to Patea and go into camp, tents and camp equipment being served out to us for that purpose.

EVERY BULLET HAS ITS BILLET

Chapter 8

"And We Die, and None Can Tell Them Where We Died."—Kipling

We reached Patea and formed a standing camp, for as great political changes were on the *tapis* the campaign for a period marked time. During our absence the forces remaining behind under Colonel Butler had not been idle, having defeated and driven off the ground a large party of Hau Haus at a place called Katotauru, while the *Kupapas* had also rendered good service.

It was now generally known that the regular troops were to be withdrawn from the country, so that the action at Katotauru was the last engagement in which they took part, though they were still employed for a short time to garrison certain places.

It is not a pleasant thing to say, but it is the truth, that during the past six years their efforts had been futile, although all the colonial fighting men allowed that had Sir Trevor Chute been in command from the start of the war things would have been very different.

It was at this time that Colonel Haultain, the Colonial Defence Minister, determining to carry out a bold policy, gave directions to occupy the confiscated land situated between the Waitotara and Waingangora Rivers, and issued orders that all the west coast colonial troops, many of whom were at that time serving on the east coast, should return and rendezvous at Patea. In the meantime things were a bit quiet with us. When I say "quiet" I use the word in the sense that we had no fighting at least, with the Hau Haus, for a time, for no one could call the Rangers' camp peaceful nor reposeful, nor was it a place in which a man given to sedentary pursuits would care to linger or dwell.

I was now to experience the great curse of the colony, for I regret to say the majority of our men, rough and uncouth as they were, but who had been quiet and tractable enough in the field, now became a prey to the grog-seller, and the scenes of foul, drunken debauchery were disgusting to the last degree. This was only to be expected from the majority of our crew, as there were many among them who were the flotsam and jetsam of the South Seas and Pacific slope, but what surprised and disgusted me was that many of our worst cases were men whom I knew to have been at one time gentlemen.

Of course I had seen plenty of hard drinking at home (a man in the wild parts of the world, although colonial born, always speaks of the British Isles as "home"), but then the vice was accompanied with music, excitement and fun, when a man carried off his legs by conviviality might be excused for temporarily forgetting himself, and the crime was disguised by its surroundings; but here it was not even vulgar, it was bestial, and for days our camp was a pandemonium, filled with drunken, blaspheming fiends who, without any joviality, wit or humour, scarcely with even an attempt at a sing-song, gulped down vile doctored rum till they collapsed and wallowed in their degradation.

I was puritanically inclined, or a devotee to an extravagant belief in teetotalism; far from it, for I was myself as wild as a hawk and as reckless a spendthrift as ever Ould Ireland produced, but what I could not stand was the foul, bestial manners and language brought out by the accursed poison sold as rum.

Still there was some excuse for the men, as you must bear in mind these fellows, accustomed to long spells of hardship in the bush, cut off from woman's or any other civilising society, and undergoing long periods of enforced abstinence, were, when they did touch the fringe of civilisation, mad for some change, and had but little wherewith to amuse themselves.

Very many of them had never played a game such as cricket or football in their lives; they had no papers, books nor periodicals, even had they cared to read them; and there was not a theatre, music hall or anything of that sort to entertain them; no, not even a woman, whose presence would have quickly shamed them to decency, for there is nothing that sobers up and tames a wild upcountry man more than the wholesome presence of a respectable female. No, there was nothing but this infernal rum, and they wallowed in it.

The day we reached Patea I had been looking after Tim, and it was not till evening, when I had seen him snug in hospital, I reached our tent, and the scene there was far from pleasant for a tired, hungry man.

Outside squatted Buck, grilling some meat on the embers of a small fire, while a couple of pannikins stood in the same, and a loaf of ammunition bread lay on a blanket beside him. So far so good, but where was Pierre and his *batterie de cuisine?* We were in camp. Sutlers with stores were plentiful, and all morning Pierre had been gassing about the wonderful dinner he was going to give us, and I had looked forward to it.

"Come on, Dick," quoth Buck, "I'm getting some tucker ready for you and me. I guess the others won't sup tonight; shove your swag down here and let's fall to."

"But where are the rest of the boys?" I said. "I've just seen Tim put away all right, and the surgeon-major told me he would do well and be fit for duty in next door to no time."

"Oh! I'm glad Tim's O.K.," answered Buck, "but if you want the rest of the boys you'll find them in the tent. I've just humped the last of them up from the damned grog shop, and a ruddy job I've had of it, but it won't do to let one's mates lie aroun' uncared for. Wish to goodness you'd have come along a bit earlier so as to give a hand, darned if I don't."

I looked into the tent and there I saw my comrades lying in a distorted heap, mixed up with loaves of bread, blankets, and all the camping paraphernalia, every one of them putrid drunk.

This for a moment upset me, as I regarded Hutton as more than a passing acquaintance, and I could not understand how he, a gentleman by birth and education, could have sunk his pride so as to have got drunk in such companionship as our mates. Old Jack I also liked, but his was a different case, as nothing better could be expected from him, Pierre or George than a pirates' debauch; and I had but small respect for Smith, who, notwithstanding his culture, had somehow never seemed to ring true.

However, I could do nothing for them, so squatted down and enjoyed the meat and bread Buck had so kindly prepared for me. Fortunately the night was a fine one, so after a yarn by the fire we made down our blankets and slept in the open, leaving the tent to the votaries of Bacchus.

The following day, as the bust was still being kept up, I attended a sale of captured loot, cattle, horses, etc., and bought for ten pounds a very fine horse, getting also a nearly new saddle and bridle of the best Australian make for two pounds. The nag was a very well-bred one and had evidently been bred by some settler looted by the Maoris, and was more than half wild, besides which he was in very poor condition; but he was only four years old, well topped, with splendid quarters, legs and feet, and I made up my mind to set to work to break him in and get him into good condition.

As I was overlooking my purchase Mr Roach strolled up.

"Well, Burke," he said, "so you've started a stable, have you? Well, you've made a deuced good start. I know the breed of that horse, and the man who bred him never bred a wrong 'un," and he pointed at the two *tomahawks'* brand on the near shoulder. "He is by Cid out of a Duchess mare, and is as near thoroughbred as they make them. You have a cheap lot, but, by George! you may have a job to break him, although once you have done it you'll find he's all right, as there is not a particle of vice in the breed. Come along and let's see you back him. But have you ever tried to back a buckjumper before? What sort of a hand are you in the pigskin?"

I told him I was all right in the hunting-field, having ridden from childhood, but had never broken in a horse, nor ever seen a buckjumper in my life.

"Then," said he, "I advise you to let one of those defence force fellows do it. There are plenty of rough-riding stockmen among them."

"Well, sir," I answered, "I'm determined to tackle him myself, especially as I want to train him afterwards, and if I remain in the colony I must sooner or later come across a buckjumper."

"True," he replied. "I'll give you a hand with the saddle, but bring him into the paddock so that if he pips you we can round him up easily. One thing's in your favour, he is very poor, so that you may have a chance of breaking him before he regains his full strength."

Buck had by this time joined us, and with their assistance I managed to bridle and saddle the horse, a job that gave us some trouble and attracted many idle troopers, so that when I led him into the paddock I had a big gallery.

The English cut of my riding breeches and boots had given me away to the onlookers as a new chum, and there were plenty of men offering odds that the tenderfoot would be pipped in less than a minute.

Patting and talking to him I led him about for a few moments up and down the paddock, which was a field of some ten acres, surrounded with a five-foot post-and-rail fence. Mr Roach now took his head and placed his hand over his near eye, while Buck held the off-stirrup ready to place on my foot.

In a moment I was in the saddle and gave the word to let go when Buck, having placed the stirrup, together with Mr Roach, sprang clear, leaving myself and horse to fight it out. For a few seconds he stood still, then gave himself an angry shake or two, then kicked viciously, rearing between each kick as if he wished to throw himself backwards, when, finding this did not move me, he stood still and snorted as if he remarked to himself: "Well, I am damned." All at once he seemed to have made up his mind, for he made a determined snatch at his bit, and although I was on the lookout for him he dragged the reins through my fingers, and, like a flash of lightning, down went his head, while his back seemed to bend and give under me, but in a moment he shot up into the air, all four feet leaving the ground at once, bending his back up, arched like that of an angry cat, and returning to the ground with a jar that nearly drove my spine through the roof of my head. The same jar seemed to send him aloft again like an india-rubber ball bouncing, when after it has been thrown up into the air it returns to the ground only to bound up again.

This exercise went on for some minutes, and though it was far from pleasant yet I felt I could stick it all right, the worst part being that when in the air it seemed as if I were sitting on the end of an egg, as, bar a tuft of hair in front of the gullet plate of my saddle, devil a bit of the horse could I see at all.

Presently he stopped dead, and cheers rose from the onlookers. "Well sat, new chum!" "Gad! the chap can ride a bit!" and other laudatory remarks, so that I began to think that the game was won, when I heard Mr Roach's voice shout: "Look out, Burke. He is going to side-buck."

What side-bucking meant I had no idea, but I was soon to find out, as without the slightest warning he again started, but this time he did not spring straight ahead but sideways, at the same time making his body wriggle like a snake, while the jumps came so quickly I could not get the chance to regain my grip, which the first side-buck had loosened. More and more I was shifted from my hold, and although I did my best, yet I could not save myself, and I am sure some subtle instinct told the horse he was getting the better of me, for he seemed to redouble his efforts, and with one mighty plunge sent me flying over his near wither. I fell heavily, but was up in a moment, a bit shaken though not hurt, and amid the cheers of the men again mounted.

No sooner was I in my seat and the men helping me sprung clear than he started with the side-bucking, but this time I knew what to expect, and was on the lookout, so was able, albeit with difficulty, to retain my seat, and after some twenty minutes' game tussle forced him to walk and canter round and round the paddock, having fairly conquered him, which I should not have done so easily had it not been for his starved condition.

This I set to work to rectify with good grooming and feeding, riding him twice a day and passing all my spare time talking to him and training him. On two occasions only he again tried bucking, but as he failed to get me off he gave it up, quickly learning to know me and picking up flesh and manners in a wonderful way, so that before a month was over I possessed a really valuable mount, one that in the future was to carry me through some tough jobs and warm corners.

In this way I passed my time till my comrades had finished their bust, which was not concluded till their last shilling had been spent, and I also, with Mr Roach's kindly assistance, began to study the Maori language, which, thanks to my knowledge of French, came very easy to me.

As soon as they had spent all their money my tent mates began to sober up, and it was a pitiful sight watching them taper off. For a day or two they were all mad for more drink and suffered dreadfully, and acting on Buck's advice I began to doctor them.

On the first day I procured and issued to the poor broken-nerved wretches five tots apiece; on the second, four; on the third, three; and so on till, by the time it came to one tot, with the exception of Smith, they were all right and swore off bar rations.

Smith, I regret to say, was not satisfied with this regimen, and for days continued to loaf around the camp trying to cadge drinks, and would go to any mean extreme to procure one.

Pierre and George, when fit, returned to their scouting, and Mr Roach kindly gave me leave to accompany them so as to pick up what I could of the trade.

These two worthies at first were by no means keen to take me, as they did not consider I was hard enough, but I managed to overcome their scruples, and when they found I soon became as hard and untiring as themselves they quickly began to instruct me in their wonderful bush lore.

Yes, and bush lore is a very wonderful science, and to be mastered by no one who does not give himself up heart and soul to its study.

First of all there are so many things a new chum must learn and remember, and it must be impressed on him that the bush is revengeful and if treated with disrespect is apt to exact a mortal punishment. Let me enumerate a very few of the things a man must thoroughly master before he can call himself a scout: He must learn to use his senses to un unnatural degree. His eye must get accustomed to see and note everything, although he is giving his attention to something else.

At the same time his senses of smell, hearing and feeling must also always be on deck, while his memory must retain every mortal thing his senses have discovered and noted. He must be able to pass through the bush day or night as noiselessly as a bat and in as straight a line as a bee, although in crossing it he will surely be encountered by many obstacles, which he must be able to get over, get under, or get round and pick up again his straight line. He must be able to approximately tell the time, day or night, and also to steer his course without compass, sun or stars. He must learn the different call and note of every day or night bird and be able to distinguish them so as to be sure that any bird is calling with its natural note at its proper time and in its correct locality.

These are only a few of the things a tyro has to learn and digest, or if he does not do so don't let him go scouting when Hau Haus are hostile.

I am not going to turn this chapter into an article on scouting, but have simply told you a few of the subjects I had to learn, and which I did learn, and digested so carefully that at last I became, and mark you it was after long and weary work, cognisant that I owned another sense or instinct that informed me if I was going right or wrong and eventually became so acute that in some ways it warned me of approaching danger.

All this was not learned in a day or without undergoing great hardship, but I stuck at it, wandering through the rough country with my queer companions, and gradually mastering some of their marvellous skill and bush-craft.

Our duty chiefly consisted in searching for *pahs* in the most inaccessible parts of the country, for although the fighting had, for a time, ceased, yet we were well aware that the natives were still hostile, and in fact so long as they clung to the Hau Hau or Pai Marire faith they must continue to remain so.

The regular troops were at this time being withdrawn, and Colonel McDonnell, although he had not yet assumed the command of the west coast, was anxious to make a move so as to get the men out of the camp and strike another blow at the Hau Hau. The *Kupapas* had returned to Wanganui, so he issued orders for three companies of the Forest Rangers to make a night's march up the Waingangora and beat up the enemy, who were in force in that district, and it was on this patrol that death was to be brought home to me.

We left camp at sunset, loaded as usual, but each company had to carry four stretchers as we had no hospital men with us, so that we had to take turn and turn about with the butchers' trays, as the men called them, and we marched all through the night, resting for two hours before day-light. We were moving in three separate bodies, and were destined to get a lesson on how difficult a matter it is for combined movements to be carried out successfully when working in a rough, bushed country, especially when no communication can be held by the various units.

Our company was to make the frontal attack; the other two, making detours, were to try and envelop, or at least outflank, the enemy's position, Mr Roach's orders being to advance to the attack as soon as it was light enough for a man to be able to see his fore sight. This we did, taking every care and precaution in our advance, and found the enemy, far outnumbering us, posted in a very strong position.

We, however, in accordance with orders, gaily began the fight, expecting our flankers to chip in every moment, but they had been delayed on their march and did not do so, and soon the Hau Haus began to outflank us, so that Mr Roach was forced to give the order to retire, an order we carried out as coolly as if on parade, disputing every fathom of ground and daring the enemy to rush us. Still we must fall back or allow the natives to outflank and eventually surround us, which spells being cut to pieces in bush fighting, so we were retiring very steadily by alternate groups of four, my four consisting of myself, Hutton, Jack and Buck.

The bush was an open one—that is, it consisted of the usual huge trees without much undergrowth—so that we could move quickly from cover to cover but were more exposed while doing so.

Hutton and myself were together behind one tree; Jack and Buck behind another, about six yards away, and at the time were in the firing line, not more than a dozen yards away from the advancing Hau Haus, who were yelling like a lot of fiends newly let loose from the pit.

We were firing alternately—that is, I had laid down and fired from the right-hand side of the tree, then had slipped behind it, letting Hutton take my place while I loaded under cover. Hutton had fixed and had sprung to his feet as we were about to vacate our cover and run back so as to pass through the groups that had taken up their position some twenty yards to our rear, and were ready to cover our retreat; in fact, I had started to race back, when I heard beside me the thud a bullet makes when it strikes flesh, and Hutton, with a gasping cry, fell against me, nearly knocking me off my feet.

In a moment I had hold of him, dragged him back to the tree, and had grasped my carbine, just in the nick of time, to meet the rush of a big Maori who, *tomahawk* in hand, had charged in to finish off his victim. He was in fact not more than three yards from me when my bullet crashed into his head, when, throwing up his arms, his knees gave way and he fell dead at my feet, this being the first Hau Hau that I could be positive of having put out of mess up to date.

He had hardly reached the ground before I had seized Hutton's carbine, handing him mine, saying: "Try and load this, old chap," which, although he was coughing up blood, he managed to do.

At the same instant Jack and Buck were alongside of us. "'Ere, what's all this?" howled the former, his blue eyes on fire and his face as hard as a stone.

"Leave me alone," gasped Hutton; "the other fellows have all fallen back and you'll be cut off. I'm done for."

"Leave yer alone," growled Jack; "that be damned for a yarn; white-livered you must think us 'uns to leave yer alone. 'Ere, Dick, you and Buck cover me. I'll carry our mate out. Bring along all the carbines and give the ruddy scum hell if they try to rush. Come on, now," and exerting his enormous strength the foul-mouthed old pirate lifted Hutton, big man as he was, and bore him tenderly, like a mother carrying a sick infant, to the rear.

Buck and myself now had our hands full, but I think both of our next shots must have been lucky ones, as the Hau Haus hung back for a moment from rushing us, a moment we grasped to race back under heavy fire to a tree some dozen yards away, where we turned at bay.

Again we fired, and I know my shot was a lucky one, as I got a good chance, and saw the fellow I had aimed at crumple up and fall, which gave us the opportunity to again run back to fresh cover.

No sooner had we reached it than Buck shouted, "It's all right, Dick, the flankers have come up and are twisting their tails; look out, we'll get a shot at the beggars in front of us as they bolt. Gosh, this beats cock-shooting at home."

Sure enough as he spoke I heard our fellows' volleys, together with their charging shout, and knew we were out of the fire, for at the same moment our own company came back with a rush, which we joined, and in a few minutes we had taken the position, driving the Hau Haus helter-skelter in flight.

The moment I could I made for the stretchers and asked the doctor how Hutton was.

"Dying, poor fellow," was the reply. "It will be all over with him in less than an hour. Go to him, he has asked for you several times. I expect he will remain conscious to the end."

In a moment I was kneeling by my poor pal's side, close to whom squatted old Jack, who was swearing softly and tying a bandage round his own leg.

"How goes it, old chap?" I asked, taking his hand.

"Dick, dear boy," he gasped, "I'm glad you wiped out the beggar who shot me. Those are not Christian sentiments, I know, but very human, still, let him slide. Listen, old chap. Your mother knows Lady —— well. I'm her son Eustace. Yes, old chap, I've never told you my yarn, but now you know it, as you must have heard it, although the affair took place years before your time. Dick, on the honour of a dying man, I was innocent. Would to God I could prove it to the old regiment. I knew your mother well. Now promise to write to her and get her to break the news to my mother, and let her tell her that as I lay dying I swore to you I was innocent of that crime, and that if I've lived like a waster I've died like a man; and, Dick, when I'm dead take the locket from my neck and send it to your mother, she'll know whom to give it to; and, Dick, dear boy, get home out of this hell of drink and brutality; there is nothing in it, only a wasted life and a death without honour like mine."

All this had been gasped out in short sentences, and to try and cheer him up I said: "But, Hutton, old pal, you don't die without honour; you got your death-wound fighting bravely for Queen and flag."

He smiled like a child and muttered: "Yes, Dick, Queen and flag, God bless them. Queen and flag."

For some time he lay still, while I wiped away the bloody froth from his lips, administering now and then some weak rum and water, and vainly tried to remember some prayer, if only to counteract the awful oaths rumbled out by old Jack, who had by now taken post on the other side of the dying man.

"Say, Dick," growled the old pirate, as he expectorated a worn-out chew of tobacco, "don't yer think our shipmate's parted his moorings?" And he swore with due solemnity. "Coz I feels inclined to go back to the ruddy bush and see as if I can't do something to square this 'ere blooming account. Yo've done your bit, you have, when yer lifted the hatch off that swine's head, but I guess I feel as if I wants to do a bit myself." And the old fellow made to rise from the ground, but sank back as Hutton again opened his eyes and gasped out:

"Thanks, Jack; goodbye, old ship," and then, after a pause, turning his fading eyes towards mine, he whispered: "*Une vie manqué, une vie manqué*, but thank God finished like a gentleman, for Queen and flag. God bless them, Queen and flag. So-long, Dick, go home." And as he muttered the last word he closed his eyes, and with a smile on his face his gallant spirit left its clay to answer the eternal roll-call.

There is no time for lamentation, and but little for mourning, in the bush, so that as soon as the doctor had pronounced our poor pal dead old Jack and myself set about his obsequies. I first of all removed from his neck the locket, which was sewn up in leather, and looked through his poor sordid pack in case there might be any letters or papers to take care of; but there were none.

"'Ere, chuck me that blanket, mate," growled my fellow-undertaker. "No, mine's a new one. We'll start him aloft in that, seems more respectful like," and the kind-hearted old filibuster substituted his own brand-new blanket for Hutton's tattered one, at the same time producing a small canvas ditty-bag, out of which he extracted a sailmaker's palm, needle and twine. "Yer see, Dick," he continued, "I always like to give a mate his last chuck, so long as I've got time, respectful like. So that he's no call to feel shame when he toes the line afore Davy Jones. Now you turn to and dig the hole, while I sew him up shipshape and Bristol fashion, coz t'other mates will be 'ere soon and we may have to hoof it."

This was very true, so leaving Jack to sew up the still warm remains I started in with *tomahawk* and hands to scoop out a shallow resting-place for my dead pal.

I had not more than half finished when I was joined by Mr Roach and the rest of the company, some of whom helped me to complete the grave, and when it was ready his tent-mates lifted, with rough though revering hands, the shapeless form, and bore it slowly to its last resting-place. There we laid him down, shovelling the soft soil over him with our hands, and concealing the spot so that no wandering Hau Hau could discover and desecrate the remains of our gallant comrade.

Yes, there, alone he lay, without a prayer having been said over him, without a bugle having been blown, or without a parting shot having been fired, and with only a mob of rough, sin-stained men to, for a few minutes, mourn for him, yet I guess that as horny hands wiped away a salt drop or two, and deep voices muttered oaths and threats of revenge, none of his noble ancestors resting under the old abbey roof at home were more sorrowed for or rest better than their hapless kinsman killed in a forgotten, nameless skirmish and buried by his wild and reckless comrades in a hidden grave on a lonely fern ridge among the wilds of the New Zealand bush. R.I.P.

No sooner was poor Hutton planted than we fell in, moving off to continue the patrol, and I told Mr Roach about the locket and message in case I might be rubbed out, for I was new to the game then and my poor pal's death gave me the hump. However, we were to have no more fighting that patrol, and returned to camp after two more days of bushwhacking.

On our return I found Tim had been returned fit for duty, and I was glad of it, as my light-hearted follower always cheered up the tent. The hump was still bearing heavy upon me, and as it was now the beginning of June and my period of service terminated at the end of the month I had to make up my mind whether I would sign on again or return home, as my poor dead pal had begged me to do.

I was tired of camp life, for although I enjoyed my scouting trips, and knew there would be heaps of good fighting to be got through in the near future, still the glamour of the Rangers had worn off. There was another pay-day to be faced on the 5th July, and much as I liked some of my comrades, yet I had no desire to associate again with the foul, drunken, swearing mob that pay-day would turn my companions into. No; I would quit it. There was no middle course that I could see, so I would return to Europe.

Man proposes but *Kismet* decides, for just as I had come to the above determination Mr Roach called me and told me to go to the colonel's tent as he wished to see me, and of course I at once reported there, where I found him hard at work, but he at once called me in.

"Burke," said he, "I hear you have worked very hard to pick up a knowledge of bush work, that you are a good horseman and leave the rum-bottle alone. Moreover your company commander in-forms me he has the greatest confidence in you. Do you know anything of mounted drill?"

I answered in the affirmative and he continued:

"Well, I am in great want of an officer to take over the adjutancy of the Mounted Defence Force. I know of course you are a gentleman, well educated and all that, so I offer you the position. The war will breeze up again shortly and you'll get plenty of fighting."

Naturally I was much gratified by the offer, though I explained to the colonel that I was at present on the horns of a dilemma as to whether I ought not to return home.

He, however, laughed, and said: "Well, Burke, seeing you travelled fifteen thousand miles to see some fighting it would seem a pity to return all that distance with such a short experience."

My late resolutions all seemed to fade away, so after some more palaver I agreed to sign on as a commissioned officer for three years, or longer, if required.

As the interview terminated he drew out an official document, which he handed to me with a laugh, saying: "I was so sure of you that I sent to Wellington a month ago for your commission, and have much pleasure in now handing it you. You will appear in orders this evening. Come and dine with me tonight."

As I strode away from the H. Q. lines I cogitated over the new aspect of my affairs; but the thing was done, all my determination of returning home had blown to the deuce and I had signed on for another three years. I felt rather mad, but solaced myself with the thought that anyhow there would be plenty of good fighting in the near future. Of course I had mentioned to the colonel that my promotion would necessitate Egan's transfer, and he had at once directed that the worthy Tim should be transferred in that day's orders, so I wended my way back to my tent to say goodbye to my mates and see to the moving of my kit over to the mounted men's lines, situated about a mile from the Rangers' camp.

My news was received by my comrades in various ways. Tim's wild ebullition of joy at the idea I was to be an officer and that he was going to be my own man once more was tempered by the regrets of the others at my leaving them, while old Jack's pungent remarks, such as "What the hell do yer want to fight aboard a ruddy 'oss for? Ain't yer legs good enough? Course yer ort to be on the ruddy poop, I know that," etc., etc., were rumbled out in the best grumbling style, accompanied with his very choicest selection of bad words. Pierre and George were also sorrowful, declaring that the Rangers were losing their best scout, but their lamentations I cut short by slipping a couple of sovereigns into Pierre's hands, telling him to go to the sutler's and procure materials for the very best repast he could manage to serve up.

This he did, and a wonderful repast it was, so that when it was over, and the farewells said, old Jack himself confessed: "Things did not look so dirty to wind'ard after all," and insisted on helping Tim to carry our kits over to our new camp, while I mounted my horse and rode over to report myself to my new O.C.

CHAPTER 9

I Join the Troopers

I was very kindly received by my brother officers on joining, all of whom were fine fellows, but sadly deficient in their knowledge of drill, so I had to turn to at once and knock them into shape.

Our duties chiefly consisted in patrolling, escorting strings of pack-horses or drays, where practicable, loaded with rations, etc., and despatch-riding, the latter a very arduous and dangerous work indeed, of which I shall say more *anon*, though of course we had to do our share of bushwhacking, when we discarded the breeches and boots for shawls.

The troopers were the perfection of irregular mounted men, being taken mostly from young colonial fellows who had been stock-riders, but there was a good leaven of broken-down gentlemen and remittance men, so, taking them altogether, they were a hard-riding, hard-fighting, hard-swearing and hard-drinking crowd.

You may have some difficulty in understanding why troopers should of necessity be hard swearers. Let me explain. The bad habit comes from driving pack-horses, most of which beasts of burden are mules, and pack-mules, like transport oxen, will not do their work without being comforted and encouraged by the most awful language, stock whips by themselves being useless; so even the most religiously brought-up young men acquire this habit and stick to it.

It was in the beginning of July that Colonel McDonnell assumed supreme command and it was officially announced that the regular troops were to render no further service in the field, but were to evacuate the country at their earliest convenience.

We now therefore began to look out for sharp work, as our O.C. was not the man to let the fern sprout without doing something, and although it was winter, and bitterly cold, we knew that his theory of native warfare was to fight winter and summer, wet or fine, cold or hot, day or night, until the resistance of the Hau Haus should be overcome.

In this he was quite right, for although it entailed great hardships on us, with probably a heavy loss of men, still it would cause more loss to the enemy, as the fighting would be in their country. Their *pahs* and villages would be burnt, their food-supplies would be looted and destroyed, their women and children would have to starve in the bush, and they would also lose a lot of men. This they could not afford to do and we could; for, should we lose a hundred men in an engagement, we could enlist a hundred more, but should they lose a hundred they had no surplus stock from which to replace them.

The colonel knew the Hau Haus well. He knew it must be war to the knife and that no peace was possible with mad fanatics whose one belief was to slay every white man and even all their own countrymen who refused to accept the absurd Pai Marire faith.

There is no doubt that had the colonel been allowed to carry out this policy the colony would have been spared at least two years of bloodshed and expense, but in every country where the Union Jack flies there is always a gang of rotters, peace-at-any-price men, nigger lovers, pro-Boers, pro anything, so long as it is against their own flag, and New Zealand, like all others, was cursed with such a mob.

However I had nothing to do with politics and was delighted when the colonel, a few days after he had taken over the command, moved his headquarters and the bulk of the forces to Manawapou, some fifteen miles nearer our old battle-grounds.

Towards the end of the month the colonel, escorted by a small party of troopers, rode to the Waingangora River, to interview We Hukanui, a neutral chief, so that he could ascertain through his medium whether the Hau Hau tribes wanted peace or war.

Of course we all knew peace was the last thing they desired, but according to Maori etiquette it was the correct thing to do, and the interview was both novel and entertaining.

As it was by no means certain what sort of a reception we were going to receive we advanced to the trysting-place, a *kainga* (open village), taking every precaution, and found some thirty Maoris squatting down in a semicircle, waiting for us. My first move was to leave two troopers, who were to remain mounted, as videttes, some hundred and fifty yards to our rear, so as to prevent any attempt to surprise us from that quarter, and this act received great praise from the colonel, who rode straight up to the squatting natives and dismounted.

After the customary salutations had been gone through many speeches were made and various proposals suggested, among them one, moved by We Hukanui, that the colonel, alone and unarmed, should accompany him and call on the Hau Hau chiefs, was declined without discussion, as it was too risky even for our gallant O.C., the fate of the last Peace Commissioner who had called on them being of far too recent a date to make him risk the same end. (*Note.*—Mr Broughton, Chief Native Commissioner, had a few months previously, at their own request, visited the Hau Haus alone and unarmed for the purpose of discussing peace and had been foully murdered in the presence of the chiefs without being allowed to say a word.)

So the colonel, as an amendment, handed the Rt.-Hon. We Hukanui a cartridge and a white handkerchief, directing him to convey them to the Hau Haus as symbols of war and peace. The chiefs were to choose which symbol they preferred, returning the other to the colonel, who also sent them the polite message that should they choose the cartridge they would at once advise him when and where they would like the fight to take place. This ended the *runanga* and we rode back to camp.

On the following day a letter was brought in from the Hau Hau chiefs, requesting an interview, so again we rode out to meet them, taking this time only twelve troopers, though we left fifty Rangers in a very strong position on the bank of the Waingangora River.

At the rendezvous we met several chiefs and a large number of their followers, whose absurd gesticulations, together with the gibberish they talked, pretending it was English, for they declared that the angel Gabriel had served them out with the gift of all tongues, excited the risibility of our men to such an extent we could scarcely restrain bursts of laughter, which would have been highly indecorous on such a grave occasion.

After the chiefs had made many speeches, in which they declared they wanted peace, the colonel replied: "It is good. Bring all the chiefs to the Waingangora tomorrow; we will ratify peace there. If you do not come, I shall know you want war."

The following day we waited at the Waingangora, but no Hau Haus came; we were not disappointed, as none of us expected they would, and at nightfall we returned to camp.

Our O.C. now determined, as there was no chance of peace, to strike a rapid blow, so on the evening of the 1st of August he moved out of camp with a strong force to surprise the village of Pokaikai.

The night was a fine one, though the cold was so intense that it numbed our thin-clad men to the bone, while the stirrups and scabbards of us mounted men were quite thick with frost. Cold as it was we had to face it, and before daylight had reached our positions, halted and dismounted.

Shortly after we had halted Pierre and George came in with wonderful information, which was that they had crawled so close up to the Hau Hau pickets as to be able to overhear their conversation, the tenor of which was that they, the Hau Haus, considering there was no possibility of being attacked on such a dreadfully cold night, had decided that bed was the best place for them, and so had taken themselves off to their virtuous, or otherwise, couches; also that the village was an open one, that they had penetrated into the middle of it, and that all the natives were asleep in the arms of Morpheus or their own various ladies.

This was a piece of unprecedented luck, nor was our O.C. the man to let such a chance slip, and the new orders he gave were excellent. He had at his disposal one company of military settlers armed with rifles and bayonets, the remainder of the outfit carrying carbines and revolvers, so this company he ordered to silently fix bayonets, enter the village and post themselves at the doors of the various *whares* (huts) so as to imprison the inmates. He also gave orders that on no account was a shot to be fired, as he now had great hopes of being able to surprise an adjacent village, hive its inhabitants in the same way, and so kill two birds with the one stone.

The movement was a plain and straightforward one, so simple, in fact, that no one doubted its successful termination, but, as Bobby Burns asserts, "*The best-laid plans of mice and men often run crooked,*" and it was to be so on this occasion.

It has often been the lot of an unfortunate commander, after a long and harassing night's march, to have his well-thought-out plans utterly ruined by some crass idiot discharging his rifle, lighting his pipe, or committing some other wicked act of folly or culpable clumsiness, and unfortunately the military settlers had in their ranks a half-baked rotter, whose nerves, getting overwound, let go a cheer just as the company was about to enter the village. The cheer was taken up by his comrades, which gave the alarm to the sleeping enemy, who rushed out of their huts and took to headlong flight.

As the whole show was now spoilt, the military settlers opened fire and charged, knocking over some of the fugitives, and bayoneting a few of the late starters, but the O.C. had to content himself with the meagre spoil of some dozen women, while, had it not been for the misconduct of the aforesaid infernal idiot, he would have scooped up all the principal Hau Hau chiefs and probably have ended the war: which shows what a tremendous lot of harm one fool can cause.

We had, however, made a valuable capture, and one that entailed great loss to the enemy—namely, some forty stand of rifles, together with a large supply of ammunition and other arms that fell into our hands. During this affair we lost only one man, and he was killed in rather a queer way.

At the end of the engagement one of the military settlers entered a *whare* for the purpose of bringing out a dead Hau Hau, and was still inside when a party of Rangers, who were searching the huts for any of the enemy possibly concealed, came up to it. Hearing someone inside the hut they demanded who was there, and received the answer: "A white man."

Now it was believed that the infamous deserter, Kimball Bent, was with this gang of Hau Haus, and the men had all previously been cautioned to this effect, so that the Rangers fancied they had at last hived the scoundrel that every man had sworn should receive no quarter. Had poor Spain (the military settler) answered: "Friend," more questions would have been asked; but as he simply replied to the challenge, "A white man," the Rangers, convinced they had the villain in their clutches, fired on him, thereby shooting their own comrade.

By this time the loot had been collected and all the huts, with the exception of one, had been destroyed. (*Note.*—The principal reason for burning huts was to destroy the large quantities of powder or ammunition concealed in the thatch.) It was broad daylight, and as, thanks to the aforementioned fool, there was no further chance of doing anything, we returned to the camp at Manawapou where, I regret to state. Colonel McDonnell could not see his way clear to hanging the nervous ass who had spoilt our day's work.

I am not writing a history of the New Zealand wars, and it would be only wearisome for people nowadays to read of the forgotten, innumerable skirmishes, night marches and encounters, with their attendant hardships, the colonial irregulars went through.

For many years the district over which we then marched and fought has been the most fruitful one in New Zealand, where thousands of smiling homesteads now stand on the sites of our old bivouacs on which we shivered and starved, and I often wonder if a single individual of the happy and peaceful population who now occupy them ever give a thought to the bands of reckless ne'er-do-wells who, by the expenditure of their blood and health, rendered that land safe for their present occupants.

The British Empire has been largely built up by the same class of men, who have rolled out its frontiers farther and farther, and then held them against savage enemies in spite of deadly malaria, fever, starvation and horrible discomfort.

Would it therefore be an impertinent question for me to ask if any one of the yapping gas-bags in the home or the colonial Houses of Parliament has ever given a thought to the welfare of these rolling stones after they have been worn out by their unrequited work? However, it's no use asking silly questions, so let's return to our mutton.

The skirmish at Pokaikai put the fear of the Lord into the Hau Haus, the chiefs of whom were so fully cognisant of their narrow escape that for a long time they hardly dare sleep inside a *whare*, which the quick, continuous movements of McDonnell, who, unlike the regulars in the past, marched without pack-horses or impedimenta of any kind, did not allay. Our O.C. kept his own counsel, no one knowing when, where or how the next move was to be made, and many a night I have been roused out from under my blankets to start away on a bitter cold march for the purpose of beating up some congregation of Hau Haus.

Scouting and patrolling was also reduced to a science little dreamt of in British armies of today, (as at time of first publication), so that the Maoris were kept ever on the *qui vive;* in fact the colonel employed their own tactics against them, and they did not like it, as village after village was attacked, stores of food were destroyed, till at last the Hau Haus became so harried that tribe after tribe weakened on it and gave in, until only two tribes remained in arms against us, and had the Government only had the sense to allow McDonnell a free hand, the war would have terminated in a few months. But it was not to be.

The first set-back our gallant commandant received was engineered by a worm called Parris, a man whom Sir Trevor Chute had ordered out of his camp, and this thing saw fit to invent and promulgate charges against the Colonel and his men for committing outrages and murdering women at Pokaikai, and a commission, consisting of Sir Cracroft Wilson, Colonel Cargill and Mr Graham inquired into the whole matter.

At this commission both Hau Haus and friendly natives were examined, and although Mr Graham did his best to help Parris to substantiate the latter's lies, it was all without avail, as every charge was ignominiously dismissed, the only foundation on which the mountain of falsehood had been raised being as follows:—

You must remember that it was dark when our men entered the village, and that on the alarm being prematurely given there was a general stampede of the natives. In the rush and dim light it is hard to tell man from woman, so one of the latter received a bayonet-thrust by mistake.

The wound was not a bad one, and after it had been dressed the colonel interviewed her, offering to have her carried on a stretcher to hospital. To this she objected, requesting instead to be left in a hut, asserting her friends would soon find her. This was done. She was made comfortable in a hut that was not burnt on her account, and we had not left the place an hour when her relations returned, so that at the time of the inquiry she was well and hearty.

History of course repeats itself, and the British House of Parliament is, at the present time, still disgraced by some of the foul liars who invented charges against the British troops in the Transvaal, and these treacherous hounds, posing as religious, honourable men, still have a big following in the country.

The same was the case in New Zealand, as Parris, who was commissioner for the district, was allowed still to retain his post, and did all in his power to thwart and hamper the Colonel, declaring the natives wished for peace, recommending the disbandment of the field force—in fact, played the part of a Little Englander with a Nonconformist conscience to perfection; and this man, owing to the criminal folly of the Government, was the cause of the discomfiture and defeat of the colonial forces.

To give you some idea of the folly the New Zealand Government perpetrated I must again digress.

In the House was a very strong peace party, mostly composed of members representing the Middle Island, in which there had been no war, and whose inhabitants begrudged paying the cost of the prolonged struggle, and whose desire to develop the resources of the colony made them ardently long for peace, so much so that they gave ready credence to the reports of Parris, while they ignored those of McDonnell; and bitterly they were to rue it in the near future.

At the time the colonel assumed command he had at his disposal an adequate field force of splendidly trained bush fighters who by continual warfare had not only learned their work but also to place the utmost confidence in their officers, their comrades and themselves. Alas, this was to end!

The major part of this force were military settlers who had contracted with the Government to serve for three years, their remuneration to be a grant of land, and it so fell out that at the very moment their services were most needed the time expired of one hundred and fifty of the very best men.

This placed the Government somewhat in a dilemma, as the Hau Haus were still in possession of the land that should have been surveyed, ready to parcel out to these fellows, and as this had not been done they could not keep their part of the contract. Still the men were quite willing to re-engage, provided the Government would guarantee ten more acres of land *per annum* for each year they continued to serve. This was the most modest demand, and the colonel permitted one of their officers to proceed to Wellington to lay the matter before the ministry, who not only refused to accede to it but treated the officer with quite undeserved insolence, going so far as to return the message that if the military settlers did not care to serve without another grant of land they could leave the service, which they promptly did, in disgust, the majority of them making off to the southern goldfields, and the district, thanks to the insolent ignorance of a pack of lawyers and counter skippers, lost forever the services of its best defenders.

Other corps had also been disbanded, and one fine day the colonel, thanks to the besotted stupidity of the Government, found himself with only one hundred and sixty men, including officers, to hold a district and carry out a campaign—duties that a few months previous had found ample occupation for nearly four thousand men. Yet our gallant O.C. was not the man to be daunted. True he had not enough men to garrison the posts which the Hau Haus, now emboldened by our paucity of numbers, not only threatened with attack, but also they ambushed every road, attempting to cut off, and if successful cut up, our despatch-riders and ration convoys. No; he would hit back, as he knew that passive resistance was no use in savage warfare, and although he had to withdraw nearly every man from all the posts to obtain a striking force, even then by no means an adequate one, still he did so.

Just previous to this headquarters had been moved forward to Waihe, where an old *pah* had been reconstructed into a small but strong fort, the building of which had been begun, carried on and completed under fire, so that we continually had to drop tools and take up arms to resist attacks.

At this time you might say we lived under fire, as all day long the natives fired at us from the bush, and it was now I played in the most extraordinary cricket match that I think ever took place.

The game was inaugurated in honour of the completion of the work, and was Pigskin Polishers (troopers) *v*. Footsloggers (rangers), and was looked forward to with much excitement by both corps. Naturally the players were all out of practice, their dress far from accurate, and the pitch, well, damnable; but we turned to with *élan*, though to bat, bowl, or even field, belted as each man was with his revolver and fifty rounds of carbine ammunition, was very trying.

Moreover the side in the field had to pick up their carbines when they changed places at the call of "Over!" and the umpires held the batsmen's guns as in this country they sometimes hold their coats. In fact the whole get-up was *outré* in the extreme, and I fear ordinary spectators of English cricket would not have been highly gratified unless they had regarded it as a charity burlesque.

Now the main bush, in which the gay and festive Hau Hau lived and gambolled, was about one thousand yards away from the fort, but there were big patches of bush up to within four hundred yards of it, and any amount of *manuka* and fern scrub, that afforded good cover to an enemy wishing to pass from one to the other of these patches, so that, notwithstanding all our vigilance, scouts, or even considerable numbers of Hau Haus, could get quite close up to the stockade.

Well, the game commenced, and of course attracted the attention of the gentle savage. Word was quickly passed into the recesses of the bush that the white man was up to some new and inexplicable devilment, so before long we had a highly interested if not appreciative gallery, who, emerging from the bush, squatted down, and for a time behaved itself with decorum.

To this we did not object, and had they continued to behave they might have remained there to the end, but perhaps they were overcritical, and the play, as I have already stated, not being first class, they may have considered they were entitled to show their disapproval of it.

Now we could have made allowances for their ignorance or their want of appreciation, although they were self-invited and had paid no gate money, even should they have gone so far as to hiss, but I main-

FIELDING UNDER DIFFICULTIES—LOST BALL

tain that paying spectators should restrain themselves from heaving at the players such things as dead cats, antiquated eggs, or ginger-beer bottles, but when it comes to expressing dissatisfaction with *tuparas* (double-barrelled guns) and Enfield rifles it is high time for the performers to skip or clear the ground.

Now the play was not good, that I allow, and also it is very doubtful what the Hau Haus thought had occasioned this entertainment and extravagant display of energy on the part of the hated white man. As most of them had been Christians they knew it was not a religious ceremony, neither was it a war-dance, white men not being civilised up to the merits of the war-dance. Perhaps they put it down to witchcraft, or some sort of an extra insulting challenge issued by men who had just built a *pah* in spite of the lavish expenditure of powder they had seen fit to waste in their attempts to obstruct its completion.

Anyhow it was something important, or wherefore those cheers and hand-clapping from the other white men who lined the parapet or reclined on the ground, and as such must be counteracted.

First of all they danced a war-dance, and as no attention was paid to that they proceeded to take more active measures.

In the meantime the game had been progressing steadily. The troopers had had their first innings and had scored one hundred runs and the rangers had scored ninety with the loss of nine wickets.

The excitement was intense, "Well bowled," "Well hit," "Oh, well fielded" being howled by the enraptured lookers-on after every delivery, while ribald chaff, banter and badinage were being exchanged by troopers and rangers that would have shocked the spectators of a modern test match.

The last hope of the Footsloggers was a leviathan sergeant, an old Varsity blue, but his partner was a very fragile reed, who only required one straight ball to finish.

Could the sergeant keep the bowling to himself? That was the question, and men hugged themselves with excitement. He has it now, and the fielders retire farther out. By gad! he gets a loose one, and opening his shoulders he smacks it over Long-on's head. Big as the hit is he will only get three or perhaps four for it, as on that tussocky ground where a ball pitches there it stops, and Long-on is far out. Still the hit is a big one and is cheered by his delighted friends. "Well hit," "Oh, well hit," "Run it out," "Oh, run it out." Nor are the troopers behindhand with their shouts. "Double up, oh, double up," "Sling it in, oh, sling it in," as Long-on has turned and, weighed down by revolver and ammunition pouches, darts after the leather sphere. Yes, there it is lying on that bit of open ground less than a hundred yards from that patch of scrub. Spurred on by the wild turmoil of shouts—"Oh, hurry up; for God's sake hurry up," "Chuck her in now—smart," "There, run three, run it out; allow one for the throw," etc., etc.—he rushes at the ball.

But what's the matter? Of a sudden the wild yells terminate into the pious ejaculation of "Oh, hell!" while the eager fielder throws himself on his nose, hunting cover, and drawing his revolver lets go the agonising shout of *"Lost ball!"*

Well this is what the matter was. As the questing fielder rushes to secure the ball that lies in full view in front of him and throw it in, out of that patch of *manuka* scrub darts several spurts of flame and smoke, and a number of balls of a different nature whistle round his head, and I ask you present-day cricketers which of you would have cared to have fielded that ball and slung it in to the expectant wicket-keeper? Or would you have hunted cover and howled, *"Lost ball!"* as that Pigskin Polisher did?

"Damn such interruptions," shouts the umpire, who was the colonel at that; "drive the beggars off the field." And in a moment batsmen, fielders, umpires, scorers and onlookers grab their weapons and charge that patch of *manuka* scrub. We reach and tear through it just in time to see a party of Hau Haus disappear into a clump of bush some way farther off, then, laughing and cussing, return to our game as the friendly natives good-naturedly offer to keep the ground for us.

The continuation of the game evidently mortified the Hau Haus, for they lined the four-hundred-yard bush and fired volleys at us. Did we allow them to stop the game? Not a bit of it. It was far too important a one to allow a gang of measly Hau Haus to interfere with, for was not that night grog night? And had not every trooper wagered his tot in backing his side? And had not every ranger done the same? Stop play; indeed no! They would play it out to the bitter end. So the game went on.

Now it is rather trying to most men to stand up against fast, erratic bowling on a more than bumpy pitch, but should the batsman's attention be distracted while watching the ball by the whistle of an Enfield bullet past his nose, or by seeing the pitch torn up by a similar missile, it becomes too exciting for anyone.

Again, it is rather conducive to wild bowling for a bowler to have to submit to the same ordeal preparatory to his delivering a ball, nor can even an umpire give the amount of attention the game requires to his important functions when half his time has to be devoted to dodging ricochets. So that the colonel, a sportsman to his finger-tips, ordered all the available men not playing to assist the friendly natives in keeping order in the free seats. This they did, though not without a smart skirmish, which ended in the rowdy interrupters being driven off the field with the loss of several men, which served them right for trying to interfere with sport.

This well-merited chastisement did not, however, satisfy the contumacious bounders, for they took post in the big bush and continued to lob bullets at us from the distance of a thousand yards, but of these we took no notice, for although now and again a bullet would announce itself with an angry hum, or drop nearly plump into the ground, yet they afforded a man a good excuse should he butter a catch or make a duck. Anyhow we played the match out, and I am delighted to say the troopers won by the narrow margin of seven runs, although I regret to add I contributed but little towards the winning score.

CHAPTER 10

How Maoris Should Be Fought

I mentioned in the last chapter that our paucity of men allowed the Hau Haus the opportunity of making things warm for us, and they lost no time in taking advantage of it; for one day they had the cheek to ambuscade, within half-a-mile of the fort, a dray loaded with rations. Now there was a standing order that a ration dray should be escorted by twelve troopers, but as the unfortunate O.C. of the post from whence the dray started had only twelve men for all duties he could only send three, and the Hau Haus thought this far too good a chance to be lost. The dray was drawn by two horses driven tandem fashion, and when it had reached within half-a-mile of Waihi, and within view of the camp, a party of natives lurking in the scrub fired a volley at the escort and charged with their *tomahawks*. One trooper, named Haggarty, went down, horse and man, but the driver managed to unhook his lead horse, jumped on its back and with the remaining two troopers won through to the fort, from whence a party of Rangers had already sallied.

These soon reached the spot, where they found the empty dray and the remains of the poor chap chopped to pieces, but the rations and the shaft-horse taken away. Now this vexed the colonel, and more than irritated the rest of us, as rations were very scarce indeed, and we were quite pleased when the O.C. determined to return them a Roland for their Oliver; so next day another dray, apparently heavily loaded, with an absurdly small escort, was despatched from the fort.

Some hours, however, previous to its departure, a party of Rangers and friendly natives had been despatched to do a bit of ambuscading on our behalf, and proved themselves worthy of the trust placed in them; for when the Hau Haus, having spotted the sham escort, came down from the bush to gobble it up they fell into the trap so skilfully planted by the Rangers, who knocked the immortal stuffin' out of them, sending them back to the bush hungry and howling, having on this occasion received *toko* instead of tucker.

This lesson, though a severe one, the O.C. did not think quite adequate, so he determined to strike another blow to teach them better manners for the future, and to leave his men's rations alone. He therefore with the greatest secrecy called in men from the other posts, which was a very dangerous thing to do, as it left them for the time quite defenceless, but he had no other course to pursue, and Fortune favours the bold player. Still, after scraping every man together, he could muster only one hundred and thirteen men of all ranks, and it was a very, very risky game he intended to play, and one he would never have attempted had he not had the greatest confidence in his officers and men.

Of course a body of men as large as this one was bound to be spotted leaving camp, so that to mislead the enemy's scouts he first marched to the fort on the Waingangora River and pretended to start work there, but at ten p.m. we silently left there, crossed the river, and made for an old deserted *pah* where our scouts had come across a well-defined track running inland. This track they had scouted until it had ended in a clearing, but could penetrate no farther as the enemy's scouts were too much on the alert. However, he hoped that he had blinded them by what we had done at Waingangora.

Well, we started, passed the deserted *pah*, moved carefully on till we came to the clearing, and then, as we were ignorant of the actual position of the Hau Haus, we lay down and waited. Presently we heard, not far off, some cocks crow, which giving us the desired information we moved off in their direction, and had not proceeded a mile when, just as day broke, we came to a long, narrow clearing with a lot of huts scattered all the way up it. As there was no possibility of surrounding the place our O.C., without a pause, led us right up it, leaving a few men at the door of each hut as we passed, who, with carbines loaded and cocked, stood at them without making a sound. The movement, quickly conceived as it was, was admirably carried out, for although before it was quite completed an alarm was given, yet very few natives escaped, nor was there the least confusion as the men, all of whom were old hands, stood ready without saying a word.

When the arrangements were finished to his satisfaction the colonel posted himself in front of the largest and most central hut, and delivered his ultimatum, shouting out: "Will ye, O Ngatiruanui, who are now surrounded, surrender yourselves as prisoners of war or be shot?"

The query was a brief one; the answer was still briefer, for it came in the shape of a volley fired from all the huts that dropped a lot of our men, although it would have been better for the inmates had they considered their answer more carefully, as Rangers are not men with whom to bandy words. For in a moment fire was applied to every *whare*, which, being built of dry *raupo* as inflammable as petrol, burst into sheets of flame that transformed the quiet village into an animated hell.

Out from the flaming *whares* rushed men, half mad, with scorched hides and blazing hair, only to be blown off their feet by shots fired from a few yards distant, while the flames, smoke, explosions of powder, yells, cheers and shots, together with the roar and crackling of the burning huts, made a service that sunny Sabbath morning that must have delighted Old Nick himself.

This part of the day's performance did not last long, as in less than ten minutes every hut but one was consumed, and every Maori dead with the exception of that one's occupants. Unfortunately the hut remaining was a big *whare puni* made of thick slabs of wood covered with earth, at the door of which lay the dead body of one of our men, and as no fire would touch this little fortress there was nothing to be done but dig out the garrison. We at once set to work at this job, and had nearly unearthed them when we were attacked from three sides by an overwhelming party of Hau Haus.

It was evidently high time to clear out of that, but our colonel was not the man to be balked of his prey. There was no time for more digging, so he again called on those inside to surrender, promising to spare their lives if they did so at once.

To this they consented, and one of them came out, but he had no sooner shown himself than a number of friendly natives standing close by recognised the unfortunate Johnny as one of their bitterest tribal enemies, so let drive a volley at him, nearly blowing the poor wretch to smithereens. This low-down conduct drove the colonel hopping mad, and he cussed the delinquents with so much unction that the tone of his cuss words reassured the Hau Haus to that extent they at once came out and surrendered.

It was now high time for us to skip, and we promptly made ready to do so, as we had already lost three men killed and seven men badly wounded; this for a small force like ours was bad enough, but casualties in savage warfare mean a much greater loss than the actual number of men hit.

You see it is this way: A man gets wounded in civilised warfare; well, his side only loses the use of one player for that match. As for the wounded Johnny, he just makes himself as comfortable as circumstances permit and quietly awaits the arrival of the first ambulance, be it friend or foe, when he is picked up and taken care of.

This, however, was not a rule of the game as played in New Zealand. If a man got wounded there his own friends must get him away smart, for if the Hau Haus got him, so far from making his wound whole they would make him into a whole wound by torturing him in a way not fit to write about, and as it took at least four men to carry the poor chap along the rough bush paths we lost the use of five men's rifles instead of losing only one.

Then again it was considered very bad form to leave a dead man behind, for doing so not only supplied the enemy with a quantity of fresh meat rations, but the capture of one was considered to be a great triumph to them and an equal disgrace to ourselves. It therefore amounted to this, that as we had ten men *hors de combat* it left us with only-sixty-three rifles to withstand the onslaught of the infuriated Hau Haus, besides which we had nine prisoners to shepherd.

Nevertheless we must skip, so were just moving off when Pierre rushed up and reported the enemy had seized and were holding the only path we knew leading out of the confounded clearing.

Even this Job's comforter did not daunt our gallant O.C, who at once summoned the prisoners and demanded if there was any other path leading out of the place we could make use of, at the same time politely informing them that if there was not, much as he regretted the necessity, he would be forced to order their immediate execution.

This reasoning they saw was sound, and they at once promptly replied that there was another road, and that rather than linger any longer on that in-salubrious spot they would guide us out by it.

Now this was real kind of them, so we carried the wounded off, leaving a rear-guard of only thirty-five men to cover our retreat, and it was fortunate, not only for themselves, but for the whole of us, that they were a splendid lot of well-trained old hands who were conversant with every wrinkle in bush fighting, and moreover had as commander one of the bravest and most experienced officers in the country.

Nor were we going to have a very rosy time of it, as carrying a heavy man in a blanket along a narrow, crooked path running through dense bush and over a terribly rough and broken country is no child's play. Remember that on a bush footpath stretchers are of no use, the unfortunate wounded must therefore be lugged along either in men's arms or doubled up in a blanket; that we had none of those drugs nor appliances that now rob the battlefield and hospital of half their terrors and that even on reaching camp a fern bed with a rolled-up blanket for a pillow was the only accommodation a wounded man could hope for.

At the front there was no chloroform, medical comforts nor nurses, so that the lot of a wounded man was by no means a happy one. Well, we were nearly clear of the bush when the colonel called me and pointing out a low rough hill said: "Burke, you see that hill, the path runs half way round its base and we shall be in open ground when we get past it, but if the enemy gain possession of it we shall lose heavily. Now, I want you to take ten men, make for the top of it as fast as ever you can, and hold it till Northcroft and the rear-guard win past."

Hastily summoning the first available ten men, among whom were old Jack, Pierre, George, Buck and Tim, the rest of them being friendly Maoris, we pushed for the hill as fast as we could get over the ground, reaching the top of it just in the nick of time, for as we surmounted its crest we ran bang into a dozen Hau Haus who were struggling up the other side.

There was no time for speech-making nor tactics, so we just jumped at one another, and I had no sooner fired my carbine than I saw a big native with his tongue protruding and the whites of his eyes turned up spring at me through the smoke, twirling a long-handled *tomahawk* around his head, as if it had been a shillelagh in the hands of one of my own countrymen at home, and moreover had barely time to throw up my carbine, so as to guard a swashing cut he was good enough to deliver at the left side of my head. Troth and it was no fool of a cut either, for it drove my carbine in until the muzzle of it came against my left shoulder, which fortunately prevented my guard from being quite broken, though the razor-edged blade at the business end of the six-foot flexible *manuka* handle, whipping over my carbine barrel, cut my left ear in two, scarred my cheek, and gashed my eyebrow so deeply that the flap of the wound fell over, which besides deluging me with blood quite obstructed the sight of my left eye, so much so that I thought I was blinded.

This thought transmogrified me into a raging fiend, so I let go my carbine, and, without even pausing to say damn your soul, flew at his throat like a wild cat, which I was fortunate enough to get a firm hold of with my right hand.

Well was it for me at that moment that I had devoted so many hours of my young life to the gymnasium and *salle d'armes*, and that my great natural strength had been increased by culture to an almost phenomenal extent, for now it was to be tried to its very utmost, and my wiry, well-trained thews and sinews tested to their breaking point. Well was it, also, for me, that by the quick fury of my wild-cat attack I had at once made good my hold on his bull throat, a hold I swore to maintain till death parted us. Gad, I was very angry, for the thought of having lost my eye was more than I could tolerate, and I saw scarlet.

My opponent was a big, powerful fellow, standing fully six feet and well proportioned, who, although inclined to run to flesh, was still very active, and a most formidable antagonist for a young man who measured only five feet seven inches and weighed under eleven stone. He was, moreover, a noted warrior and a past master in the use of native hand-to-hand weapons. Therefore, failing firearms, it was the very best thing I could have done to grapple with him, and it was to my immense advantage having caught the first hold.

The moment I had closed with him he dropped his long-handled weapon and strove with all his might to tear away my grip on his throat with his left hand, while with his right he attempted to seize mine, but I successfully guarded it and, although he repeatedly struck me with his right hand, we were too closely locked for him to do me much harm, while I was surely if slowly choking him.

The struggle seemed to last for hours, in reality it did not last for five minutes, but it was a hot five minutes, and one to be remembered a lifetime. For a few seconds we tugged and heaved at one another, and twice he swung me off my legs into the air, but I hung on and landed on my feet. In vain he tried to sink his nails into my right forearm, but the muscles, hardened by years of fencing, cricket and gymnastics, were as rigid as iron, for although he scratched and scored the skin yet he could make no impression on the arm itself, the nervous fingers of which were nearly buried round his windpipe.

I now began to feel I was getting the best of it, besides which, although still animated by the determination to kill, I was becoming cooler and cooler, and watched for any opportunity so that I could profit by it.

Again and again he made desperate efforts to throw me off, and after one prolonged, furious struggle, in which I thought my sinews must give way, his feet got caught by a vine and we fell heavily sideways to the ground; when with one tremendous heave I gained the upper hand and drove my right knee into the lower part of his breast-bone. Oh, but it was a glorious feeling of exultation that rushed through my brain as I tightened, if possible, my clutch on his windpipe and, using the leverage of my knee, tugged and tugged again.

One more despairing effort made and thwarted convinced me he was beaten as he perceptibly grew weaker and weaker, and although I never relaxed my attention to my own particular quarry I glanced round to see, if possible, how the game was progressing with my comrades, as with the exception of one or two pistol shots everyone had fought mute, and the grim match had been played with tomahawk, knife and hand.

The first I spotted was Tim, on his feet, wrestling furiously with a big Maori, and at the same glance saw George glide up and bury his huge knife in the native's back, who at once relaxed his hold, when Tim, throwing the dead body clear, yelled out: "Mr Dick, where are ye, sor? Oh, holy Jesus, Where's the master?" Jack I could also see kneeling in the stunted fern evidently top dog, for I caught the flash of his swinging *tomahawk* and heard the crushing thud as the blow descended. I could also hear the grunts and deep sobbing gasps and see the fern trembling where men still fought in their death struggles, but I had now no anxiety for the future as we had at least three hale men on their feet and temporarily out of employment, so I started in to finish off my man.

My man was by now almost passive, so much so indeed that I could have easily drawn my knife with my left hand, but somehow the thought of sticking a man like a pig revolted me. No; it had been up to now a fair fought fight, hand against hand, so let the hand finish it; nor did he require much more attention, as after one or two convulsive heaves he lay quite quiet and I knew I had finished him.

I was just on the point of rising when up rushed Tim swinging a *tomahawk* over his head, who with his eyes blazing yelled out: "Hould on, Mr Dick, hould on, sor," and before I could say a word sank his weapon into the dead man's head, sending the contents of it spurting all over me.

"Faugh, Tim," I said, starting to my feet. "It's a dirty fighter you are; give me something to wipe my face with."

"Och, be the howly Saint Bridget, it's kilt ye are, Mr Dick; oh, wura, wura, where's the doctor, bad luck to him," whined Tim.

"Killed be d——d," said I. "But he has blinded my left eye." And seeing the row was over I quickly gave the order: "Load all the carbines, boys, and take cover."

No sooner was this done than Tim was alongside me with a couple of bandages and a pannikin of water, when, tenderly raising the flap of flesh that hung over my eye, in a moment I knew that the sight of it was all right and the relief of mind was immense.

It did not take my kind-hearted comrade more than a minute to replace the flap and twist a bandage round my head, when I was quite fit to attend to my duty.

First of all I looked out for any enemy; there was none in sight though the noise of the rear-guard action was drawing much closer, and I was delighted to see the colonel's party already past the danger point as I was now able to judge how lucky we had been in capturing the hill, for our loss must have been very heavy had the enemy succeeded in gaining it, because the hill completely commanded the only footpath.

I next turned my attention to our own casualties; one friendly native was dead, poor Buck, wounded desperately, was lying on his back with his head on a blanket, and as I knelt down beside him, taking his hand, he opened his eyes and murmured: "Goodbye, Master Burke, struck bed-rock, panned out, shift my pegs," and with a sigh or two the gallant English yeoman drew his pegs and started for another gold rush. The remainder of us, although more or less chipped, were all fit for another scrap if called upon to face one, while nine dead Hau Haus cumbered the ground.

Setting Jack to sew up our poor comrade in his blanket, while Tim and one of the Maoris dug his last claim, with the rest of the men I was keeping a bright lookout, when the colonel with thirty men joined me.

"Well done, Burke," said he, "by gad, you fellows have done well. Not much hurt I trust? Well, my boy, you wanted to gain bush-fighting experience, gad, you are getting it. I'll leave you six more men and take the others on to the rear-guard. In case you are attacked hold this place to the last, but retreat when the rear-guard get round that corner, we shall be able then to cover you. So-long," and he was off.

I, however, was not called on to hold the hill, as Lieutenant Northcroft made such a masterly retreat, and his men fought so well, that the enemy, seeing we had possession of the position and rightly judging that their own party, sent to grab it, had been cut to pieces, after harmlessly burning an immense quantity of ammunition at long range, drew off, allowing our men to disentangle themselves from the bush, and to retire back to camp in peace.

Chapter 11

Sport à la Lost Legion

I have previously asserted that this yarn is not meant to be a history of New Zealand wars, nor do I wish to harrow the tender hearts of gentle readers, should I be fortunate enough to secure any, by stories of savage bloodshed or by describing gruesome details of war to the knife. Yet, taking into consideration the astounding ignorance of most well-educated English men and women concerning the history of the principal colonies that now form the greater portion of the mighty British Empire, I think I may be pardoned for recounting a few scenes of the events, battles and hardships, willingly endured by the men who actually won those colonies and rendered them habitable for a civilised people. Nor do I think the men, rough, wild, undesirable ne'er-do-wells as they mostly were, who recklessly risked their lives for that purpose, should be entirely forgotten.

These scenes are not imaginary ones, evolved from my own brain, but real occurrences; and the men, whom I am trying to describe, actually lived, fought, drank, and were killed in the way I relate; alas, would that I had a more gifted pen and a more artistic touch to depict them, their reckless lives and their hard deaths.

However, as my pen is neither artistic nor gifted, nor even a particularly good one to write with, I must jog on as best I can, in the same way my gallant O.C. did, when, short of men and with plenty of malignant, backbiting enemies in both Government and district, he made head against the hostile Hau Haus.

After the fight at Pungarehu, fortune seemed for a considerable time to have deserted us, which was not to be wondered at, for although the Government provided more men, and we were reinforced by various parties of volunteers, yet these recruits were, for the most part, new chums of a very inferior quality. Indeed, most of them, having been enlisted from among the scum and riff-raff of the big Australian cities, were naturally very different from those old hands whose services the idiotic Government had so cavalierly dispensed with, or who had been lost through the wastage of war; and I was soon to learn the awful difference of going into action with a lot of untrained, half-baked, raw hands, instead of well-trained, reliable men.

Again the newcomers could not stand the physical hardships of the work. They knocked up when marching and were not by any means dependable shots or bush men. So that the campaign dragged, for although we made many attempts we never again succeeded in catching the enemy on the hop as we had done at Pungarehu. In fact, on one or two occasions, we received more than we gave, and although we did not, as yet, meet with any calamitous disaster, yet, at times, we had to quit the bush faster than we went in, having failed to do that which we went in to attempt, and these failures so bucked up the Hau Haus that it enabled Titokowaru, a savage and very fanatical chief, to draw numbers of them to his flag, with whom for over two years he successfully opposed us, during which period he administered two very serious defeats to the colonial forces.

It was while on one of these numerous excursions I witnessed a somewhat extraordinary instance of presentiment of death, which, owing to the fact of the man who received the impression taking advantage of it, thereby dodged the catastrophe. Here's the yarn, deduct what moral you will.

Among the friendly natives was one named Winiata, who was distinguished for his great courage; and when, among a race noted for their bravery, a man becomes so distinguished, there can be no doubt of his intrepidity. In fact, not only by his own comrades, but also by the white men, and even by the Hau Haus, no mean judges of courage, he was regarded as the very incarnation of valour.

Now Winiata always led the van, and was the rear of the rear-guard in a retreat, and his numerous acts of dare-devil recklessness were the talk of both camps. Well, on one occasion, we were advancing to attack a place, when to everyone's astonishment Winiata hung back, and instead of being leading man enacted the part of a timid skulker. This surprised the O.C. so much that he asked the man what was the matter. Winiata, without hesitation replied: "I dreamt last night I was leading the van as usual, when we were ambuscaded and I was killed, the bullet striking me on one hip and coming out at the other, so today I remain in the rear."

THOKOWAKU

The column, at the time, was moving through dense bush, along a footpath so narrow we could only proceed in single file, and a short time after Winiata had unbosomed himself the enemy poured a volley into the head of it, killing the leading file. Whereupon Winiata rushed to the front and, pointing to the dead man, said to the O.C.: "Ah, that's the bullet which meant to kill me," and true enough the death wound that had killed his substitute was exactly similar to the one he had dreamt was to have finished himself off. After this all the other natives declared that Winiata's god was a very powerful one and that his *mana* (luck) was great.

I have, up till now, said but very little of the various ways in which we tried to amuse ourselves when resting in camp or, as we now were, marking time in our Hau Hau tail-twisting operations. True, we were much scattered, being located in different forts, but our O.C, fully recognising the necessity of allowing the men recreation, *as all work and no play makes Jack a dull boy*, eagerly grasped every opportunity of affording the men any amusement that lay in his power. So that we indulged in an occasional cricket match, race meeting and athletic sports, with now and then a camp fire and sing-songs.

Some of the competitions were very good, as amongst such a mixed crowd as ours there were naturally some really good athletes, not only among the white men but also among the friendly natives, all of whom took a very keen interest in the events.

Of course, after one or two trials the crack men were discovered, but we had such clever handicappers that the interest in the various events was always kept up to the required excitement pitch, so necessary to render this form of sport attractive to the looker-on, and as there was much healthy rivalry between the various posts there was no chance of the general interest in these sports flagging.

It was through taking a very keen interest in my post's chances for distinction that I discovered a man who, had he been taken in hand and been well trained and taught in his youth, would I am sure have turned out to be one of the greatest athletes the world has ever possessed.

Strange to say the man himself, a London Cockney, was profoundly ignorant of his own capabilities, and it was quite by accident I discovered them. The way it was done is as follows.

A big athletic meeting was to be held at headquarters on Christmas Day, at which each station was to be represented, and the rivalry was not so much between individuals as it was between the various stations, one garrison against another, also trooper *v.* footslogger, and the men at my post were very keen.

We were, however, sadly in want of a sprinter and high leaper. I could run and jump a bit, but then I had been beaten so easily on a previous occasion at all these events that it was hopeless to expect me to win on the coming one. True, we had a most reliable man in Tim for the mile and the long jump, and although he also had been defeated before, still, on that occasion he had been unfit, while now he was in splendid trim, so that we had great hopes of him pulling off his events, but I could offer no such excuses as I had been in splendid fettle and had done my very best, but had not succeeded in getting placed, as I had been fairly beaten by better men, and as I was by a long way the best man at the post things looked very black for us, and our hearts were very dark indeed.

Now among my men was one named Bright, who had been enlisted not so much for his fighting capabilities, for he was no good either in the pig-skin or in the bush, but as a baker, and even as such he was a bad one. Up to date I had never taken much notice of the fellow, except perhaps on a muster parade, when I invariably had to check him for general untidiness, in fact the wooden way he slouched about the camp rather got on my nerves, and then his bread was often damnable.

One day, however, I happened to notice him on a bathing parade and was much struck by the muscular development of his legs and thighs, which without being abnormal had yet every appearance of possessing extraordinary nervous powers.

That evening we were practising sprinting, at which he was simply looking on, when turning to him I said: "How is it. Bright, you never compete with the others?" to which he answered:

"Well, sir, I never tried to run or jump in my life."

"Then," said I, "it's high time you did. Come and run over the hundred yard course with me and do your best so as to try and push me."

It could not have been called a fair race, as I was dressed in flannels and canvas shoes, while he was togged in overalls with ammunition boots, and of course my experience gave me an immense advantage at the start, as when we jumped off I must have gained over three yards. I was ahead, as I expected to be, when I had covered fifty yards, and I expected to win easily, but all of a sudden he whizzed past me as if I had been standing still, and although I strained every nerve he ran clean away from me, beating me by fifteen yards or more. I was simply thunderstruck. I had run and been beaten often before by men whom I knew to be good men, but never had I been beaten like this, and turning to one of the sergeants, an old public schoolboy, I asked him how he accounted for it? To which he replied:

"There is only one way to account for it, sir. This fellow Bright is a perfect wonder. Why, sir, when you had covered forty yards he was ten yards behind you, then all of a sudden he seemed to start going and appeared to go faster and faster every yard he ran. By Jove! sir, if we had him at Lillie Bridge how he would astonish the world."

Here was the chance of our winning the short races at the approaching Christmas sports, so we promptly took him in hand to teach him to start, run straight and all the other wrinkles of the running track.

Then happy thought! Why the blazes should not this ignorant lout be able to jump as well as run? Faith it was worth while trying him, so I bullied him till he did so, and found out he jumped like a seasick kangaroo, with body and legs nearly straight. Teach the bounder to jump like a Christian we could not, but by teaching him where to take off, and keeping him hard at it, by the time the sports drew near he could clear five feet six inches, which was good enough.

Well, this Johnny we kept dark, and all the men at my station saved their money and formulated plans to get a bit of their own back, as they all had lost heavily at the last sports, and they meant this time to plunder the Amalekites.

The man who was first favourite for the hundred yards and the quarter of a mile was a very smart young Australian who had run in good company over in Victoria. He had won both events at the last contest and as he, as well as two or three others, had beaten me easily then, and as all hands fancied I was still the best man at my station, the foot gangers thought we could have no chance, and were ready to plank their bottom dollar against our winning a single event.

The long-looked-for Christmas Day at length arrived, and as the Hau Haus were quiet all the men who could be spared from garrisoning the forts gathered together at headquarters. Now, the rule was that only two men from each station should enter for each separate event, so that when myself and Bright entered for the hundred yards, quarter of a mile and high jump it was considered our chance was nil, long odds being wagered against us. In fact Bright's slouching wooden appearance caused unbounded merriment with much rough banter.

The troopers, so as not to spoil the market, had deputed one of their number, who was supposed to possess great acumen and almost Satanic finesse, to transact the wagering business on their behalf, those of them being present strolling about bewailing their station's lack of chance, and the wily-one received very long odds against our winning a single event, being so cute that he filled his book before the sports started.

The hundred yards race was the first on the programme, for which event ten competitors toed the mark, and there was much chaff at the clumsy way Bright took his place. The pistol was fired, and we jumped off, Bright, of course, last of all, but before the ruck in which I was had covered thirty yards he rushed past us like an express engine, and at seventy-five yards had overhauled the leading man and challenged the young Australian, Duff, who, running first and thinking himself quite safe, was saving himself as much as possible for his other races. In a flash Bright took the lead from him and, to the unbounded astonishment of all hands, breasted the tape quite three yards clear in advance of Duff, who, when he had recovered from his amazement sufficiently to speak, ejaculated the word "D—n!"

Of course the footsloggers all swore it was a fluke and tried to account for their champion's defeat in various ways, with much vivid language, while Duff allowed he had been caught napping, and asserted that before such a thing should occur again he would jolly well go to—well, a warmer climate than even that of Australia—and that in the quarter of a mile he would make the ruddy dough-puncher long to immolate himself in his own blasted oven.

Just before the race I scratched, as I wanted to see it run, as did most of the other men. It was Duff's best distance and we all knew he would try his utmost, and although I had great faith in my neophyte, yet it was a big order to expect him to beat a man with a known record such as Duff had.

Well, the pistol cracked and Duff gained a lot of ground at the start; nor did Bright, for the first fifty yards, seem to be able to set himself going, but then he all at once appeared to get into his stride. His pace increased in a marvellous manner, and he seemed to run up to the others with an ease and rapidity I have never seen approached, while before they reached the hundred-yard peg he had collared Duff, who was leading. The latter made a game effort to retain his place, and for perhaps ten yards or more did so, when Bright shot ahead, going faster and faster, and without an effort ran right away, winning easily by at least thirty yards.

This was a glorious victory, and when he had won the high jump, clearing five feet seven inches, one grim old Maori chief gravely asked me if I had imported the devil, and proposed that he should kill him off-hand, as in his opinion no such common personage as a cook or baker had any right to beat warriors or chiefs. He also stated he had for some time entertained grave doubts of Bright's respectability, as some hot bread he had eaten of Bright's making had given him a most infernal pain in the stomach, so at any rate he thought he might *tomahawk* him just a little bit in the way of *utu* (payment or revenge) for his dose of indigestion. But then again on second thoughts his tummy-ache was a thing of the past, his present need was tobacco, and as the fellow was one of my slaves, perhaps if I handed him over a plug it might be as well to forgive and forget. Needless to say he received his plug.

That day was a big day for the troopers, as Tim won both the mile and the long jump, so after a good dinner my men returned to our fort weighed down with plunder which the wily one had extracted from the pouches of the footsloggers, and all confessed that even a rotten bad baker may sometimes prove useful.

Among a crowd like ours there were, of course, some very queer fish, men from every grade of society and every walk of life. To very many of these, society had said goodbye without regret, and yet we had men in our ranks who, but for a single failing, were fit to occupy any position in the *beau-monde* they had quitted forever. Nor had they all been wrong uns; far from it, as many, like myself, had simply been born unlucky or had not the means to retain the positions in which they had been born.

One of the queerest of these fallen angels was a man who called himself Barney Fisher, or the Arapipi spider. Who or what he had been the Lord only knew, but he possessed gifts that would have made him a welcome guest in any country house in the world. A superb horseman and good at every outdoor game, he was equally proficient in those indoor pastimes that make a man like himself so valuable to a hostess, who finds it so hard to find amusement for a houseful of people on a wet day. He could paint a picture worth looking at, write a song and sing it, although the *libretto*, if similar to the topical chants he composed for his comrades' benefit, would not have been tolerated for a moment, dance a breakdown or jig and drink ration rum by the quart without turning a hair, besides all which he could talk fluently on any subject in the world in most of the European languages and was as good-natured and obliging as it is possible for a man to be.

Over and over again he received heavy remittances to take him home and on more than one occasion took his discharge for that purpose, but it was no good, he never got farther than the nearest town, where he could cash his draft, which being done he would paint that town crimson until his last shilling was blued and then return to the troop.

So used were we to these periodical absences that his horse and equipments were kept ready for him and he would be received back with open arms, one reason for which being that the said horse was such a fiend that no other man cared to groom him, much less ride him, although with Barney he was as quiet as a lamb.

Yes; the Arapipi spider was a queer fish, but we had one queerer still; a tall, thin slab of a fellow who called himself Limbs, and was yclept by his comrades the Duke of Limbs.

Standing over six feet three, he wore a close-shaved face, long as a child's coffin, the features of which always seemed set with such a look of intense melancholic disappointment that the observer would at once come to the conclusion that the wretched man had just murdered his father for his wealth, and had then only found wild-cat securities. Still he was a cheery chap in his own sorrowful way, and although he was never known to laugh, or even smile, yet by his inadvertences he would cause amusement, or sometimes even trouble, by perpetrating acts which, if committed by an ordinary individual, would have stamped him as a malignant *farceur* or a practical joker suffering from liver.

He was, moreover, most good-natured, he would give away anything, but like the gifts of the Greeks his donations at times were dangerous to their recipients. Did he not on one occasion present old Paukino with a Tongeriro (a seidlitz powder, so called by the natives after a burning mountain that is always vomiting a column of steam), directing the ancient warrior to first swallow the powders and then drink a pannikin of water, a process that turned the respectable old man-eater into a human volcano of the most active description, and cost me a gallon of rum to pacify his infuriated relations, all of whom swore, and not without reason, that his Grace had bewitched the old fellow.

His Grace's strong suit, however, were his limbs, of which he had the most perfect control (hence his title), he being the most wonderful contortionist I have ever seen in my life, and he would frequently raise a laugh on parade, while sitting rigid in his saddle, by scratching the back of his head with his spurs, or by tying himself into a knot on some equally inappropriate occasion. He was checked frequently, but was such a good fellow, and made such splendid excuses when carpeted in the office tent, that he escaped without dire punishment, especially as the O.C., considering the men's lives were quite hard enough to be endured, set his face dead against drastic punishments which would make them harder; but one day his Grace played a trick that might have caused serious trouble. It happened in this way.

I have mentioned in a previous chapter how, during the shindy at Pungarehu, we had captured nine prisoners, or rather nine Hau Haus had surrendered to the O.C. on his promise that their lives should be spared, and as it was a nuisance keeping these Johnnies alive in a frontier post it was decided to send them, for safe keeping, to Wanganui.

On the first night of their journey, themselves and escort were to sleep in our fort, at which the colonel happened to be sojourning on the same night. Well, my guard took them over from the travelling escort, and they were confined inside a somewhat flimsy hut in the centre of the fort with a sentry inside to watch them, for which purpose a stable lamp was suspended from the roof.

This was by no means a safe prison, but, as all the rest of the detachment slept in the open surrounding them, there was no chance of escape, especially as they well knew if they tried to play monkey tricks it would be paramount to ordering their own funerals, besides which, they had sworn to the colonel that they would make no effort to do so.

Well, the night waxed late; the camp, prisoners and everyone, with the exception of the guard, the colonel, myself and two other officers being fast asleep. We officers were writing and drawing, in fact assisting the O.C. with despatches that had to be forwarded next day, when all at once we were disturbed by yells of terror and consternation. To seize our revolvers and dash out of the tent was the work of a moment, and we were in time to see the men spring to their arms, while out through the flimsy walls of the *raupo*-built hut burst the yelling Hau Haus.

In a moment they were seized, in fact they made not the slightest attempt to run away, and in a few minutes were paraded before the indignant O.C., who sternly demanded, "What the Hades they meant by making such an infernal clamour and trying to escape?"

To the charge of attempting to get away, a hoary-headed old cannibal offered an indignant denial, and as for the clamour and hut-breaking, that he declared was the colonel's own fault, as why had he shut them up with the devil.

This defence amounting almost to a counter-charge, made the colonel open his eyes. He was essentially a just man, and his great knowledge of Maori character at once led him to believe that something out of the common must have happened, so he ordered the sentry to be called, who turned out to be the Duke of Limbs. On his stepping forth, the O.C. demanded the reason of the turmoil.

Now the colonel was quite ignorant of the duke's gifts, and he started back, rubbing his eyes, but saying nothing, for, as he afterwards confided to me, he thought he must have been mistaken when in the dim light it appeared to him that the trooper, standing rigidly to attention, all of a sudden elevated his right leg and scratched the back of his head with his spur, at the same time answering in a most lugubrious voice:

"Sir, I went on sentry at ten p.m. as second relief. I counted the prisoners, saw the lamp was trimmed and then as the roof of the *whare* was too low for me to stand upright I seated myself with my back to the door and watched the natives. At eleven-thirty, sir, that old man woke up and looked at me, when he immediately started yelling, which roused the rest of the heathens, who all started yelling, jumping up at the same time and bursting through the walls of the hut. I gave the alarm and caught one by the leg, but he back-kicked me so hard in the midriff I was forced to let him go. I did not use my weapons as I feared injuring my own comrades, whom I knew to be outside, and whose presence rendered escape impossible."

"Quite right," quoth the colonel, but after listening to a long speech from the ancient man-eater he continued: "It's very extraordinary, but the natives swear you are the devil and frightened them. What have you got to say to that?"

"Simply, sir," answered the unabashed trooper, "that their assertions are neither complimentary nor truthful, as if I was his Satanic Majesty I could find more congenial employment than being a trooper, and as for frightening them, I assure you, sir, I never moved from the moment I sat down."

Again the O.C. interpreted to the still trembling natives, and again an eloquent speech from one of them, at the end of which the colonel, turning to Limbs, said:

"Sit down at once in the same manner you seated yourself in the hut."

His Grace, looking if possible more doleful than ever, sank down on his hams, crossing his feet behind his head, so that one foot stuck out on either side of it, and then crossed his hands, still holding his carbine in front of him, while with mournful eyes looking at his commandant he said, "I always sit like this, sir, when resting."

At once the Maoris yelled and tried to push their way through the grinning troopers who hemmed them in, while the astonished O.C, who by the way had never seen a circus in his life, threw himself back in his chair and gasped.

"Sit down like that when you want to rest, do you? Then, in the name of all that is righteous, how do you recline when you want to sleep?"

Without a word, and seemingly without an effort, the noble duke gave himself a twist and in the snap of a cap reversed himself so that he stood on his feet, with his western parts elevated in the air and his long, melancholic face upside down framed between his legs.

This transformation scene was greeted by another yell from the Maoris, while the perplexed O.C, opening eyes and mouth, ejaculated:

"Well, I am damned. For God's sake, man, get straight if you can," and then aside, "I wonder what in Hades he will look like when he's dead." For in a moment a respectable, if sorrowful-looking, trooper was standing rigidly to attention before him. "Well," continued the commandant, "I can't punish the natives, that's clear, nor can a camp be alarmed for nothing, so, Mr Burke, be good enough to see this man does nine days' pack drill, and if that does not keep him straight then lash a spare tent pole up and down his back bone—I fancy that will fix him; and now, sergeant-major, relieve this tired sentry, let the prisoners be taken back to the hut. Fall away, men; come, gentlemen, let us finish our work."

DESPATCH RIDER

CHAPTER 11

The Year of the Lamb

During the latter part of 1866 and the early part of 1867 the war on the west coast of New Zealand languished; Colonel McDonnell had for a time been sent over to the east coast and had straightened things out at Rotorua, while we who remained behind marked time. The truth being we had no men to take the field with.

The Maoris, only too glad to get a spell so that they could plant fresh crops and repair damages, sat tight and did nothing to excite active retaliation, while Parliament, especially the South Island members, howled for peace and retrenchment, and although we all knew there was absolutely no hope of a lasting peace, yet, of course, the Government had the say, and more men were disbanded.

We, however, who held the frontier lived in a semi-state of war, and although patrols and scouting was all we could do, yet I had great opportunities of improving myself in bushcraft and scouting.

Towards the end of 1866 Toi, the principal Hau Hau chief, visited headquarters, bringing with him twelve men, and this deputation demanded peace.

"Very good," answered McDonnell, "it is the earnest desire of the white man to live in peace. Therefore bring in all the Hau Hau chiefs of the district and we will ratify peace."

The deputation left, promising to do so, but never returned. Pungarehu had evidently instilled the fear of the Lord into the Hau Haus, for Toi complained against the colonel's method of fighting.

"The soldiers," quoth he, "always gave us notice of their approach. They blew bugles and made plenty of noise so we might be ready to receive them, but you and your men slip through the bush by night like rats and we can't sleep for apprehension."

"Yes," answered the colonel, "we fight in your own manner and you don't like it."

"No," said Toi, "let this sort of work cease, or we shall soon be unable to continue the war." And having lodged a dignified protest the old cannibal retired.

There is no doubt that Toi, himself, really wanted peace, but he was sinking into obscurity, as now Titokowaru took the lead, and everyone conversant with Maori nature knew that so long as he lived and ruled the roost there was no possibility for peace.

This man had always been a bitter enemy to the white man, and his hatred had been enhanced by the new fanatical religion to which he had become one of the very first converts, being one of those who, in April 1864, had made the insane attack on Sentry Hill, under the leadership of the Hau Hau apostle, Hepanaia. In this fight the apostle Hepanaia and most of the leading chiefs were killed and Titokowaru himself lost an eye. Now as the prophet and apostle Hepanaia had promised his disciples a bloodless victory, but had not only been killed himself and his men defeated with dreadful slaughter, anyone would think that a sane man would have chucked up such a rotten religion, especially should he also have lost an eye through his devotion to it; but not so Titokowaru, who became more than ever embittered towards the white men. In fact, as Tim put it, he had turned from being a Fenian into an Invincible, and wanted hanging. This was quite true, but, unfortunately, you must catch your hare before you can cook him, and Tito was too wily a bird to be caught.

It was in May 1867 that the last of the military settlers were disbanded and handed over their land-scrip, but most of them, not wishing to be murdered, and possessing a far greater knowledge of the true state of affairs in the district than the Government, sold their rights for what they would fetch, and either left the country or went to the gold-diggings, which were now booming, as the great Coromandel and Thames gold rushes were in full swing.

The volunteers had also completed their period of service and, owing to the crazy manner in which the Government, mad for retrenchment, acted, no others were enlisted, so the district was almost without defenders.

Now there was some excuse for the members of Parliament representing the South Island, who knew nothing about the circumstances of the case nor the customs of the Maoris, but there was no excuse for anyone on the ground, much less for the damned commissioner, who not only wilfully misled the Government but did everything in his power to thwart and hamper McDonnell.

It may have been true that the Maoris wanted peace for a time, or rather a truce, as we had so rattled them, destroying their crops, villages, stores of food, etc., that they must either gain time to recuperate or give in, and they completely hoodwinked the Government. For even Titokowaru with some of his men visited Waihi early in June 1867 and announced that this was the year of the lamb, meaning that it was to be a year of peace, but he said nothing about what animal was to represent the coming year.

Again, shortly after this visit, another hostile of importance, Whare Matangi, chief of the Paka Kohi tribe, visited Patea, he also declaring this was to be the year of the lamb, but likewise refraining from mentioning what the following year was to be; and the astute natives so utterly blinded the Government, who, longing for peace themselves, persuaded themselves they had obtained it, that they refrained from grasping the opportunities pointed out by McDonnell; and the festive Hau Hau planted and garnered his crops in security, laid in provisions and ammunition for future use, rebuilt his *pahs*, furbished up his firelock and sharpened his tomahawk, for are not these the pursuits meet to follow during the piping times of peace?

This relaxation of hostilities also gave time to Titokowaru to consolidate his party of irreconcilables, and he was joined by very many hot-heads of other tribes, which soon gave him greater standing in the country.

Anyhow, it was not long before the natives showed their real inclinations, as the very same Paka Kohi tribe which the commissioner had declared to be so desirous for peace forcibly stopped the survey of the Whenua Kura block and although they did not murder the survey party, still they drove them off the land.

The colonel managed to quiet this trouble, and one or two other disturbances the starting of which further convinced him that the natives, now that they had saved their crops, meant to fight, but this opinion the commissioner laughed at, and just at the moment when his services were most required the O.C. was sent with sixty of us to suppress a fancied Fenian rising on the gold-fields of Hokitika.

Naturally we looked forward to this trip with delight, as it would afford us a most agreeable change in the somewhat monotonous life we had been leading for the last few months, besides which the gold-fields contained many opportunities for indulgence in vices our monasticism on the frontier did not permit.

Hokitika is situated on the west coast of the South Island, and was what is known as a poor man's diggin's—*i.e.* a goldfield that a man with no capital can win gold from by his own labour. The New Zealand goldfields were never such rowdy ones as the Californian nor the Australian, being free, with few exceptions, from bushrangers and the murderous riff-raff that congregated at the American mines. Yet they were rough, and a strong party of Irishmen, known as the Micks, were apt, especially when under the influence of whisky, to make themselves objectionable.

It must be remembered that at this epoch things were very stormy in Ireland, and even in England, and the Micks instigated by whisky had held meetings and talked a lot of infernal rot, from which the warden of the goldfields, a nervous ass, had imagined possibilities of Fenian risings, insurrections, civil war and the Lord only knows what other catastrophes; hence the reason for withdrawing the O.C. and the greater portion of his reliable men from the west coast of the North Island just when their services were most required.

However, we who composed the party looked on the whole trip as a joke, and a pleasant interlude to the hard work and short rations we had had for so long to endure. As for any fighting with Fenians that none of us believed, although Tim and myself conjectured there might be some heads broken by way of a frolic.

It was in this spirit we took ship and went to sea, eventually reaching Hokitika, where we had to land in surf boats, through a very bad surf indeed.

We, however, passed through it in safety, when we were joined by the colonel, who had gone ashore previously. The authorities had begged him to land us with loaded arms, and had prophesied all sorts of bloody happenings, but the colonel had very rightly taken their wailings with a pinch of salt, so we reached the shore in the most unostentatious manner, at a time when the Micks were sleeping off their previous night's debauch, and we were quickly marched up to a spot the colonel had selected, where we expeditiously made ourselves safe and snug.

This artful move on the part of the O.C. completely out-generalled the Micks, as the sons of Ould Ireland, God bless her, were by no means in a state to have resisted our landing had they wished to do so, and by the time they were awake, and ready to renew their potations and politics, we were in possession of the strongest position overawing the town. This fact may have induced them to take up another Hue of defence against the bloody Saxons, and they may have determined to kill by hospitality those they feared to attack with force. For their deputation waited on us, not with pick-handles, revolvers and fowling-pieces, but with cases of champagne and John Jameson's whisky, and I verily believe they would have defeated us had we remained much longer with them.

The west coast diggings were at that time booming, any man caring to work a few hours a day being able to make his eight to ten pounds per week, some of course far more, so that it was a marvel to me why men cared to serve a government, risk his life and undergo the awful hardships our men did, for six shillings a day.

It was during this epoch in New Zealand I could have, had I chosen to look after my own interests, made my pile. I had plenty of money, and could have got plenty more had I asked for it, and as I before stated the late military settlers were selling their land-scrip for what they could get, so that as I was on the spot I could have purchased blocks of the finest land in New Zealand for a song, but I did not, and I want to warn young Lost Legionaries not to follow on my spoor.

I had made the Crown and flag my fetish from early childhood, and in my own stupid and conceited mind reckoned it to be my bounden duty to fight for them, and that so long as the war continued I must continue to serve, no matter what it cost me in pecuniary and personal losses. This infatuation has stuck to me all my life, and is as quick now as it was then, my life in consequence, so far as gaining the good things of this world goes, being a wretched failure.

I therefore want to warn the rising generation against it, so that all of you young fellows who are thinking of leading a frontier life take the advice of an old hand. "Fight certainly and fight like the devil, but don't be carried away by any sentimental rot."

"God save the King" is a very fine tune, and the Union Jack a very pretty object flying at the mast-head, but neither king nor flag can come to your aid when you are old and stranded on the pebbles, while as for your country, represented as it is by a gang of greedy, self-seeking politicians, you may starve in the gutter or rot in the workhouse. Therefore, my romantic new chum, when you see the chance to make money on the one hand and fighting for your country on the other, you go for the money. There are plenty of bally fools such as I have been to do the fighting. Your paltry services won't be missed, and you will be thought much more of by the people of the self-same country.

We remained three weeks at Hokitika, and were then fortunately sent back from our Capua to sterner work, landing at Patea just barely in time for the colonel to quiet another shindy, as the natives had stopped the survey on the Makoia Block, and although he managed, by his vast knowledge of Maori manners, to tide over this trouble, yet it was evident the billy was boiling and must soon boil over, for now everyone could see, with the exception of those wilfully blind, that war was imminent, as the natives now commenced openly to steal every horse and head of stock they could lay their hands on; so the early months of 1868 passed.

Some very foolish acts on the part of the resident magistrate and commissioner hurried on the inevitable climax, but yet the perpetrators of these follies still swore the sham peace would be a lasting one and objected to order in the few settlers who had the temerity to cling to their farms.

It would take too long to relate the wretched details of that miserable time, but eventually they culminated in the cold-blooded and brutal murder on 9th June of three harmless bushmen while peaceably at work.

Colonel McDonnell was at the moment in Wanganui, from whence he at once returned, and did all in his power to secure the safety of the district, but we were so short-handed that, even with the forts inadequately garrisoned to an alarming extent, he had not one man to take the field with. He therefore made a flying visit to Wellington to try and instil some glimmer of reason into the wilful numskulls who formed the ministry, receiving, after much persuasion, leave to enlist three hundred white men, together with one hundred Maoris, for a service of not longer than three months.

Now the men were wanted for immediate service, so that there was no time to pick or choose them, nor was there time to train them when chosen, and it must be remembered that the population of New Zealand forty odd years ago was much smaller than it is now, also that the goldfields were booming and really good men scarce. Yet even then, in the towns, there were numbers of loafers and riff-raff who, too lazy to go in for hard colonial work, hung about the cities waiting for what they call a suitable billet to turn up, and it was from the ranks of these useless unemployed that the great majority of the three hundred white men were enlisted.

I do not suppose a more useless gang were ever got together, but then on paper they represent three hundred men. Well, the colonel had asked for them, the Parliament had granted them, the town magistrates had enlisted them; and as the lawyers, merchants and others, who constitute a parliament, are quite ignorant of the requirements of a war, they are apt to imagine one man to be as good as another, so that you have only got to put a uniform on his back, and clap a rifle into his hand, when the miserable scarecrow must be able to at once do the duties of a well-trained soldier, or even a highly skilled bush fighter.

In the meantime more settlers had been murdered, more farms burnt and cattle looted, so that Titokowaru and his tribe, the Ngatiruanui, having saved their crops, and being well rationed with stolen oxen, considered it was high time to begin hostilities on a larger scale.

It was on the 9th June the aforementioned bushmen were murdered, and on the following day every one of our forts were more or less invested, so that it was dangerous to leave the shelter of the parapet, as on the 10th, a trooper, named Smith, having left the fort to catch his horse, was killed and cut to pieces before the eyes of his comrades, who were only able to recover his two legs, the rest of him being taken into the bush and eaten.

The Hau Haus also made it lively for the despatch riders, making numerous attempts to cut them off, capture or kill them, while on the 20th June sixty of them made a desperate attack on the ration dray, escorted by a sergeant and ten troopers, at the same place where Haggarty had been killed previously. The escort, however, made a stout resistance, and being relieved smartly from the fort the assailants were beaten off with loss.

I think I may here give you a personal experience of the pleasures of despatch riding, such as were enjoyed by the mounted portion of the colonial forces when engaged on that necessary occupation. It must be remembered that in those days we had no heliographs, and therefore all orders, letters or news had to be transmitted by horsemen riding from fort to fort, and the Hau Haus looked on it as great sport, trying to cut off, kill or capture the unfortunate whose duty it was to carry them.

Of course their chief ambition was to catch the despatch rider alive, as then it would afford them much amusement in torturing him to death, though failing capture he was of value to them dead, as they looted his arms, and also procured good meat rations from his remains. Anyhow it was good sport, so, as they knew we were far too weak in numbers to attack them, they made up hunting parties to catch us. Fortunately most of the main road ran along the sea-beach and was fairly open, but when it was necessary to ride inland you had to pass through scrub, bush and long fern, in which they laid their ambushes, and it behoved the horseman to have all his wits on deck.

Well, one day I had to carry despatches up to Waihi, a distance of some fifteen miles. I was well mounted on the horse I had first bought, who had turned out a slashing charger, very fast, with great staying powers, very sure-footed and a grand swimmer, the latter such a necessary accomplishment in a country abounding with tidal rivers and no bridges. It was a lovely afternoon, and I rode with stripped saddle, carrying only a brace of revolvers. The road ran for some miles along the beach, the tide being out, and I enjoyed my canter over the hard, firm sand although I had two rivers to cross, one of which I had to swim; these, however, were negotiated comfortably and I turned inland, where the track ran through *manuka* scrub, patches of bush and fern.

I at once started a bright lookout, but saw nothing to guard against until I came to a place where the track ran through a natural clearing about a mile in length, and no more than one hundred yards across. (*Note.*—These natural clearings are common enough in New Zealand scrub, especially on the Taupo and Kaingaroa plains. How formed no one knows.) The road ran up the centre of the clearing, which was covered with short tussocky grass that grew in little detached knobs like the wool on a nigger's head. I had just entered this clearing when my eye caught the gleam of something bright that sparkled for a moment in the scrub more than half way along the length of it, and knew it was caused by the sunshine flashing on the head of a *tomahawk* or the barrel of a firelock. Catching hold of my horse's head I slightly increased the pace, at the same time dropping my right hand on the butt of my revolver and preparing for a lively time.

I may have ridden a third of the way up the clearing, when *bizz* came a bullet past my nose, followed up by perhaps a score more. Thank the Lord a Maori could not shoot for toffee, and I saw at least forty natives at the far end of the clearing jump out of the scrub and make for the road, to try and cut me off, while yells from my rear told me retreat would be worse than going on, and I knew there was nothing for it but to break through or be caught; in which case even suppose I was not shot dead I must shoot myself, as it would never do to fall alive into the hands of these fiends. I therefore let my willing horse break into a gallop, and charged along the road as if Old Nick had kicked me.

Fortunately the noble beast I bestrode was as bold as he was handsome, and never winced nor shied from the yelling devils who, with waving *tomahawks* and mats, tried to frighten and check him, but just extended himself, and obedient to my hand and knee pressure swung to whichever side I wanted him to go. In fact he seemed to be guided by my will and understood my wishes as soon as the ideas were formulated in my own brain. Oh, what a splendid gift Providence presented to man when he gave him the horse, and what a friend the noble beast is to you, when you treat him as a pal and not as a slave.

Some such thought rushed through my mind as, pistol in hand, I sent him at the crowd of howling savages, a few of whom had already reached the road, two of whom I spotted as being the most dangerous.

These two bounders had taken up positions on either side of the track, the one on the left side being armed with a long-handled *tomahawk*, with which he evidently intended to maim my horse's legs, the other stood empty-handed, whose plan, plain enough to surmise, was to grab the horse's bridle and pull the wounded beast down, or, in case he fell, to seize me and put a stop to any resistance I might offer.

Backing these fellows up, and running to support them, were a scattered mob of others, armed with guns and *tomahawks*, but I had no time to notice these critters, as, uttering a yell that must have been inherited from some far-back old Milesian ancestor, I charged straight at my would-be body-snatchers.

It was clear to me that the man with the *tomahawk* was my principal danger, as should his cut at my horse's legs be successful down we must both come in a heap, and it would be a case of Kingdom Come for the pair of us. So aiming at his midriff as well as I could, when I was within ten yards of him, I fired, and to my delight saw him collapse in a heap.

I had barely fired when I was badly shaken in my saddle, as my horse seemed to stop dead, make a half rear, and strike out savagely with his forefeet. 'Twas only for a tick of time, for with a plunge and bound he regained his stride, and I caught a glimpse of the smashed head, face and shoulders of a man writhing on the ground, as my horse leapt over him; so it was not difficult to understand that the native had sprung at the bridle and been struck down by my noble charger, by which meritorious act he had gained *utu* (revenge) for the brutal treatment he had received from the Maoris whilst he was a captive and slave in their hands.

Anyhow we had broken through them, and although a shower of bullets followed us, two of which touched my gallant pal, while one knocked the heel and spur from my right boot, we were safe, and I cantered along to the fort talking to my horse, and praising him for the bold way he had behaved, while he, playfully reaching at his bit, now and then snorted back as much as to say, "Right, Boss, we euchred those ruddy jossers, didn't we?"

Earnestly the reinforcements were looked out for, as the garrisons of most of the forts were so weak that it was more than doubtful whether they could offer a successful resistance against a determined attack. Moreover, trusty spies brought in information that Titokowaru contemplated making such attacks as he was very desirous of obtaining a supply of rifles wherewith to arm the numerous recruits who had lately flocked to his standard.

Nor was the information false, for on the morning of the 12th July he attempted to capture the redoubt at Turu Turu Mokai, and very nearly succeeded in doing so.

This redoubt was an old work that had been constructed by the 18th Regiment at a time when there were thirty men to do the work now allotted to one, and though it had been built on an important tactical situation, yet the site had been badly chosen, nor was the work itself of any strength. This did not matter when the district swarmed with defenders, but now we were so weak it was considered extremely vulnerable. Moreover, for a long time, while the sun shone on our side of the fence, it had been abandoned; the berm had in places been washed away by the heavy rain, and in places the much damaged parapet almost tottered over the ditch; still, the importance of its situation was so great that the O.C. had to now make use of it in his scheme of defence.

This tumbledown structure was garrisoned by twenty-five men under the command of a very fine officer, Captain Ross, who had done everything in his power to make the place defensible, but had only succeeded in making the weak spots more apparent.

The site of the work itself was so bad that it necessitated a flying sentry to watch a gully that could not be overlooked from the fort, up which a storming party could easily creep, and there being no room for the O.C.'s tent inside he had to have it pitched outside, near the drawbridge, which consisted of two narrow planks that spanned the ditch.

On the night of the 11th a civilian came to the fort and claimed protection, which was at once granted, so that there were twenty-seven white men at Turu Turu Mokai that night. During the night the flying sentry reported a flock of strayed sheep had disturbed him, and there is no doubt that under cover of these animals two parties of Hau Haus, numbering forty men each, crawled through the fern, close up to the fort, lay down and waited for the right moment to rush the tumbledown work.

The flying sentry who had the morning relief, however, spotted some dark figures, and discharged his rifle at them, receiving in return a volley which wounded him badly, though he still had strength to crawl into the long fern where he hid until relieved.

The storming party at once charged, making for the gate, which in the dark they missed and ran all round the work looking for it, a pause that gave Captain Ross the chance of getting inside and defending the entrance. He had no sooner got to the gateway—there was no gate—than the storming party rushed him, led by a noted fighting chief named Tautai, who, missing his footing on the narrow planks, tumbled end over end into the ditch, an accident that saved his life, as the bullet, that should have sent him whooping to perdition, killed the man following him.

Two more Hau Haus, the gallant captain, disputing the narrow way, despatched to their father Satan, when the remainder, not relishing their reception, jumped into the ditch after their chief, and at the same moment the second party rushed up.

Captain Ross was still in the gateway, doing his best to give the newcomers a hearty and warm welcome, when one of the scallywags in the ditch crawled up under the bridge and discharged his gun into the unfortunate officer's body; at the same moment another of them sank the head of his long-handled *tomahawk* into his chest, and dragged the desperately wounded man down into the ditch, where he was soon hacked to pieces.

His fall caused some confusion in the already scanty garrison, and that in rather a queer manner, as when wounded he shouted: "Take care of yourselves, boys. I am done for."

On hearing which four men, interpreting the order to mean that each man should try and save himself, mounted to the top of the parapet, and, jumping over the Hau Hau's heads who were in the ditch, sought to save themselves by breaking through the other assailants and hiding in the fern. Three of them succeeded in doing so, the fourth being killed.

The defenders were now reduced in numbers to twenty-one, Sergeant M'Fadden taking command, occupying the post of danger left vacant by the death of his gallant officer, where bravely he sustained the fight until he was shot dead, when Corporal Blake stepped into the breach and post of honour, only to fall in the same manner; thus the gallant fellows held out, defending their trust until eight of them lay dead and six of them desperately wounded in the blood-stained gateway, the civilian also being killed.

Six men only were now left to continue the fight, but their comrades had not died uselessly having, previous to their departure to that Valhalla designed by Providence for the reception of Lost Legionaries, administered such punishment to their enemies that the latter withdrew from the attack on the gateway to positions from which the whole interior of the work, with the exception of one bastion, could be searched by a plunging fire.

To this bastion the six dauntless fellows now retired, determining to make their last stand and die there. It was the best spot in the untenable work, the gorge being masked by a flimsy wooden hut, that was not bullet proof, although it prevented the Maori sharpshooters from seeing the defenders and aiming at them.

Their greatest danger was the parapet that here, as I mentioned previously, simply tottered over the ditch, and which the Hau Haus at once set to work to undermine.

They were now in a desperate strait, but never lost heart. Relief was bound to come. Could they hold out long enough? They gained time by a clever ruse. The Maoris feared mounted men more than anything, so the defenders with one accord started cheering, at the same time shouting: "Hurrah, the cavalry are coming!" Whereupon the sappers left off their work, preparing for a bolt.

This trick was played two or three times, but the nervous Maoris were always rallied and forced to return to their work by the infamous scoundrel, Kimball Bent, whose voice, cursing the Hau Haus for their cowardice and urging them on to make further efforts, was distinctly heard and recognised.

At last the relief did come, though not by the efforts of the troopers, who for some inexplicable reason were left behind, Major Von Tempsky, then in temporary command, selecting infantry to go to the rescue and leaving twenty troopers standing by their horses without orders.

He, however, arrived just in the nick of time, as the enemy had not desisted from their work and retired more than a minute when the crumbling parapet fell bodily into the ditch which, had it done so a few moments sooner, would have left its six gallant defenders, all more or less hurt, to the mercy of their savage opponents, but they, by their splendid defence, not only saved their own lives, but prevented a large amount of arms and ammunition falling into the hands of Titokowaru and the baffled Hau Haus.

The relief of Turu Turu Mokai, although successful, was the origin of a most miserable squabble which ended in a sad tragedy, as it was the cause of as gallant an officer as ever drew sword throwing away his life in attempting to regain a reputation for courage which in the opinion of every man worth his salt should never have been doubted.

It happened this way. When the garrison at Waihi were alarmed by the sound of heavy firing, both troopers and infantry at once turned out. The former, twenty in number, were a very smart body of men indeed, always ready at a moment's notice to tackle any job that might come along. They were under the command of Major Hunter, who was also second in command to Major Von Tempsky (temporary O.C. of the district), who was a splendid though very jealous officer.

Hunter, the moment the alarm was given, ran round the fort to see that the sentries were on the alert, and when he had done so found that Von Tempsky had started with his own men, the infantry, leaving no orders for the mounted men nor for himself.

This placed him in a dilemma. It was clear the headquarters fort, containing large supplies of arms and ammunition, could not be left in charge of a guard of six men. It was also clear that the mounted men were the proper men to have gone to their comrades' assistance, but as his senior officer had left them behind without orders it was clear he must utilise them to hold the fort. He therefore gave orders to lead the horses back to their stables and for the troopers to man the bastions.

Now the troopers were as keen as mustard, and had been ready for duty even before the infantry, for although they did not, like the bold garrison of Branxholm Castle, drink their wine through their helmets barred, it was only because they had no wine to drink nor tin pots to wear on their heads, but they drank their ration rum, when they could get it, under their forage caps, and they always lay down to sleep fully accoutred, breeched, booted, belted and spurred, while their horses stood all night in their stalls saddled and bridled, with their heads round, ready to be led out and mounted in a moment.

It was so on this occasion. In fact they were standing by their horses before the foot men fell in, so it was through no fault of theirs they were not employed .

Now the troopers were well aware that they were the men who should have been selected to have gone, as they could have reached their endangered comrades at least half-an-hour before the foot-sloggers could hope to do so, and the fact of their being left behind drove them hopping mad, while on receiving the order to man the bastions the sergeant-major used language most reprehensible and unwarrantable, for which he should have been most severely punished. As the delay caused by using foot instead of mounted men was responsible for at least half the casualties, great irritation was felt not only through the force but also through the country, and the newspapers, getting to hear of the sergeant-major's hasty words, immediately started to disseminate their garbled reports, it even pleasing the ink-slinging stool-polishers, who write them, to shower abuse and cast doubts on the courage of a brave officer whose boots they were not worthy to black.

The synopsis of the wretched affair was this. Major Von Tempsky was the senior officer whose undoubted duty it was to take steps to immediately relieve the besieged fort. Well, he chose to go himself, taking his own men, infantry, with him, and leaving the mounted men and their officer behind without orders.

This action on his part clearly shows he was instigated by one of two ideas: either he considered the infantry most suitable to effect his purpose or he wished to gain all the credit of the relief for himself and men regardless of the danger the other fort ran through not receiving speedier assistance. Most certainly Major Hunter could not have followed on and left the headquarters fort unprotected.

Anyhow poor Hunter, a most high-spirited and sensitive man, unable to endure the slurs cast at him by a scum of newspaper men, threw away his life a few months afterwards at Moturoa in giving the lie to his cowardly detractors.

CHAPTER 13

Te Ngutu-O-Te-Manu

Colonel McDonnell returned to the district on the same day as the fight at Turu Turu Mokai took place, reaching the bloodstained ruin at noon.

There was, however, nothing to be done but wait for the reinforcements, which, as they arrived, were licked into shape as rapidly as possible, although it was not till the 21st of August they were deemed fit to be introduced to the Hau Haus.

On this date a strong patrol was sent to have a look what Titokowaru was doing, but that nobleman, not caring to have his privacy intruded upon, hunted the new chums out of the bush, killing four and wounding eight of them. So the disgusted O.C. decided to await the arrival of the Wanganui warriors, whose enlistment was being delayed by our old friend. Mete Kingi.

At last seventy splendid Wanganui Maoris reached Waihi, under the command of their gallant chief, Te Kepa, when the colonel determined to make an effort, as if the new levies were to be used at all they must be used at once. There was no more time to train them; they had been enlisted for only three months, and their time of service would shortly expire.

It was therefore now or never. The country simply howled for him to wipe out Titokowaru; our Wanganui natives were hungry for a fight, so that although himself and all his officers knew well that the new chums were not to be trusted in the bush, still he made up his mind to march out and attack Titokowaru in his vaunted stronghold.

Now, before I begin the yarn of this most disastrous expedition let me inform you that at this period I do not think our gallant and much respected O.C. was at his best, nor was this to be wondered at. For nearly two years he had been struggling, not only against the Hau Haus but also against an obtuse Government, who had listened to his bitterest detractors and enemies, while they wilfully closed their eyes to the obvious requirements of the district, and who, regardless of his expostulations, had reduced his fighting strength to an absurdly inadequate force, and even now, when his prognostications had been proved correct, suffered the very men whose lying reports had misled them to remain in office and hamper the endeavours he was making to straighten out the desperate muddle for which they were responsible.

Again he had at present under his command for a very limited space of time a field force on the bulk of which neither himself nor his officers could rely, and with which he was expected to work immediate miracles, and, as if all these circumstances were not enough to worry him to distraction, just at the moment his services were most in demand his only trusty spy, Katene, deserted and joined the Hau Haus, so that he was left without any reliable information to guide his movements. Therefore I am sure that several of the decisions he came to and acted upon would have been otherwise had not his keen judgement been obscured by manifold anxieties and worries more than even his strong and brave spirit could tolerate, and that on this occasion he was not in full possession of his brilliant fighting faculties.

Anyhow, as something had to be done, he issued orders that a field force composed of two hundred white men and the seventy friendly natives should parade on the night of the 6th of September 1868.

During the day every preparation was made, but alas when night fell the *tohungas* (medicine men) discovered something had gone wrong with the moon and a star, an unfortunate occurrence, as it denoted the overthrow of the expedition, and the Maoris, who up to that time had been in a state of huge delight at the chance of a scrap, now hung back.

In a moment the whole aspect of affairs was changed, as even Te Kepa and his best warriors begged the O.C. to postpone the *taua* (war party) for twenty-four hours. On any other occasion I am sure he would have done so, as the colonel was always most anxious not to run counter with the superstitions of our valuable allies, but the irritated, overdriven man was inexorable, and issued orders that the expedition should start that very night, let the moon and star shine as unpropitiously as they darned well pleased.

At this decision the hearts of the Maori warriors became very dark indeed, and they held a meeting so as to discuss what on earth should be done. They were all keen for a fight, but it was flying in the face of Providence and courting disaster for themselves should they neglect such pregnant warning; so things looked very black, as should the

Maoris refuse to march it was quite clear to all of us the impossibility of our proceeding.

At last, after many speeches, a grim old warrior of great experience got on his hind-legs. Quoth he: "Men of Wanganui, we have done all in our power to persuade the white chief not to go, but he insists on doing so, notwithstanding the predictions of certain disaster we have received. We are bound by honour to accompany him; besides, we languish for a fight. The *taua* will be defeated and the white men cut to pieces, which will serve them right for neglecting this warning. But we, my children, having protested against such godless profanity, will escape without injury, and as we go in honour we shall, provided we fight bravely, all return safe with our honour enhanced." This speech ended the meeting and the friendlies determined to come with us.

Now you good people who live at home at ease may laugh at a white man believing, or even tolerating, the prophecies of a savage devil-dodger, but very many experienced frontiersmen, in the course of their pilgrimage through wild countries and among wild races, come across so many queer and uncanny incidents quite inexplicable to their philosophy, therefore they are not so ready to laugh at or deny that which they cannot understand.

Consequently many of our old hands believed in the sombre prognostications of the *tohungas*, and perhaps were not wrong in doing so, for if the proof of the pudding is in the eating of it, surely the value of a prophecy is in the veracity of its fulfilment, and on this occasion the soothsayers certainly scored the straight tip, as on the next day the friendly natives, although they fought with a reckless gallantry never surpassed in the annals of war, and while covering our retreat exposed themselves in a manner that even astonished the fanatical Hau Haus, yet, during the whole disastrous affair, they had not one single man scratched, while what happened to us white men I shall now relate.

Well, this difficulty being satisfactorily overcome, we paraded at ten-thirty p.m. on the 6th, two hundred white men and seventy Maoris, a force quite sufficient had the former been of the same calibre as the old rangers and military settlers, but alas, out of the two hundred, not more than forty men had ever been in the bush before, and these old hands had no confidence in their inexperienced comrades; in fact, the old joyous devil-may-care spirit so noticeable in the ranks when starting on past expeditions was on this parade entirely wanting, and the old war-dogs looked more as if they were attending their grand-mother's funeral than starting for a jolly romp with the

COLONEL WHITMORE

Hau Haus in the bush.

Anyhow we started, the night being bitterly cold, with a very heavy frost that gave our nearly naked allies jip, laming their bare feet to such an extent that some of them were crippled for weeks afterwards, so that even they did not escape scot-free, but were in some way punished for accompanying their ungodly and incredulous white comrades.

Two miles had been covered when we came to the flooded Waingangora River, whose icy waters rose breast-high as we forded it linked arm in arm so as to prevent being swept away. Oh, scissors! it was cold, my shawl and jumper being frozen as stiff as boards five minutes after I had crossed! We, however, pushed on, and when daylight came we were deep into the bush on the western slopes of Mount Egmont.

Now we had no idea where the Hau Haus really were, as all the information the colonel had received since Katene's desertion had been conflicting, some reports stating that Titokowaru had fallen back to an inland *pah* called Ruaruru, the position of which was quite unknown, and as the so-called peace had given him plenty of time to build a dozen new *pahs*, provided he had a mind to do so, he might be anywhere within fifty miles of us.

We had therefore to follow the old bushwhackers' plan—*viz.* enter the bush and cross it in a straight line, and if you cut a well-defined track follow it in the most likely direction to the bitter end.

This we did until one-thirty p.m. on the 7th, when we cut a well-worn path which ran nearly north and south. This was a streak of luck, and at a short council of war it was decided we should follow the track in a southerly direction towards the sea.

After a short halt and a bite of cold, sodden food, for of course no fires could be lighted and our rations had been soaked in the waters of the Waingangora, we moved on for nearly an hour, when another halt was called and Te Kepa ordered one of his men to climb a gigantic *rata*-tree so as to obtain an outlook and try if he could spot any smoke rising or see any indications of a clearing in the adjacent bush.

The fellow ran up one of the huge pendent vines like a monkey, being soon lost to sight among the lichens, orchids and parasites that draped the branches. He had not been gone over a few minutes when down he slid, reporting he could see plenty of smoke not more than half-a-mile down the track, and could plainly hear the sound of a *haka* (indecent dances accompanied by unprintable *libretto*). This was a real slice of luck, as if the Hau Haus were *hakaing* they could not be aware of our vicinity, and we might catch them on the hop.

Another council of war was held, when Te Kepa gave the soundest advice, which I am certain would have been followed by the O.C. had he been in his normal state, although there is no doubt that the reasons he assigned for the action he took were very weighty.

The chief's advice was as follows:—

> We are here without the Hau Haus suspecting us, but we ourselves are ignorant what sort of a *pah* we have to attack or where it is exactly situated. Now therefore let the white men, many of whom are tired, retire a short distance off into the bush, where, keeping perfectly quiet, they can lie down and rest. I will place my men in ambush along the track, so as to *tomahawk* any one of the enemy who may pass without noise, though I do not expect any of them to do so. Then when it is dark I and my picked scouts will go and reconnoitre the Hau Haus' position, so that at daylight tomorrow morning we shall know what to do and fight with our eyes open.

Now there was much wisdom in this counsel, and had the colonel followed it we should have at one blow knocked Titokowaru out of the running, but the O.C. decided otherwise, asserting the great danger we ran of the Hau Hau scouts cutting our trail, when the enemy would either clear out or prepare themselves to resist our attack. Accordingly he gave orders for us to immediately advance in the following formation:—

Te Kepa with his seventy men led the van, followed by Major Von Tempsky with one hundred white men, while the colonel, commanding the remaining hundred white men, brought up the rear; the column to move in close order and as rapidly as possible.

Te Kepa's men had not marched more than a quarter of a mile when they came to a tent with a woman standing outside it, who directly she saw the advance-guard ran down the track screaming at the top of her voice, with a few of the friendlies in close pursuit, but they did not succeed in overtaking and despatching her before she raised a hullabaloo that would have alarmed the dead.

As the pursuing natives passed the tent a man and two children jumped out, who were at once shot, though another child was saved, one of Te Kepa's men carrying it on his back all through the subsequent engagement.

The screams of the woman, together with the firing, had of course alarmed the Hau Haus; the singing of the *haka* at once ceased, and as there was now no possible hope of surprising them we pushed on rapidly, though with all due caution, until we came to a large clearing.

Here we halted for a few minutes, while the O.C. made his final arrangements. Not a vestige of a pah *was* visible, nor, as a matter of fact, did any one of us catch a glimpse of the *pah* on that day. In front of us was a patch of dense, heavy bush containing huge trees, and we knew that somewhere among these was the lurking-place of Titokowaru.

The colonel's orders were concise. Te Kepa was to deploy his men in extended order to the left, so as to surround the *pah* on that side; Von Tempsky was to execute the same movement to the right; and his own party were to advance in extended order to the front.

So far so good, and as soon as Te Kepa and Von Tempsky had cleared our front—I was with the colonel's party—we deployed and extended, but directly we began to advance our troubles began, as the new chums would keep on closing in instead of moving forward in open order.

This inclination to crowd into a mob became worse as we entered the bush, so that, notwithstanding all the efforts of us officers, and the objurgations of the old hands, all formation was speedily lost.

Passing through a narrow strip of bush we came to a deep and broad creek, whose steep banks were covered with dense undergrowth. This we had to cross, and as we descended the bank the left of Von Tempsky's party surged into the right of ours.

In vain we raved at them, even going so far as to strike some of them and threaten others with our revolvers, but it was no good, the wretched conscripts had a bad attack of bush funk and would not obey orders.

As we struggled down into the creek I fell over Tim, who said to me: "For the blessed Virgin's sake, take care of yourself this day, Mr Dick, sure these damned hooligans will land us up to our necks in the bog. May Satan scrape ye wid red-hot oyster shells, ye narvous spalpeens, mil ye extend or will ye march to hell in subdivisions," he howled, while doing his best to second my efforts, but it was all of no avail, and we started to cross that creek, so as to ascend the far side, in a disorganised rabble.

Up to this time dead silence had brooded over the bush, but when we reached the centre of the creek's bed a terrific war yell was raised and a tremendous volley, of at least three hundred rifles and guns, was poured into us, from a distance of not more than ten yards; which, tearing our disorganised mob into tatters, transformed the bed of that forest, fern-embowered creek into a bloody shambles.

This reception was far too stern a one for our nervous new chums, over forty of whom at once scrambled out of the creek and bolted, never pausing in their flight until they reached the crossing place of the Waingangora River.

In vain with the old hands and those of the new chums who had the pluck to stand, though not the sense to extend, we made a rush and attempted to charge.

We failed at once, for the cunning enemy had woven the ground vines and undergrowth on their bank so closely together that nothing except an elephant could have broken through, while from the lofty *rata*-trees, in whose branches the best shots of the Hau Haus had been placed, came a plunging fire that knocked over man after man, so that we could do nothing but lie down and return the fire of our invisible enemies.

The casualties among our officers had been very heavy. Lieutenant Hunter had been killed; Dr Best and Lieutenant Rowan, badly wounded by the first volley, had been carried out of action, while Captain Palmer and Lieutenant Hastings, both badly wounded, had subsequently to be abandoned to the awful fate of falling alive into the hands of the ferocious Hau Haus.

In the meantime, Te Kepa had fared much better, for with his warriors well in hand he had worked round the left of the clearing, and with a rattling charge had swept away the party of Hau Haus sent to oppose him, subsequently taking up a strong position ready to storm the *pah* when ordered to do so.

Our plight, however, was now hopeless, as the enemy manned a low, well-bushed hill, the fire from which enfiladed the creek, rendering our position in the bed of it more untenable than ever. Still I am convinced that, had our men all been old hands, our gallant O.C. would have pulled us out of the mess, and we should have won the day, but nothing could be done with the raw new chums, most of whom seemed to be paralysed by the slaughter and the bloodcurdling yells of the Hau Haus.

This being the case, Colonel McDonnell saw that the only way to preserve the remainder of his force was to order an immediate retreat; so, directing us to carry out the wounded, he despatched his brother, Captain McDonnell, to Von Tempsky with orders for him to at once withdraw his men out of action and join his own party, Te Kepa offering to cover the retreat of our shattered force.

We had brought ten stretchers with us: these had been rapidly filled, and as we had now not more than sixty men, officers and privates, left, we were just able to handle fourteen wounded men, four being carried on rifles, as it required at least four men to carry a stretcher and six men to carry a man on rifles through the rough bush, so that all the remaining dead and wounded men had to be abandoned.

This abandonment of our wounded comrades was a heart-rending calamity, but nothing else could have been done under the circumstances, although we knew well the dreadful fate that awaited the unfortunates.

It takes time to write an account of a scrimmage of this sort, but in reality not ten minutes had elapsed from the moment we had descended into that infernal creek until we started to get out of it, during which period, out of the two hundred white men, one-fourth of our force had bolted, and out of those that had remained over one-third of their number lay dead or dying in the bed of it.

We had just succeeded in extricating the fourteen wretched sufferers when Captain McDonnell returned with the information that he had taken the order to Von Tempsky, who demurred at obeying it as he was of opinion that another charge might succeed, but while moving a step or two, so as to try to get a look at the *pah*, he had been shot dead. He had then given the order to the next senior officer, Captain Buck, who promised to at once obey it, when he returned to the O.C., who ordered him to take some friendly natives and secure the dangerous defile at a place, on the line of retreat, called Te Maru, so as to prevent the Hau Haus taking possession of it, which if they had done would have sealed the fate of the broken force.

This order he carried out splendidly, as just when he reached the place he fell in with, and utterly destroyed, the party the enemy had despatched to seize the defile, so that, thanks to the colonel's foresight and his brother's gallant action, our retreat was secured.

As soon as we had got the wounded up the bank the retreat began, Te Kepa forming the rear-guard and also protecting our right flank from the swarm of Hau Haus who now, with triumphant yells, rushed out of the *pah* and attacked us furiously, shouting out their intention to kill and eat the whole outfit. But they had tough nuts to crack in Te Kepa and his warriors, who, answering them yell for yell and shot for shot, challenged them to fight hand to hand, taunting them at the same time with cowardice, insomuch that they feared to charge and finish off a beaten *taua*, and reminding them of defunct ancestors who had been killed and eaten in old-time wars; so with great expenditure of ammunition and much bad language the miserable retreat continued.

Now it is no pleasant duty for a tired man to struggle through a New Zealand bush under the most favourable circumstances, but when he has to form one of a stretcher party to carry a heavy wounded man through the said bush, his troubles are increased many times, especially should he be blazed at every yard of the journey, as was our case while retreating from Te Ngutu-o-te-Manu to Te Maru, men being frequently hit all along the route, although we were fortunate enough not to lose any more killed, and so were able, when, thanks to Captain McDonnell, we had crossed the gorge in safety, to drop our stretchers, turn about, and give our pursuers such a grilling as to make them turn tail and leave us alone.

It was now ascertained that Captain Buck with his party had not joined up, nor did any of us know what had become of them, the truth being that every officer and man had been so fully employed that no one had had time to devote a single thought to the absentees.

Colonel McDonnell, who was much cut up, proposed to return and look for them, but Te Kepa pointed out that in every probability they had retreated some other way, and as there was no doubt that the great majority of the enemy had followed us, it therefore stood to reason Buck's people were better off than ourselves.

This argument the Colonel was forced to admit, and when he was informed that six of Te Kepa's most experienced warriors had, previous to the retreat being ordered, joined Buck, he reluctantly gave orders for our retreat to be continued.

The sun had set as we reached Te Maru, so, as we had abandoned our packs and haversacks, we had to toil, hungry and worn out, through the bush, carrying our suffering wounded, at which heart-breaking job Te Kepa and his glorious warriors took turn and turn about, so that we reached camp at two a.m. on the morning of the 8th.

Here we found everything in a state of chaos, as the d——d runaways, who had arrived there hours before, had spread the bloodcurdling report that the whole outfit had been cut to pieces and killed, themselves being the only survivors. Oh, but they received *toko* from fist, boot and belt of the infuriated old hands.

There was, however, no news of Buck and his party, which greatly disturbed our much troubled O.C. and again gave the gallant Te Kepa another opportunity of displaying his worth, for he immediately volunteered to start with his men at daylight and search for them.

This he did, but had only proceeded two miles when he met them returning dead beat, under the command of Captain Roberts. This officer reported that no sooner had Captain McDonnell given Captain Buck the orders, and returned to his brother, than Captain Buck, without telling anyone else of the orders he had received, made the attempt to recover Von Tempsky's body but was shot dead in trying to do so.

Captain Roberts then assumed the command, but, as he was in ignorance of any order to retreat, continued to hold his ground until he was informed by his own men that the colonel had retreated.

Fortunately he had just been joined by Te Kepa's six men, one of whom, a noted war chief, recommended him to retreat in the direction of the sea, which he did, and although his new chums behaved very badly, yet with the few old hands and the friendly natives he managed to beat off the attacks of the Hau Haus till dark, when after firing a farewell volley they drew off. He now halted his party till the moon rose, during which halt two of his men died from cold and exhaustion, and then, under the guidance of the old chief, extricated his men from the bush and reached camp as I have already described.

So ended the unfortunate expedition against Titokowaru in his stronghold at Te Ngutu-o-te-Manu.

CHAPTER 14

Moturoa

Our defeat caused consternation through the country, bitter recrimination flying like hail before a southerly buster, while it added greatly to Titokowaru's prestige, who was at once joined by every wavering native in the district. He had moreover captured from us over fifty rifles and carbines, as well as revolvers and ammunition, which enabled him to arm his recruits.

We, on the other hand, had lost heavily, for not only had fifty men been killed or severely wounded, but out of the other men who had been engaged more than half their number had been more or less wounded, and very many of them were not fit for further active service, while the remainder of the new chums became so utterly disorganised that it was not even safe to let them do a sentry-go.

The state of the camp at Waihi was deplorable. The hospital overcrowded with sick and wounded had not sufficient means of treating the patients, while it was absolutely suicide for anyone to move beyond rifle range of the fort. Moreover with such a reduced force of efficient men it was more than manifestly impossible to maintain the out-lying forts, to escort food and forage supplies and also to provide a force to meet the enemy in the field.

The Wanganui natives also demanded to go home, as their great chief Hori Kingi Te Anaua had just died and it was necessary for them to attend the *tangi* (wake), a ceremony of the most sacred importance to the Maoris. We also received indubitable intelligence that Titokowaru meant to move southward through the bush, cut off our communications, and threaten Wanganui.

Under these circumstances Colonel McDonnell and the Defence Minister, who had come up to the front, decided that the only thing to be done was to abandon Waihi, with all the frontier forts, and fall back to Patea, which could be supplied by water transport. Of course relief had been sent to us, and Colonel Whitmore with a splendid division of the Armed Constabulary quickly arrived from the east coast.

With these and our own reliable men we at once moved out to reconnoitre the Hau Hau position, but although we numbered three hundred men and found the enemy, yet for some reasons I never understood we fell back after skirmishing to within less than three hundred yards of them, and that without firing a shot.

Three days after this reconnaissance the retrograde movement to Patea was commenced, and was very well carried out, for notwithstanding the scarcity of transport the frontier garrisons were withdrawn, and the wounded, with nearly all the stores, safely escorted to the same camp ground from which we had so gaily advanced, nearly three years before, so that all the toil, bloodshed and hardships endured during that period had been borne for nothing. In fact we were far worse circumstanced, for Titokowaru had moved through the bush in a parallel line to our retreat, had forced the Paka Kohi tribes to join him, and had taken up his headquarters at Hukatere, on the head waters of the Patea River, and shortly forced us to abandon our principal outpost at Kakaramea; then moving still farther south he established himself at Moturoa, well to our right rear.

These movements put the fear of the Lord into the Wanganui settlers, who fled to the town for protection, where, although they could muster fifteen hundred militia, they squealed so lustily for assistance that the Government, now trembling in their shoes, sent two companies of the 18th R.I., who were still in the country, to take care of them.

It was at this time that Colonel McDonnell resigned the command of the district in disgust, and Colonel Whitmore was appointed in his place—a change of commanding officers that gave us no pleasure, for, although we knew him to be a brilliant soldier, yet he lacked tact, his manners being decidedly against his ever becoming a popular officer. Furthermore, although he had gained a good reputation in the Crimea, he was ignorant of both the manners and customs of the Maoris, and quite failed to raise any enthusiasm in the hearts of his colonial irregulars. Still, as he was always ready to fight, and was quite heedless of fatigue and privations, they tolerated him, though they never respected nor loved him as they did Fighting Mac.

Titokowaru now became very active, for although he was too knowing to attack strong posts, yet he swept off every head of cattle, burned every house, ambushed every track, murdered a few settlers and killed several despatch-riders and scouts.

The authorities, however, had not been idle. Major Roberts who had been sent to the goldfields to try and re-enlist old hands now re-joined, having persuaded over one hundred good men to accompany him, these being further supplemented by another draft of a hundred, the majority of whom were Irishmen who had taken their discharges from the 57th Regiment, then on its way home, and all of whom were picked men. Again, Te Kepa had joined with four hundred Wanganui *Kupapas*, so that Whitmore was able to hunt out and disband all the riff-raff of undesirable wasters we had previously been hampered with.

This was nuts to our old hands, for now everyone felt we could again put up a fight that would not disgrace us, so the hearts of the Lost Legionaries grew light and cheerful.

Our organisation had also greatly improved, as all the permanent fighting men had been embodied into one corps, which for the future was to be known as the New Zealand Armed Constabulary, and which soon became a picked body of men, second to none in His Majesty's dominions, and as they were all trained bush fighters were invaluable for the work they were called on to perform.

It was now high time to put a limit to Titokowaru's capers, so the colonel therefore ordered a field force to pay him a visit on the 6th November, the said force to consist of Nos. 1, 2, 3 and 6 Divisions of the Armed Constabulary, two small parties of the Patea volunteers, together with the *Kupapas*, a nice, handy *taua* (war party), being about two hundred and fifty white men and four hundred natives.

At six a.m. on the morning of the 7th we found ourselves outside the bush within which at a distance of about four hundred yards we expected to find the stronghold of the Hau Haus, and we had been informed that it only consisted of a simple stockade. This was false, as we afterwards discovered it to be one of the strongest and most cunningly constructed works ever built by Maoris.

The O.C. orders were that Te Kepa with twenty-five men of No. 1 Division and one hundred *Kupapas* should work his way through the bush to the right rear of the *pah*; an hour being allowed him to carry out this movement.

The order was successfully obeyed, Te Kepa penetrating to the point assigned him, and lying down within forty yards of the *pah* itself.

It was now a regrettable incident happened through Colonel Whitmore's ignorance of Maori customs, for he involuntarily or otherwise insulted an important Maori chief, upon which the remaining *Kupapas* refused to enter the bush or fight, thereby preventing the surrounding of the *pahs*, and the shutting up of Titokowaru inside it, which, had it been done, would have forced him to surrender notwithstanding the defeat of our storming party, as we afterwards ascertained the Hau Haus had neglected to provision their stronghold and must have been starved out in three days. But then Colonel Whitmore, notwithstanding the fact that he was a brilliant soldier, greatly lacked tact, and seemed to take a delight in, or at all events to be utterly callous about, injuring the feelings of his subordinates, a failing that more than once cost us dearly, anyhow it was to do so on this occasion.

As soon as the allotted time had expired Major Hunter was ordered, with fifty of No. 3 Division and some other details, to advance as a storming party, myself and Tim being in the crowd, and attack the front of the *pah*, which we believed to be a simple stockade, and quite four hundred yards if not farther in the bush.

A well-defined dray road led straight into the forest, along which we marched in close order, and before we had proceeded two hundred yards we came to a clearing. This clearing was only a narrow one, perhaps sixty yards across, but what made it look ominous was that all the tree stumps had been extracted, leaving no cover for a rabbit, while the undergrowth on the far side seemed unnaturally dense. However Major Hunter, who led in person, gave the order to double and we dashed across it.

The morning was a damp and slightly foggy one in early summer, a light mist rising from the ground in spiral wreaths and curling away among the trees looked very beautiful in the rising sun.

We could see nothing of a stockade, in fact I do not think Major Hunter realised we had reached the *pah*, and it was afterwards ascertained that on this side of the *pah* there was no palisading at all, but that the Hau Haus had made a breastwork by rolling the logs of huge trees into a line, over which they fired, while in front they had made with the branches interwoven with undergrowth and ground vines an impenetrable abatis. They had also masked the work most cleverly, and as a dead silence brooded over their position there was nothing to show that the scrub was occupied.

At a steady double we crossed the clearing, reaching within fifteen yards of the far side, when a single shot rang out, followed quickly by two more.

"Charge," shouted Hunter, but before we could quicken our pace up went a terrific war yell, a sheet of flame and smoke met us full in the face, a sheet of lead tore through our ranks and the roar of over two hundred rifles and guns went echoing among the trees.

Down in a heap fell a third of our number, but the groans and cries of the wounded were smothered by the frantic cheer of us men left on our feet as we made a wild rush at the undergrowth, so as to get to hand-grip with our enemies. It was in vain, the network of well-woven vines and creepers was impervious, while their elasticity simply bounced us back, when in desperation we hurled our bodies against them.

"Out *tomahawk*," I howled. "Here, Tim, you and half-a-dozen men cover us," and my subdivision sprang at the entanglement, trying to chop our way through the tough *lianas* so as to open a path for the rest.

The distance between ourselves and the yelling Hau Haus was not great, not more than twelve feet, but we could not win through, for resting their gun barrels on the boles of the fallen trees they discharged them right in our faces, mine being severely scorched by the flash from one of them.

In a moment the four men who had followed me with their tomahawks were shot dead, and Major Hunter ordered me back, directing me to retire my men a few yards, lie down and open fire.

This we did, and although much hampered by dead and wounded comrades, for more than half of our men were by this time *hors de combat*, we lay down ten yards from the bush in extended order and opened a well-directed fire, aiming at the line of the enemy's flashes.

It was now the saddest event of the day happened. We had been firing for some minutes, and had already caused the enemy's fire to slacken and grow wilder, when Major Hunter walked up and down our line, an action quite unnecessary, as our men were behaving, if not talking, like angels.

"Lie down, sir, for God's sake, lie down," shouted some of the men, who all loved him dearly. "There is no need to expose yourself, sir; we'll stand by you, sir, to the last grip."

But he refused to do so, saying: "No, no, boys; I must show the world today I am no coward."

Under such circumstances the end could not be long delayed, and he fell mortally wounded, having sacrificed his life, giving the lie to the scum of unjust accusers who had thrown mud at him after the fight at Turu Turu Mokai; he was carried out but died immediately.

Well, there we of the storming party lay out in the open, and although more than half our men were dead or wounded, still we were determined to hold our grip on the position, even if we could not succeed in getting into the work.

Heavy firing was going on round the *pah*, perhaps some other party might have better luck, anyhow we were not going to budge until we received further orders.

We had hung on like this for more than half-an-hour when the enemy's fire slackened off, and of course ours followed suit, and we were wondering what was to be the next move, when all at once a stark-naked Hau Hau, probably mad with fanaticism and wishing to give an exhibition of his invulnerability, jumped on to the top of their breastwork, exposing his whole person to us from his knees upwards, and of course standing up as he was he could also see us lying down within ten yards off from where he stood, and began to go through his incantations, holding his hand, palm turned towards us, at the full stretch of his arm and barking the words *Hau Hau* at us like a dog.

Poor fool, he had either not learned the right incantation, or something else must have been amiss, or at all events he was wrong in his conjectures *re* invulnerability, as our men, who had all been waiting for a chance, let drive a volley at him that simply lifted him off his feet, so that if he finished his formula at all he must have completed the peroration in a hotter climate.

It was just after this interlude the fire breezed up again, and Tim, who was lying close to me, said, "Begorra, Mr Dick, here comes the boys to help us. Do you not think, sor, we may bate the beggars yet? Sure isn't it a trate to have rale men beside ye? Look to the rear, sor, sure they're splendid."

I turned on my side and looked, and there I saw the colonel—I hated the diminutive beast, but, by gad! he could handle men—leading No. 6 Division (most of whom had been 57th men and Irish at that) out of the bush. They were advancing in extended order as if on parade, and at once drew the enemy's fire from us, at the same time our call and the retire were sounded.

These calls, loath as we were to quit, we obeyed, carrying with us, however, all our wounded and, with the exception of the four men who had been shot in the undergrowth, all our dead. These four bodies it was certain death to approach, nor had we sufficient men left to have carried them had any of us succeeded in getting hold of them; as it was most of us had to carry each his man as far as the bush. Strange enough to say the wounded man I individually carried out was an old school-fellow of mine who had been in the same house as myself.

Retiring in perfect order, though as fast as we could, we passed through the files of No. 6 Division, and in a short space of time reached the dray track, where we deposited our loads and lined the bush to cover the retreat of No. 6. No sooner were we safe than our gallant rescuers fell back as if on parade, and the Hau Haus, poor misguided miscreants, fancying they had got us on toast, leaving the *pah*, rushed after us, thinking they were going to enjoy a high old time cutting up a beaten *taua*; but here they made a blooming error, for no sooner had No. 6 reached the bush than they also halted and joined us.

Howling with exultation and mad with fanaticism the Hau Haus rushed across the clearing to *tomahawk* the men whom their prophet had promised them that the angel Gabriel would deliver into their hands, and possibly, had we been a mob of half-baked new chums, he might have done so, but as we were not we waited quietly for the colonel's order, who, good little man, though he was a beast, allowed them to come within twenty yards of our ambuscade.

Then out rang his word of command: "Give them Hades, boys," the last word being lost in a volley that knocked the immortal stuffing out of them and sent them howling back to their *pah*.

Now it is my firm belief that had Colonel McDonnell been in command he would have followed up this success with another charge, as our men were full of fight and well in hand, but Colonel Whitmore thought otherwise, and give the wee devil his due he never lacked for pluck or enterprise, so maybe he was right.

Anyhow, picking up our dead and wounded we slowly retreated to Nukumaru, and next day took up a new line of defence on the Kaiiwi, as it was the best position to defend the town of Wanganui.

A few days afterwards we received the intelligence of the massacre of Poverty Bay, and it was decided to despatch Colonel Whitmore with two hundred picked men to the east coast. It was, however, first necessary to provision Patea, and the strong redoubt at Te Wairoa. This was done, and then, handing over the lines of defence to local militia, with one hundred Armed Constabulary to give them backbone, the little colonel in an infernal temper embarked, on the 2nd December 1868, with two hundred and twelve men for Poverty Bay, and I bade farewell to the west coast for a time.

PART 2

CHAPTER 1

War on the East Coast of New Zealand—Yarn of the Gate Pah

After a voyage during which nothing happened worth recounting We landed at Tauranga, a pretty little township with a good harbour situated on the Bay of Plenty; but before I proceed with my own personal yarn I think I might give you some idea of the fighting that had taken place on the east coast previous to our arrival there, and also a brief account of the extraordinary ruffian, Te Kooti, we were about to encounter.

It is very difficult to write an account of New Zealand warfare, as it was mainly a jumble of innumerable skirmishes dotted here and there with an engagement that by stretching a point might be termed a battle. Again so many different tribes took part in the twelve years' continuous fighting, while the various campaigns would often partially die away only to flare up again, and so many separate expeditions took place at one and the same time as to render it almost impossible to write an account of the long war so that it could be understood, much less be made interesting to an ordinary reader, who would quickly become confused and bored by a superfluity of dates and of the Maori names of trivial combats, although each of them was necessary and cost the men engaged therein much hardship and bloodshed.

When the war originally broke out in 1860 the east coast tribes sat tight and did not join the Taranaki and Waikato natives, but at the end of 1863 they had in a great measure joined the coalition of the tribes under the newly elected Maori king, and in 1864 a large percentage of them, abandoning Christianity, adopted the crazy Hau Hau faith.

At this period, many settlers having been murdered, General Sir

Duncan Cameron proceeded to Tauranga in April 1864, with a field force of two thousand men well supplied with artillery, having moreover at his disposal a splendid naval brigade drawn from five ships, and with this fine body of men attempted to overawe and subdue the rebellious district.

Two considerable tribes, however, the Arawa and the greater part of the Ngatiporou, had refused to join the Hau Haus, and threw in their lot with the Europeans. The former of these proved them-selves to be the most useless allies, being the only New Zealand native tribe of a cowardly disposition; they were also prone to overvalue themselves and give trouble to the white officers sent to command them, for which reason I suppose the Government pampered them to an inordinate extent, thereby making them more useless and insolent than ever Providence intended them to be. The Ngatiporou, however, were a splendid fighting race, who, under their glorious war chief Rapata-te-Waha-waha, rendered most valuable services.

The New Zealand wars brought to the front many colonial officers, some of whom had previously served in the regular army, while others had acquired their training and experience through long years of active service, making up for any lack of theory and barrack-square knowledge by their sterling commonsense, their acquaintanceship with Maori customs and the ready way they adapted themselves to the exigencies of bush fighting.

Names such as Whitmore, Tuke, McDonnell, St John, Von Tempsky and many others, men never heard of in England, should be treasured in New Zealand, and with these every colonial boy should be taught the names of the two gallant Maori chiefs, Rapata-te-Waha-waha and Meiha-Kepa-Te-Rangi-Hiwinui, whose splendid courage and devout loyalty did so much to bring the long, weary war to a successful termination.

General Cameron with his forces arrived at Tauranga in April 1864, and at once took the field, commencing operations by an attack on the Gate Pah, at which place he was badly beaten. Many and varied are the accounts I have heard about this disastrous action, both from old soldiers who took part in it, and also from natives who fought there against them, and after weighing the pros and cons the only conclusion that I can come to is that the defeat was due to the crass stupidity and folly of the general and his staff, who had neglected to scout or make any reconnaissance of the so-called *pah*.

If you care to read an account of how two thousand seasoned British troops plus a strong naval brigade amply supplied with artillery and supported by the broadsides of three ships of war were defeated by one hundred and thirty Maoris, the majority of these being youths, badly armed with old muskets, double-barrelled guns and *tomahawks*, I will give you a native version of the affair as recounted to me by one of the few seasoned warriors who defended the place.

Tourists proceeding in the mail-coach from Tauranga to Ohinemutu may be shown close to the road an old earthwork, and the coach-driver will gravely inform them this is the remains of the Gate Pah; but this is not a fact as they are the ruins of a redoubt built by the troops subsequent to the disaster. The spot where the light actually took place lies close to the sea-beach on the Tauranga side of the swamp, where the ground is comparatively level and is commanded by hills on two sides, being bordered by the waters of the harbour and the aforementioned swamp. And now let me try to spin you the yarn as I was told it by my old Maori friend and quondam enemy.

I had been out *ka ka* and pigeon shooting in the big bush that lies between Tauranga and Ohinemutu, my companions consisting of three *rangatera* and some half-a-dozen lads to carry our swags, game, stores etc., and at nightfall after a most successful day's sport we had formed a snug camp in a small open glade through which ran a clear rippling creek. The *mi-mis* had been made down, we had enjoyed a scrumptious repast, and the eyes of the whilom warriors glistened when I produced from my swag a big bottle of rum, together with a liberal supply of tobacco.

A tot of the former having been disposed of, the pipes being lighted, and each old sportsman having emitted a heartfelt grunt of beatitude and satisfaction, I turned to the senior of the party and said: "Tell me about the fights you had with the Queen's soldiers at Tauranga."

"*Augh! augh!*" grunted the ancient, allowing a dense column of smoke to escape through his nostrils. "The flesh of the pigeon and *ka ka* is sweet, the warmth of the burning log is good, the taste of *waiperou* (rum—*lit*. stinking water) and tobacco are very good, but better than all these is war, and the next best thing is talking about it. Yes, I will tell you of our victory and of our defeat by the soldiers of the Great White Queen. Draw near, you boys, listen and learn, so that when your turn comes you will know how to fight so as to sustain the honour of the Ngaiterangi.

"More than ten years are now dead since we joined the coalition of tribes who had lately elected the new Maori king, we doing so not that we were so hungry to fight against the soldiers, but had we not done so we could not have withstood the anger of the Waikato and the other tribes who had elected him. About this time also we were visited by prophets who preached the new Pai Marire faith, and we who had discovered that the white missionaries were humbugs gave ear to them, and many of us joined the Hau Haus, as they promised that we should acquire much *mana* through their incantations, they also promising us immunity from wounds and death in battle; but we soon found out that they also were humbugs.

"Yes, friend, the white missionaries are humbugs and the Hau Hau prophets are humbugs, all of them talking about matters not to be understood even by themselves, as no two missionaries or prophets agree on the matters they talk about. Let these men pass you by, oh children! The best things in life are war, rum and tobacco, these a warrior can understand.

"Pass me, my white friend, the bottle, and now I have moistened my throat I will tell you first of all about our victory, and it is right that I should do so, because it happened to take place before our defeat, and it is well to speak of events in their due and proper order, also in recounting our glory I may perchance gain courage to tell you better about the way the soldiers took *utu* on the Ngaiterangi for their brothers we had killed.

"Now it fell out in this way. News had come to us of the fighting at Orakau and how the Taupo and Uriwera Maoris had cloaked themselves with glory defending that *pah*, and we all determined to do likewise provided the big white chief saw fit to honour us with war. Yes; true there had been plenty of soldiers in Tauranga for a long time, but up to this time they had remained quietly in their forts, and had not come out to molest us, we there-fore took no notice of them, but proceeded with our peaceful avocations which at that time of the year was for the young men fishing, and as the soldiers occupied Tauranga, our usual fishing ground, we occupied the *kainga* near the sea-beach, close to the spot you white men now call the Gate Pah.

"No; it was not a fighting *pah*. It had no defences, nor was the position a fit one on which to build a fighting *pah*. It was simply a few *raupo* huts surrounded by a light fence, just strong enough to keep the pigs out from destroying the fish we were drying on low stages, for, as you know well, friend, there is no timber suitable for building a *pah* or anything else within a long distance of the place. Besides, the nature of the ground was such that had we built a *pah* there the soldiers and ships with their big guns could have destroyed it at once.

"Now there were in the *kainga* one hundred and thirty Maoris, but out of that number there were only four of us who were real warriors—*i.e.* who knew from personal experience the joys and the responsibilities of war, the remainder were young men who had been entrusted to us to be taught all the arts becoming to a Maori warrior, and who were at that period learning to cure and catch fish. These young men, however, were all *rangatera* (well-born gentlemen). There were no slaves with us for it is not seemly to train *rangatera* with slave boys, and it so chanced that on this occasion these youths were to be called upon to do warriors' work before they had received their full instructions.

"Well, my friend, the fishing was progressing, and we had already caught, cured and sent to our homes very many loads of dried fish, and in a few days more we should have returned to our tribe. One day, however, we received news that some big ships with many soldiers had reached Tauranga and that the great chief himself was coming to attack us. This was a great honour, but we could not understand it, for the white men must have known that where we were fishing was not a suitable place for us to fight in, that it was only an open *kainga*, the taking of which would gain the soldiers no credit.

"Also the big white chief must have heard that the bulk of our tribe were at that very time building large entrenchments at Te Ranga, which when complete would be suitable for him to test the courage of his warriors by attacking. Messages, however, we at once sent to our allies the Ngatiporou and Whakatohea to come to our assistance, and they did so, but were met and defeated at Maketu by the wild soldiers (the colonial irregulars) who killed very many of them; but of this we knew nothing as that fight took place on the same day as the one on which we were attacked by the real soldiers and the *Ngati Jacks* (naval brigade).

"These *Ngati Jacks* you must understand, boys, do not belong to the same tribes as the soldier, though they likewise fight for the Great White Queen. They are a strange people. I who have seen them know them well, and tell you youths to beware should you ever have the honour to fight against them. Great is the courage of the soldiers, but also very great is their folly, for they will walk up to an entrenchment in a body and suffer themselves to be shot down by our fire from under the *pekerangi* (outer fence of a *pah*), but the *Ngati Jacks* rush at the fence tumultuously, leap on one another's backs and in a breath are among you. Then, oh my sons, your hearts must be very strong should you want to stay and fight to the end.

"All the warriors of the Great White Queen swear very much when they are fighting, but *the Ngati Jacks* swear the most. Yes, my sons, they are a strange people. They have no villages, nor do they plant nor keep cattle, but live in the bowels of the ships in which they store much rum, salt pork and tobacco. Neither do these men possess wives nor women, though when they come ashore it is well to send all women and girls far away as the *Ngati Jacks* are very prone to make love in a very unceremonious manner. They also roll from side to side as they walk, drink much rum and eat tobacco.

"After we had despatched the messengers, we four warriors held a council to decide what we should do under the circumstances. It was plain we could offer no prolonged resistance in the *kainga*, yet we must fire at least one volley in honour of it, should the great white chief deem it worthy of attacking. Again, although its occupants were nearly all young men and boys, still they were born *rangatera*, and their honour and future reputation must not be jeopardised by retreating without making a show of resistance, moreover we could not insult the soldiers who had come so far to fight us by allowing them to occupy the place without being fired at.

"We had, however, heard it was the custom of the great white chief to fire many shots with his big guns before he ordered his storming party to charge, and if he did so on this occasion we, who were without entrenchments, must all be killed before we could fire one volley in honour of the *kainga*, ourselves or the soldiers, and our hearts grew dark with perplexity. It was then that our chief man spoke. He had fought against the soldiers in the Waikato and his war craft was great.

"These were his words: 'It is true, friends, we cannot defend the *kainga* against the soldiers, nor can we withstand the fire of their big guns, but it is also necessary for the sake of our honour to remain in the *kainga* and fire one volley. Come, let us do this. We can cut much *raupo* and fern, and tie it to the fence so as to make it look solid and big. The ground is soft. We will dig trenches and pits in which we can hide from the fire of the big guns, and on that small hill we will erect a high flagstaff. Perchance the men who fire the big guns will mistake it for the *pah*, as may also the *Ngati Jacks* on the ships, and by firing at it instead of at the *kainga* we shall escape the anger of the big guns. Should this plan succeed enough of us may remain alive to fire a volley at the *taua* and so save the honour of all concerned.'

"We saw his words were very good so we acted on them, and by working hard all night we completed our preparations. Next day (29th April 1864) our scouts came in with the information that the soldiers were marching out of Tauranga to attack us, and that the ships were coming up the bay, so at once we ran and concealed ourselves in the pits and trenches we had dug.

"Presently we saw the soldiers arrive on the high ground and in a short time their big guns began to fire, when to our joy we at once saw that misled by the flagstaff and flag they were aiming at the hill on which it was erected some hundred fathoms away from the *kainga*. At this our hearts grew light, for the noise of the big guns, especially those belonging to the ships, sounded like thunder, while the hill on which the flagstaff stood was shrouded in flame and smoke, and groaned with the bursting of the big power-filled balls which, had they been directed at us, must have quickly destroyed every man, so we thanked Wai Mati for his crafty foresight. For a long time the big guns thundered in their wrath while we lay hidden in our trenches, then they ceased, and Wai Mati, peeping out, called to us: 'Arise, children, the *taua* is advancing, line the fence and when I give the word fire one volley, then break and retreat through the swamp to Te Ranga.'

"We obeyed his order and when we had lined the fence we also peeped through it and saw a long line of soldiers with a line of *Ngati Jacks* in rear of them advancing to the attack. When they had reached within twenty fathoms Wai Mati gave the word and our fire darted out through the fence to meet them, then waiting no longer we ran to the rear of the *kainga* and broke through the back fence meaning to disperse in the *raupo* swamp, and each man make his way as best he might to Te Ranga.

"But as we broke through the fence for a breath we stood still with amazement, for there drawn up in line was another strong *taua* of soldiers whom the big white chief had sent round to intercept our retreat. What were we to do? We were all *rangatera* and it was not befitting to our rank to be taken prisoners, as that misfortune would reduce us to the level of slaves. No, we must conquer, escape, or die, and we felt justly angry with the want of consideration on the part of the great white chief for placing us in this dilemma.

"There was no time to delay, the loud shouts of the charging *taua* as they crashed through the fence and entered the *kainga* rang in our ears, while the intercepting soldiers were making ready to fire a volley that would destroy us should we try to break through them. We must surrender or die. Then out cried Wai Mati and his voice sounded clear above the noise: 'Back into the *kainga*, my children. Let us die there fighting like *rangatera* with our *tomahawks.*'

"In a breath we turned, and every man, *tomahawk* in hand, rushed back into the village, and threw himself on to the astonished soldiers who had already occupied the place. Now happened a strange thing. Those soldiers who had been sent to cut us off commenced firing into the *kainga*, and the men working the big guns, seeing they had been misled by the flagstaff, recommenced their fire, this time aiming at the right spot, the ships likewise doing the same. Then truly was the *mana* of the soldiers inside the *kainga* very evil. They had charged like brave warriors, and having broken through the fence and having occupied the place, they had a perfect right to think they were entitled to the consideration of the big chief and his other tribes (regiments).

"But just at the time when they thought they had finished their work they found themselves not only called upon to resist the desperate charge of enemies whose sole longing was to kill and die, but also they were subjected to the fire of their own allies and the big ships with whom they were unaware they had any quarrel whatever. Nor had they any time to make inquiries as to why they were subjected to such treatment. They were falling fast by the bullets and shell of their allies and among them raged the Maoris, who, although most of them were boys, yet regardless of deaths only tried to kill. Is it to be wondered at that their courage turned to water and their hearts grew dark?

"The soldier is a brave man, none braver, but astonished and confused as these warriors were after a feeble resistance they broke and fled from the place, rushing in their flight against the *Ngati Jacks*, whose formation they broke and who they carried away with them in their race for safety. No, we did not pursue them, but jumped into our pits to save ourselves from the fire of the big guns and the other soldiers. The big guns and the soldiers, however, did not continue firing, many bugles were blown, the fire ceased and to our astonishment on jumping out of our trenches expecting another attack, we saw all the soldiers retreating, which they continued to do although we danced a war dance, so as to show them we were not all killed but ready to furnish them with another fight should their big chief deem us worthy to be attacked again.

"This he did not do as perchance he had by this time been informed that ours was only a fishing *kainga* and not a *pah* worthy of being attacked by such a redoubtable warrior, so he with all his men returned to Tauranga, and that evening we retreated through the swamps to Te Ranga.

"Be still, oh boy, and ask not foolish questions. It befits youth to listen attentively to the discourse of warriors so as to acquire wisdom and knowledge without interrupting, but I answer you this one. No; the white *rangatera* did not run away when their soldiers fled. It is not their custom to do so. Like as it is with us, a white *rangatera* must conquer or die, or, if it be necessary to retreat, he must do so in a manner befitting his own honour and the authority he holds from the Great White Queen.

"On this occasion they did all that brave men could do to prevent their men from running away, and when this took place those who were left alive and unwounded faced us still, some were quickly killed or wounded by our young men whose *wakahihi* (fighting madness) was roused, before we, the trained warriors, could stop them. It is not right for *rangatera* to kill *rangatera*. When unable to resist they remain on the field of battle, restrained as they are by their sense of honour, nor can you take them prisoners, so that when we forced the young men to cease from killing, those white *rangatera*, who remained unwounded, retired slowly from the *kainga*, some of them saluting with their swords, which salute we returned, for this is a befitting thing to do between *rangatera*, be they Maoris or white men, all brave men should respect one another.

"Nor did we torture, nor even kill the wounded men left in the *kainga*, as although we had given up the missionaries and most of us had become Hau Haus, yet we had not adopted their ferocity. No, we made fern *mi-mis* for the wounded and brought them water to drink, one of their own officers, a *tohunga* (medicine man) who was unwounded, remained with them and attended their hurts; him also we did not molest, but when the evening came we departed for Te Ranga much elated by our success.

"My throat is dry and my pannikin is empty, pass therefore the bottle, my friend, and let me moisten my tongue before I tell you how we met the soldiers again at Te Ranga, and of how they took *utu* from us for their defeat.

"I have told you, my friend, that our allies were driven back at Maketu, so we for a time worked hard to complete the very strong entrenchments we were building at Te Ranga, and it would have been well for us had we finished them during the time the soldiers allowed us to do so but on hearing the big white chief had left Tauranga we relaxed our efforts thereby earning our punishment. For remember this, you boys, that those tribes that during the time of peace do not prepare for war will soon be exterminated and their home fires extinguished. Repair therefore during the time of peace the fences of your *pah*, furbish up your guns, make cartridges and sharpen your *tomahawks*, for these are the suitable pursuits for a warrior to indulge in during his days of relaxation from war.

"We, the Tauranga Maoris, neglected to finish our entrenchments although they were far advanced towards completion, and the soldiers in their courtesy allowed us ample time to do so, but when two moons were nearly dead they lost patience with our dilatoriness and marched out of Tauranga to attack us.

"Now the construction of our entrenchments was in this manner. Te Ranga, oh friend, is a long ridge of a hill both sides of which are defended by impassable swamps, so that the soldiers could not outflank or surround us, and our retreat was open. For our defences we had dug high up and across the ridge long lines of rifle pits. This was done in a very crafty way. Each pit would hold ten men, or perhaps twelve, they were dug deep though narrow, so that if the soldiers saw fit to bring their big guns, by crouching down we should be safe from their fire; also the rear lines of pits commanded those in front of it, so that, if driven out of one line, we could still hold the others.

"Now it had been our intention to erect fences in front of each line of rifle pits, so as to delay the rush of the soldiers should they charge us, and also to construct covered ways through which we could retreat with safety from one line to another; but this part of the work had not been done, although the lines of pits themselves were all completed. Two moons were nearly dead since our victory, when we heard that the soldiers under another war chief (Colonel Greer) were marching to attack us, and at the council held on receipt of this news each man blamed the other for our dilatoriness in not finishing our defences, but the time to do so was past. Nor could we blame the soldiers, the fault was ours, and we had to make the best of it. Wrangling amongst ourselves was no good, the soldiers were here, we must man the rifle pits and fight as best we could; even without the fences our position was a very strong one.

"Having plenty of time before us, as from our elevated position we could see the approaching soldiers still a long way off, we danced a war dance suitable for the occasion, and the Hau Hau prophets performed their incantations promising us victory with immunity from wounds and death, which promise made our hearts light, for, although no warrior fears death, yet it is as well to live as long as possible, as perchance some portion of the missionaries' talk may be true and no man wishes to be burnt for ever. No, it is too long a time to be passed in that manner.

"But oh, my white friend, the Hau Hau prophets were humbugs and liars, or knew not their art perfectly, as wounds and death were the lot of the Maoris that day. Give me the bottle, oh friend, it makes me athirst with anger to think of the lies of those Hau Hau prophets, and my old wounds ache and burn again when I talk of them. *Augh!* I feel better, I will continue. Our war dance and incantations being over it was time to man the rifle pits, which we did full of confidence and hope. I myself was placed in one of the advanced pits, that the soldiers must first attack, and in the same pit were ten other Ngaiterangi, all of us being tried warriors of acknowledged courage and repute.

"Our orders were not to fire a shot until the senior war chief gave the word, and then to fire all together, those of us having *tuparas* (double-barrelled guns) being ordered not to fire the second shot until the smoke cleared away and then only to do so on receipt of the order, by doing this we thought that the men armed with muskets would gain time to cast about and reload, and this order was impressed on every man.

"Situated where I was I had a good sight of the advancing soldiers who came in the order of two fish (Maori term for two columns of fours), but as they drew nearer they deployed into line, when for a brief space of time they halted, then with a rattle and flash they drew their long thin knives and fixed them on their muskets. This was done by all of them at the same breath, and the sight was a very fine one, but somehow my heart darkened, and for the space of three breaths my blood seemed to turn to icy cold water. They did not remain halted long, their chief spoke a few words to them and they uttered three loud shouts, then raising their rifles from the ground they moved on towards us, the sun flashing and playing on their long knives like it does on rippling waters.

"As they approached closer I could see their faces and the faces of the *rangatera* who led them, and I could see that each face carried on it a look of fierce determination quite different from the usual look of joyous excitement that is so becoming to a brave warrior when he advances to earn honour and renown in the glorious game of war.

"No, they had danced no war dance to excite their courage, nor had they indulged in incantations to save themselves from wounds or death, but they looked like men who, having a hard task before them, meant to see it through. They had come to exact *utu* and they received it.

"Well, friend, the soldiers advanced in the most perfect order, and, when about fifty fathoms or less from us, at the sound of a bugle, began to run, not tumultuously, but each man in his place, while we looked along the barrels of our muskets, and with beating hearts awaited the order to fire. This at last came and the thunder of our volley rumbled among the hills, but it was at that same moment the *Atua* (God or spirit) of the soldiers stood by and protected them.

"It happened in this way: about ten fathoms in front of our advanced line of rifle pits there was a natural declivity in the ground, the sides of which sloped gently, though the depth of it was perhaps four feet, and just as we received the order and fired the volley, the soldiers stepped into this declivity, so that our storm of bullets, instead of strewing the ground with dead and wounded men, went howling over their heads and injured not one of them. Oh, but the *mana* of the soldiers was very strong that day. We had no time to reload, nor even had the men with *tuparas* time to fire their second shot, for with the roar of a mighty wave bursting over a sunken reef, a long line of soldiers rushed through the smoke and flung themselves on us.

"Oh, ye boys, whose fathers all fell at Te Ranga, and who, with us few who survived, had among ourselves derided the fighting power of the soldiers, take heed and remember my word to you. If at war with the soldiers fight them in the bush or keep behind the strong fences of your *pahs*, but never, my children, let the soldiers of the Great White Queen, when they have fixed their long knives on their muskets, get so near to you as to fight chest to chest, for if you do so, your wives will soon become widows and your children orphans.

"Yes, oh friend, without a pause those white soldiers flung themselves upon us, their long knives stabbing deep, so that we fell like children before the fire of their wrath. I, as I have before related, had been posted in the advance line of pits, and having fired my musket was trying to reload it when the soldiers burst through the smoke, but before I could handle a cartridge, a white *rangatera* sprang on me, nor did he come ceremoniously, for he came head first, which may be the custom of the white *rangatera* so to do when charging an enemy, for in the act of coming he ran me through the shoulder with his sword and we both fell to the bottom of the trench.

"Here I might have gained the mastery, for he was quite a youth, but before my strength could prevail or my friends help me, his men poured in on us, they likewise coming unceremoniously, for with many curses one drove his long knife through my breast while another struck me on the head with the butt of his musket, which made me see many stars, and I fell in a corner of the trench with my head swimming and unable to move hand or foot but still conscious, though the soldiers thinking I was dead left me alone, and turned to kill my friends in the pit. This they did very expeditiously, for although the Maoris fought with the greatest courage still they could not withstand the anger of the soldiers who had come to take *utu* for their past defeat.

"Again, circumstanced as we were, we could not retreat, for as our men tried to scramble out of the pits, which were deep, those soldiers who had not jumped in on top of us slew them, and the slaughter was very great, while those soldiers, being placed opposite to the open spaces between the pits, finding no Maoris to kill there, rushed on without a pause and threw themselves into the second line of trenches, where they slew and slew, for, although the Maoris who held the trenches did all that brave warriors could do, still none of us on that day could withstand the impetuous rush of the white men, who did not pause to fire but just charged on with their long knives.

"*Augh!* I grow thirsty again talking of that disastrous day. The bottle, friend; perchance the rum may lighten my heart. Now I will finish my long story.

"Soon the fight was over and the few Maoris who escaped the fury of the soldiers had fled away into the swamp and bush. Now the white men had time to come back to examine the dead and assist the wounded Maoris, for it is the custom of the soldiers, fighting being over, to try and cure the men whom just previously they had been doing their best to kill. This, my sons, is a right and wise thing for them to do, for the Great White Queen has so many soldiers that should all of them fighting in this country be killed, still she has plenty more to send, whereas we Maoris are so few that we miss sadly every man lost, so that unless the wounded be made whole and the women and children protected it would soon come to pass that there would be no more Maoris left to fight, nor anyone to take their place to test the soldiers' courage and train them for war. This being so the white officers are very careful to repair the hurts of wounded Maoris.

"Presently a party of soldiers came to the trench in which I lay, and finding that I was the only one there to whom life still clung they lifted me carefully out and bore me on a blanket to their medicine-man, who bandaged my wounds, and after many weeks I was made whole. This was the last fight I had with the white man. No, I did not join Te Kooti, nor did I fight against you, my friend, up at Taupo, for I remained in my kainga, my wounds giving me much trouble. And now, my friend, I have told you all things and will again moisten my throat with the good rum.

"And oh, you boys, this is my word to you: think not of *utu* against the white men for the slaying of your fathers; the war is past, the soldiers have gone, and we now are all children of the Great White Queen. We must be friends with the white settlers, and, like them, obedient to the Queen's law, and perchance when you boys are full-grown she, when she sends her soldiers to war, may in her great kindness remember that she has brown children as well as white, and she may send and say:' Come, ye Maoris, and fight my battles for me beside my white soldiers.' *Augh!* that will be great honour, for perchance in those days many descendants of Maori warriors will charge side by side with the White Queen's soldiers.

"Yes, and perchance the spirits of your ancestors may be permitted to see those of their blood cut their way deeper into the ranks of the White Queen's enemies than even the soldiers can go. Stand up, you boys, raise your *tomahawks* on high and cry with loud voices: 'Hip, hip, hip, hurrah for Queen Wikitoria.' No, hold not out your pannikins; rum befits old warriors, not boys. You shall shout for her and perchance may fight for her; I who am old will drink her health. But what is this? Lo, I can see two bottles, two white friends and many Maori boys. Surely this is caused by eating too freely the flesh of pigeons, or talking of my old wounds makes my head go round, or perchance it is witchcraft. It is meet for me to retire to rest, as the whole earth and stars spin round. I spin also. God bless Queen Wikitoria. The bottle is empty, but *Kiora, Kiora, Kiora.*"

And the old warrior, chock-full of rum and loyalty, tried to get up, but pitched head first on his soft bed of fern, where the rising generation of Ngaiterangi carefully covered him up with blankets and he slept the sleep of the brave and just.

Now the trouble caused by the defeat at the Gate Pah did not end when the troops retreated to Tauranga, for recriminations, charges and counter-charges flew like hail, while the New Zealand press wrote the usual twaddle that ignorant editors generally do write on matters of war; but there was one paper in Auckland that went too far, as it accused the Naval Brigade of cowardice, an accusation as untrue as it was unjust, and the gallant *Ngati Jacks* swore they would take *utu*.

Now the *Ngati Jacks* were not given to writing to the newspapers or any tommyrot of that sort. They were men of action; they would right their own wrongs and teach the miserable ink-slinging stool-polisher decorum in their own way. They had lost a number of officers and shipmates, and it was through no fault of theirs that, after the Tommies had fallen back, they had not been allowed to take the place and finish up the job shipshape and Bristol fashion.

Well, a short time after the disaster the ships anchored in Auckland Harbour, and in due course of time liberty was given to one watch from each ship to go on shore; and no sooner had they landed than some five hundred of them paraded of their own accord, and marched quietly through the streets of Auckland until they came to the one in which the newspaper office was located. Nor had they come without suitable arguments, for they had brought with them a huge hawser and two gigantic snatch-blocks.

Now the editor's house and office were, like all the other buildings in Auckland, constructed of wood. It was an imposing two-storied edifice, and on the blue-jackets reaching it they quietly placed strong pickets at both ends of the street, made fast the blocks to old cannons sunk into the ground, passed the hawser through the editor's upper windows, and then, with one hundred men tailing on at each end of the bit of string, delivered their protest and ultimatum. The latter was short, sweet and significant. Either the editor must print at once an ample apology and own up he had lied, or down would come his whole bag of tricks.

There was no time given for palaver; there was the hawser, there Jack stood in orderly array, there stood the bos'n's mates, whistle to lip, and the thoroughly cowed editor caved in at once. Orders were quickly given, and the smartest piece of type-setting and printing ever accomplished in New Zealand was carried out. Soon sheafs of paper bills, still wet from the press, were handed out and showered from the windows, and then the *Ngati Jacks,* having received the *amende honorable,* withdrew the hawser, and, thoroughly satisfied with the *utu* they had obtained, retired themselves to more convivial pursuits, while the still trembling editor recorded a solemn oath that for the future he would curb his poetic licence, at least so far as Her Majesty's navy was concerned.

Kereopa

Chapter 2

Te Kooti

And now I must tell you something about that bounder, Te Kooti.
Every country in the world has at some time or other produced diabolically cruel villains who, under one cloak or another, religion for choice, have perpetrated horrible excesses and gratified their love for blood. Yet very often these men have been great and brainy ones. Europe has produced Tilly, Alva, Torquemada, Caesar Borgia, and many others. England has produced Cromwell and Judge Jeffreys; India, Nana Sahib; and New Zealand in like manner produced Te Kooti. Some of these men were of aristocratic birth, but others, such as Tilly, Cromwell and Te Kooti, springing from the lower middle class, had first to make their names before they could perpetrate the crimes their souls lusted for.

A number of Maori prisoners had been taken in the successful action at Waerenga-a-Hika, which followed upon the atrocious murder of the Rev. Mr Volkner by the Hau Haus.

Now these prisoners should either have been killed or, at all events, should have been well taken care of, as on two previous occasions Maori prisoners had successfully made daring escapes, one of which is worth recording.

About one hundred and fifty Maoris, prisoners of war, among whom were a few women and children, had been confined on board an old timber ship anchored far out in Wellington Harbour. They were well fed, kindly treated, and seemed well satisfied with their lot, being allowed access to the upper deck during the day, where they talked and laughed with their guard, a detachment of the 50th Regiment, while during the night they had comfortable quarters on the lower deck, all the hatchways being shut up and strictly guarded.

The old bow-port of the ship, however, had been forgotten or overlooked, and one very dark, stormy night the Maoris, who had discovered it, forced it open, when every man, woman and child slid noiselessly into the rough, shark-infested water, and swam for the shore, nearly two miles distant, where most of them landed in safety and disappeared into the bush, nor was their escape found out till next morning when the hatches were opened to serve out breakfast.

The New Zealand Government therefore determined to place the prisoners taken at Waerenga-a-Hika in a place from which they could not swim ashore, and so deported two hundred of them to the Chatham Islands, but, being of a frugal mind, they committed these two hundred fanatical, ferocious and able-bodied warriors to the care of a worn-out old officer and fifteen decrepit invalided veterans, nor did they consider it worth the expense to arm the white settlers on the island. Verily the Government were wanting in commonsense, though their cheese-paring parsimony might be worthy of a present-date Radical, (as at time of first publication).

Now during the siege of Waerenga-a-Hika a native belonging to the native contingent, named Te Kooti, had been charged by a sub-chief with holding treasonable intercourse with the enemy. He had been made a prisoner, but as there was no evidence against him he was shortly afterwards released. Subsequent to the surrender of the *pah*, Te Kooti was again charged, this time by a white settler, with communicating with the enemy, but again there was not sufficient evidence to bring him to a trial.

The great fighting chief Rapata had, however, a private grievance against him, and wished to kill him out of hand, but this the Government would not allow, an act of very short-sighted policy, as it turned out to be on their part. They, however, feared to offend Rapata, so they transported Te Kooti to the Chatham Islands with the two hundred Hau Hau prisoners. Now this was a piece of gross injustice. There had not been sufficient evidence to try him on any charge, and most certainly the Government had no right to transport a man, serving as a soldier, who had never even been tried, much less convicted.

Te Kooti was at this time a strong, daring fellow, some thirty years old, who had, fighting against the Hau Haus, acquired a small reputation for courage, but he was much disliked by the white settlers, who knew him to be a thief; nor was he respected by his own people, who regarded him as a quarrelsome *mauvais sujet* whose room was more valuable than his company. He was a man of no rank by birth, nor had he exhibited any signs of intellect likely to raise him out of the ruck of his fellows. As to whether or not he deserved punishment may be open to argument, but there is no doubt that all the atrocities committed by himself, or by his orders, were dictated by a desire of obtaining *utu* on those responsible for his deportation. Well, this fellow was deported with the other prisoners and landed in the Chatham Islands. Here Te Kooti took up the somewhat dangerous *rôle* of a prophet, and so worked on the superstitions of his fanatical companions that they rendered him unquestioned obedience.

It must not be imagined that the prisoners were shut up in jail or confined in any way; they were made comfortable and lived in huts. The burlesque guard during the night inhabited a tiny, toy sand fort in which the arms and ammunition were kept, but during the day the fort was left in charge of one of their number, the remainder being scattered over the place, employed as ration issuers, clerks, etc.

The prisoners had been landed on the Chatham Island in December 1865, and from the day of their landing till the 4th of July 1868 their conduct had been exemplary, though there can be no doubt that during all this time Te Kooti was forming his plans, and with infinite patience was awaiting a suitable opportunity for a successful attempt to escape.

On the 3rd of July 1868 the three-masted schooner, *Rifleman*, was sighted making for the island, loaded with stores for the use of the convicts, a boat-load of whom pulled off and assisted the crew of the vessel to bring her to her anchorage, also volunteering to help discharging cargo. Captain Thomas, the officer in charge of the prisoners, had been previously warned that there was mischief brewing, but the dear old soul did not believe it, or at all events took no steps to prevent the rising, which took place after this fashion.

In accordance with custom one of the old images who composed the guard was on duty in the toy fort, the remainder being scattered apart at their usual occupations, and as he pottered about he saw a strong body of the prisoners approaching him and at once demanded their business. They replied that they wanted the arms and ammunition which were stored in the fort. He answered they should not get them. They rushed him. He was a good old soldier though past work, and, promptly shooting one, tried to use his bayonet, but was immediately knocked down, his rifle wrenched out of his hand, and he finished his service by being run through and killed with his own bayonet. Truly the brave old fellow deserved a better fate.

Te Kooti, however, must not be blamed for his death, as he had given strict orders no one was to be hurt, and this was the only blood spilt during the whole affair. The Maoris also behaved with the greatest courtesy to the white settlers, depriving them of nothing except such guns and weapons as they had in their possession. No sooner had the prisoners received the arms than a boat-load of them pulled off to the *Rifleman*, boarded her, and drove the mate and crew (the captain was ashore) down below, threatening to kill anyone who resisted. They also boarded the *ketch*, *Florence*, which chanced to be lying at anchor, sent her crew ashore, and then, cutting the cable, sent their vessel after them so as to prevent her being used in any way against them.

Te Kooti had now full possession of the island, but he did not linger, as he at once embarked all the prisoners, he being the last man to leave the shore. Directly he put foot on board he summoned the crew on deck and gave them the option of either working the schooner to Poverty Bay, where he promised to hand her back to them, or to be immediately killed. They chose the former alternative and at once made sail, but a strong wind from the west prevented them from beating out, so they had to return to their former anchorage. Te Kooti took no chances, for as soon as the sails were furled he again confined the crew below, nor would he allow them to cook the food either then or on any other occasion during the voyage.

Next day they again made sail and got away from the island, but being delayed by foul winds Te Kooti ordered all the greenstone ornaments on board to be thrown into the sea as a propitiatory sacrifice to *Tangaroa* (the Maori Neptune), and as this had no beneficial result Te Kooti ordered an old man, a relation of his own, to be cast into the drink, and this, notwithstanding the old fellow's objections, was done, no one supporting nor even seconding his amendment, as it had been given out he was the delinquent who had warned Captain Thomas of the projected rising. Whether the victim was a Jonah or not, who can say, but it is certain that no sooner had the poor old sinner been launched over the lee-rail than the wind changed, so, easing sheets, they made a good land-fall at Whare-onga-onga, about fifteen miles south of the Poverty Bay settlement.

On the following day, the 10th of July, and during the whole of that night, the Maoris working like beavers, they landed some forty tons of stores, about fifty rifles and a number of other weapons, then releasing the crew Te Kooti told them to upsail and hook it. This they did, but the mate perpetrated a gross act of folly. The Port of Napier was close to him, but instead of making for it he set his course for

TE KOOTI

Wellington, and thereby lost ten days in giving the alarm.

In the meantime Te Kooti had taken up a strong position near where he had landed, and sent messengers to the adjoining tribe to come and *tangi* with him. These messages fell into the hands of Major Biggs, who could not at first believe the news, but on its confirmation mustered a force of one hundred badly armed white settlers and friendly natives, and marched against the escaped convicts. He found them strongly posted, but as the friendlies refused to attack he could do nothing. He therefore attempted to parley, trying to persuade the defiant natives to lay down their arms, but this they refused to do, and retreated inland, carrying their plunder with them to one of the most broken patches of country in New Zealand.

Now during the Year of the Lamb 1867 the infatuated New Zealand Government, longing for peace, had made up their minds they had obtained it, and, being crazy for retrenchment, had not only disbanded the Defence Force but, so as to save the expense of having a man to look after them, had removed the bulk of the arms and ammunition from the district. Major Biggs was therefore severely handicapped as the only men he had to depend upon were badly armed settlers and untrustworthy semi-friendly natives.

Owing to these circumstances Te Kooti got the best of it in the desultory fighting that took place, defeating the white men and their allies at Paparatu, while he shortly afterwards forced another column to fall back through their running out of ammunition and the desertion of the friendlies, so that his name spread through the country as a chief with a most powerful *mana*.

Colonel Whitmore, who in the meantime hurried up from Napier, followed up Te Kooti, but with his usual want of tact so disgusted the Poverty Bay volunteers that they refused to leave their own district, and Te Kooti continued to make headway, beating back an attack made on his position at Te Konaki, and also getting much the best of it in a stiff fight at Ruaki Ture. In September Colonel Whitmore left for the west coast, where he was beaten, as I have previously described, by Titokowaru at Moturoa, and Te Kooti, on the 9th of November, surprised and sacked the white settlement of Poverty Bay, where he murdered in a most atrocious manner every woman and child he could lay his hands on.

Loaded with plunder he left the devastated settlement on the 14th, and retired slowly to his lair, his rear-guard being overtaken and attacked at Makaretu on the 25th, but the Hau Haus made a good stand,

and although they lost heavily they held their ground, Te Kooti at the same time by a smart bit of generalship capturing an important convoy of ammunition and stores.

But a change was to come over the scene, for Rapata, with a party of Ngatiporou, arrived at Makaretu, and on 3rd December he, with his men, by a rattling charge carried two of the enemy's outworks, driving them back to their last line of trenches, which they deemed impregnable, but the gallant chief proved it otherwise, for he at once rushed them, and with the assistance of the other friendlies, who on this occasion fought bravely, drove out the Hau Haus with great slaughter, killing several of Te Kooti's best fighting chiefs; and they also captured the infernal villain Nama, who had been most active in torturing women and children at the late massacre. Well they got this fellow alive, and so as to try to even things up a bit the Ngatiporou roasted him alive, and "sarve him right" was the verdict given by the colonial troops, for after the Poverty Bay massacre the gloves came off and it was war to the knife.

Te Kooti now fell back, having only escaped by the skin of his teeth, to his famous stronghold Ngatapa, and Rapata moved forward to attack him, but unfortunately a quarrel about some prisoners with his allies hampered him sorely, and although he attacked with the Ngatiporou he had to fall back for want of ammunition, his allies rendering him no service whatever; he therefore, furious and disgusted, retired towards Tauranga.

I think I have now given you some vague idea of what had happened on the east coast previous to our accompanying Colonel Whitmore there, although I have not mentioned scores of skirmishes that had taken place with the various tribes during the last four years up and down the coast.

Chapter 3

Ngatapa

I think I may now trek on with my own adventures.

We landed at Tauranga in December 1868, and Colonel Whitmore at once started off to make Te Kooti sit up, taking with him three hundred well-trained and seasoned men. Near a place called Patutahi we met Rapata and his men returning to Tauranga, and Colonel Whitmore did his best to persuade the angry chief to turn back, but this he refused to do, saying: "I never break my word. I have said I would go to Waiapu and I will, but I will return with more Ngatiporou and wipe out the Ngatikahungunu, the cowardly dogs who deserted me."

This would have meant wheels within wheels, or rather a civil war within a civil war, a regular Donny-brook, and it was only after much talk that the indignant warrior could be persuaded to forgo his vengeance against the other friendlies, though he sternly refused to fight again in their company or to alter his determination to proceed to Waiapu, so, a steamer having been placed at his disposal, he departed to his home, promising to recruit more of his own tribe and to return shortly. It was on this occasion I first met this redoubtable warrior and general, when, like all other men who love a man, I greatly admired him.

Rapata Te Wahawaha had from the outbreak of the East Coast War played a very prominent part, and, one may truthfully say, had carved out in more ways than one his own path to rank and fame. He was a fine, handsome, athletic-looking man, evidently capable of enduring great hard-ships and fatigue, while you only had to look at his face to see that he had an iron will, the courage of a bulldog and the ability to command. When in repose he had all the good manners, the courteous bearing and the musical voice of a well-bred Maori, but in action the eyes blazed, the whole face hardened into a mask of granite, while his word of command was given in a voice that few who served under him cared or dared hesitate to obey.

Although of aristocratic birth, he was not a great chief by descent, nor had he up to the commencement of the war given any proof of possessing any first-rate administrative qualities, or possibly in his paternal sub-tribe he had no chance of displaying them, but from the first fight, Mangaone, in which his tribe took part, he displayed such indomitable courage and resource that by the time I met him he was not only the principal war chief, but was looked upon as quite the most prominent man in the great and powerful tribe of Ngatiporou to which his hereditary *sept* belonged. He had from the very first set his face sternly against the new faith.

The inhabitants of village after village, mission station after mission station, throwing away their Christianity, had joined the Hau Haus, but when the apostles came to Rapata's sub-tribe he sternly bade them be gone, or he would test their invulnerability with his *tomahawk*. Now several of the sub-tribes of the Ngatiporou had already perverted, and some of these sought to convert Rapata by force. Rapata, however, was taking none of that, so he waltzed out of his *pah*, and in the faction fight that ensued he fairly knocked the stuffing out of the Nonconformists, and as a proof of his determination not to stand any nonsense he shot, with his own hand, a near relation who had been taken prisoner, not, as he was careful to explain to the delinquent, because he had fought against himself, but because he had been such a fool as to join the Hau Haus against his, Rapata's, orders. He was the sealed pattern of the old-time Maori warrior, one who knew not fear or pity, and was just as ready to join in a hand-to-hand fight as to plan out a campaign or eat his dinner. Byron, singing about an old-time Dago pirate, described him as being the mildest-tempered man who ever cut a throat or scuttled ship.

Rapata was a polished Maori gentleman who with a polite and easy nonchalance could entertain the highest colonial dignitary, tomahawk a Hau Hau, or shoot a deserter with his own rifle. He was indeed a worthy ally, for had he not made the firm stand he did the whole of the powerful tribe of Ngatiporou would have been thrown in the balance against us, and the white man must for a time have been driven out of the North Island of New Zealand. And now let me break back and try to regain my spoor.

The following morning Rapata departed, still in high dudgeon, and the Colonel, selecting four scouts, sent them to find out whether or not Ngatapa had been deserted, although why Te Kooti should have deserted it was beyond my wisdom. The men he selected for the work, although good enough fighting men, were not trained scouts, nor had they ever been employed at that fascinating though dangerous game before. However, off they went while we rested in camp.

That afternoon, while lolling on my *mi-mi* with Roach, I heard a voice hail Tim, who was making ready our supper: "Here, Tim, old shipmate, where's the skipper? Lay us alongside of him, me hearty." And in two skips of a jumping cat I found my hand enveloped and crushed in the enormous fist of old Jack Williams, while a moment afterwards Pierre de Feugeron and Kantuarius were *salaaming* in front of us, Pierre showing his white teeth, shrugging his shoulders and gesticulating as only a Southern Frenchman can, while the Greek expressed his satisfaction at meeting Roach and myself again by jabbering and grinning like a demented Cheshire cat. They had come to the east coast with McDonnell in 1867, and had remained there. Jack in charge of a boat, the other two doing odd jobs in scouting.

The foreigners at once attached themselves to us, but old Jack had to return that evening to Tauranga, so that after his oaths of gladness at meeting us had rolled away like summer thunder he drank a tot out of my flask, forced me to accept a big prick of naval tobacco, and drifted away, swearing softly, to join his party.

"*Et maintenant, messieurs*," quoth Pierre, "I will do myself ze honour of taking charge of *messieurs'* cuisine."

"But, Pierre," I said, "where is the famous *batterie?*"

"Ah, *monsieur*, ze brave pot, ze poor pot; ah, *monsieur*, such misfortune, my magnificent pot lies *mort sur le champ de battaille*. Ah, *monsieur*, it was heart-rending. George and myself were retreating, and the sacred savages were coming fast behind us, but we cleared them, when *les enfants d'enfer*, seeing us escape, fired a volley, *plom* I fall on my face. George help me to rise. I am not killed nor much hurt, but my pot, my dear pot lies in pieces. I am distressed. I am enraged. Revenge. I yearn for revenge. I drop on ze knee and fire. Ah! Ah! I see one of ze canaille throw his arms on high and fall. I have my revenge. I say, '*Vive la France!*' George say, 'Damn good shot. Come, let's cut and run,' and we cut and run. So, *mon officier*, ze grand pot *est mort, mais* Pierre remains at *monsieur's* service and has ze wherewithal to prepare ze dinner for his two officers. Let *messieurs* remain tranquil. We shall see."

Messieurs remained tranquil, and in good time, instead of supping off the putrid pork and mouldy biscuits Tim had been fumbling over, we enjoyed a delicious ragout of fowls, fresh pork, potatoes and the Lord only knows what else. It is well for you, oh, my son, when on active service two scallywag foreigners, past masters in the art of looting, and owning not one ghostly idea of *meum* and *tuum*, attach themselves to you and take upon themselves the onerous duty of catering for your table. Be not inquisitive, oh, my son; ask no questions, but accept the luck Providence sends you and you will fare sumptuously.

In due course of time the scouts returned and reported that Te Kooti had abandoned Ngatapa. They had not approached the place closely, but said he had done so, because they had seen large volumes of smoke, and thought Te Kooti was burning his huts before leaving.

Now this was all tommyrot, and I marvelled at a smart soldier listening to such twaddle. In the first place a Maori does not build a hut to burn it down. Again, we had heard from Rapata that the position of Ngatapa was one of extraordinary strength. Te Kooti had expended an immense amount of labour in fortifying it. He had successfully defended it against the first attack.

Why, therefore, should he desert it? No, it seemed to me that it would be far more probable that the dense smoke the tenderfoot scouts had seen was caused by the Hau Haus clearing ground in front of their works so as to destroy cover, especially as dry fern and *raupo*, commonly used by the natives for thatch, burns with but little vapour, while undergrowth and timber, full of sap, burns with a great deal, and was therefore far more likely to be the fuel causing the great clouds of smoke reported by the scouts.

Now I happened to be present at the time the scouts reported to the colonel, and, when they had finished their yarn, ventured to state my opinions, at the same time offering to take Pierre and George, scout up to the place, and verify my theories.

It would have been better for me had I held my tongue, for I received in reply a most stinging rebuke, which was both unjust and unmerited. It is true a colonel may not be desirous of receiving advice or suggestions from a subaltern, still I had been employed on many important occasions and had earned a reputation as a scout, and, as he well knew, had put in three years' hard bush training, so even if it were presumption on my part to make a suggestion, still that suggestion was worth while taking into consideration, if not acting upon, especially as I offered to run the risk, which was by no means a small one.

Anyhow, the colonel chose to give me a most unmerciful slating for what he was pleased to term my impertinence, and also added some most caustic remarks on my general utility, and these in such a sarcastic and bitter tone that it was only my strict sense of discipline that prevented me using the whip I carried in my hand over his hide, and I was greatly delighted when I met him years afterwards, when we were both civilians, to be able to give him my plain and unvarnished opinion of his conduct both as an officer and a gentleman.

However, to return to our mutton; orders were immediately given for our return to Tauranga, which were promptly carried out, and Colonel Whitmore made arrangements to re-embark us forthwith to Wanganui; in fact No. 6 Division of the Armed Constabulary was already shipped on board the *Sturt* for the west coast, but by the merciful dispensation of Providence the skipper was absent, and the old tub, objecting to the officer temporarily in charge, sat down on a rock, which, knocking a hole in her bottom, necessitated the relanding of the men.

Now my theory *re* the smoke had been perfectly correct. It had been caused by the Hau Haus burning the scrub so as to destroy cover, and Te Kooti, informed by his scouts of our retreat from Patutahi, seized the opportunity to make one of his lightning raids, in which he murdered several settlers, and did much damage.

On the receipt of this news the little colonel went hopping mad, and without losing a moment we started off to intercept Te Kooti's retreat, but as it was impossible for the main body to move before morning he despatched Captain Newland and a party of sixteen troopers on ahead. Had he given us fifty troopers, which he very well could have done, we should have hived the artful dodger then and there, as we cut his line of retreat and did all men could do to hold him till the arrival of the colonel, but eighteen mounted men, no matter how good they are, cannot hold two hundred Maoris, especially in rough country. We however did the best we could, and had the ground been anywhere suitable we should have charged; as it was we had to draw off through the long fern, and it was only the skill of our captain, the cool pluck of our men, and the rotten bad shooting of the Hau Haus that saved us from being cut to pieces.

We had, however, been driven off the ground when Colonel Whitmore came up with Te Kooti's rear-guard and attacked them, but as his men were worn out by their long forced march over very rough country, he failed to make any impression, so Te Kooti succeeded in gaining Ngatapa, having got nine to four the best of us.

The advance, however, had begun in earnest, and at the end of the third day, the 27th of December, we took up our position on a high ridge about a mile distant from the Hau Haus' stronghold. Here the colonel received news that Rapata, with three hundred and seventy men, had landed, but refused to join up. This was a lie, for the gallant chief was coming on as fast as he could. It was, however, too good a chance for the spiteful little devil to miss of insulting our most faithful ally, and he despatched message after message of such a nature that the high-spirited Maori would not tolerate them, the last one being that if Rapata did not hurry up he would take the place himself.

On receipt of this chit Rapata immediately halted his men and returned this reply: "It is well. I have tried to take it once and failed; it is your turn now. I will camp here and await your success."

This brought the colonel to his bearings, and he saw he had gone too far, especially as some of the senior officers plainly pointed out to him that if he continued to try and bounce Rapata, that chief would return insolence for insolence, and that a quarrel with their great fighting chief would be looked upon by the Ngatiporou as a direct insult to the tribe.

Now Whitmore was a splendid soldier and no fool, notwithstanding his nasty manner and want of tact, he therefore, seeing he had gone too far, visited Rapata the next day.

"Have you taken the place?" queried the chief.

"No," replied the colonel, "I want you to help me."

"I will be with you tomorrow morning," responded Rapata, and the interview terminated.

The Ngatiporou at once broke camp and advanced, making a short halt at the Wharekopai River, where, to see that everything was all right, they danced a gaudy war dance, and as no one tumbled down during the ceremony the tribal *tohunga* and prophet declared that everything was all right and that the expedition would be successful. Thoroughly satisfied with this propitious announcement, and perhaps more so with themselves, they pushed on rapidly and joined up the same night.

The position of Ngatapa was by nature a very strong one, a high conical peak rising abruptly amidst heavily bushed hills, the face fronting our camp sloping gradually up to the summit, but the sides of the slope, although surmountable in some places, were not so in others, especially in one place, where it was so precipitous as to be quite unnegotiable, the side of the hill having slipped away, leaving a perpendicular precipice of rock quite seventy feet high, and this was the spot where the enemy eventually escaped. The ground in rear of the *pah* narrowed into a razor-backed indented ridge, the formation of which was gigantic steps, only to be descended by rope ladders, and down the ridge ran a path by which the Hau Haus hoped to escape, if driven to do so, but the path was at once blocked by our men, although for the time being we did not make use of it as a way to attack.

The front slope of the position, in fact the only one possible to march up, was defended by three lines of stoutly built earthworks with ditches in front of them and trenches in rear of them in which the defenders could take cover. Their flanks resting on the precipitous sides of the slope prevented them from being turned, while every particle of cover in front of them had been scarped away. The two lower parapets were over seven feet high, but the upper one was at least fourteen feet, being pierced with sand-bagged loopholes, and was indeed a most formidable work.

All these lines were connected by covered ways, and altogether it was what it looked, a most imposing fortification with its parapets rising one above the other on the steep slope and growing narrower as the ridge contracted. Yes, imposing it looked, in fact impregnable, or only to be taken with an immense loss of life, but it had, like most Maori *pahs*, one sad defect, it contained no water. This would have been no drawback in old-time Maori warfare, as it had never been the custom of the chivalrous sports men-like savages to prevent the women from leaving a besieged *pah* for the purpose of obtaining food and water. "For," said the old-time cannibal warrior, "how can a man's heart be strong, and how can he fight well, should he be famished for want of sustenance"

Civilised white men, however, use hunger and thirst as two of their most formidable weapons, and did so even during the most chivalrous epochs—to wit, the siege of Calais—by that mirror of chivalry, Edward III., or, coming to modern (as at time of first publication) times—*viz*. the siege of Paris—by the gospel-quoting, long-prayer-making German Emperor. How then could Te Kooti expect more consideration from that chip of the devil, Whitmore, and this was the weak joint in his armour.

At daybreak on the last day of the year 1868 we broke camp, and the whole force, by this time considerably augmented, took up a position on a conical hill some seven hundred yards in front of the *pah*, which, although a part of the same ridge, was divided from it by a deep gully, and this hill we fortified, working under a heavy fire.

Next day the Ngatiporou and some other friendlies skirmished very cautiously up the hill so as to begin the game, and, on reaching the edge of the cleared ground, came across a party of the enemy carrying water. Our men opened fire and charged, driving the Hau Haus back to the *pah* and seizing the only watering-place they possessed. Rapata at once dug, under a heavy fire, a line of rifle pits, and sent back for reinforcements, which were quickly furnished him in the shape of No. 7 Division Armed Constabulary, who, on reaching the rifle pits, immediately started a flying sap, which they drove within a distance of one hundred yards from the outer parapet, and here they formed the second parallel of attack.

The artillery division of the Armed Constabulary, assisted by some natives, had for the last few days been working like beavers to get a mortar across some miles of the most awful country, consisting chiefly of deep, rocky and precipitous ravines, every shell having to be carried on men's backs across these natural obstacles, and just as No. 7 were completing their trench the gun was brought into action, the vertical fire from which having a great moral effect upon the defenders.

On the next day the place was thoroughly invested, with the exception of the one small length of precipice I have before mentioned. This place was not overlooked, but as it was not more than seventy yards long, and perpendicular, it was deemed quite impossible that the enemy could escape down it, especially as a strong picket was placed at both ends of it, who could enfilade its face.

The attack was now pushed briskly forward, though for some days we were hampered by heavy rain that filled our trenches with mud, and added greatly to our discomfort, as we occupied them day and night. It moreover supplied the enemy with water to drink. Notwithstanding this drawback we all worked away with good hearts, though of course the risks officers and men ran, working in the flying sap, soon caused our gimcrack hospital to overflow.

I was at this time attached to Colonel Fraser's outfit that held the rear of the *pah*, and that gallant officer, not being content to look on, gave the order for us to mount the serrated ridge that led up the back of the hill. This we did; scaling ladders were quickly formed out of poles and vines. Rough constructions they were, but they served at a pinch for active, determined men, and we were all that, though perhaps not a highly moral community. We scrambled up one precipitous terrace after another under heavy fire, but covered by our sharpshooters, who, being infinitely better shots than the Hau Haus, afforded us sufficient protection, until we at last formed a rough shelter trench under the steep rock that formed the summit of the hill and the rear defence of the *pah*, so that the natives were hived in their works.

This they bitterly resented, and made sally after sally to drive us out of our hardly gained position, but we clung to it like limpets to a rock, and, although we lost many good men in the savage hand-to-hand fighting, still we managed to hold on to the end.

Colonel Whit more and Rapata now determined to storm the advance parapet, for, although we were well aware that the Hau Haus had no water, and we surmised they could have but little food, if any, still we were on less than half rations ourselves, as owing to the sinful country we were fighting in it was absolutely impossible for pack-horses, much less drays, to keep us supplied, so that many of the friendly natives, should they feel the pinch of hunger, might at any time take it into their heads they had business at home and clear out. This being so, Rapata, with fifty picked Ngatiporou, under cover of the best shots in the force, scaled the almost perpendicular sides of the slope, and, with picks and spades carried up with them, broke through the trench behind the parapet, and by doing so were able to enfilade it.

The defenders drew to that end to oppose him, and were doing their best, when with a cheer the Armed Constabulary, who were in the advanced trench of the attack, jumped out and rushed the parapet. The Hau Haus, taken in front and flank, fought bravely, but were either killed or driven pell-mell behind their second line of defences. A fresh sap was immediately commenced, the captured trench being used as a new base, and the men working like niggers, notwithstanding the heavy fire and a furious sally by the enemy had excavated by midnight sufficient cover for two hundred stormers close up to the second line.

It was now Colonel Whitmore's intention to blow up this parapet, and with a rush take the main work at daylight. Our party were also ordered to hold themselves in readiness for a last effort, and we knew something serious must happen, as that evening the enemy had made a most determined attack on us, which we had had great difficulty in beating off, and we also knew that they must be now not only short of water but also very short of food, as the bodies of the dead Hau Haus plainly showed they were on the shortest rations, while as the rain had quite cleared off they must be famished with thirst.

All that night we sat with our weapons in our hands, silently awaiting the dawn, but about two a.m. a woman in the *pah*, having relations among the Ngatiporou, called out telling them that Te Kooti had escaped. This her people would not believe, as every man of the field force was at his post and on the *qui vive*, so, thinking it might be a trap, they called to her to come out. To this she demurred, refusing to budge until her safety was guaranteed by some chief of repute. Eventually this was done, when out she came, her story being that all the unwounded Maoris had escaped, leaving their disabled men, the women and children behind them.

As day dawned we advanced cautiously into the interior of the *pah*, and found her yarn to be true; but we also plainly saw that had we made an attempt to rush the place we should most probably have been beaten back with great loss. The Ngatiporou quickly finished off the wounded men, and then, at Rapata's suggestion, started off in pursuit of the fugitives, who, as we ascertained, had been three days without water and four days without food of any sort, and were therefore not likely to be able to travel fast over such rough and broken country.

The way the bounders had escaped was truly marvellous, as they had descended the face of the precipice, and that so silently as not to have been heard by the pickets posted at either end of it, these pickets being not more than sixty yards apart.

It was not long before small parties of the Ngatiporou began to return, bringing batches of prisoners back with them, the latter being brought at once before Rapata, a stern judge, forsooth. Few and brief were the questions he asked them, and they received a short shrift and a long drop, as they were placed by squads at the edge of the highest precipice, when they were shot, their bodies toppling over and falling to the foot, and there their bones lie to the present day, (as at time of first publication).

This was a frugal way of getting rid of them, as it saved rations, burial fees and all other expenses. True it may seem to you good people who live at home under the lee of the law and the police that our conduct was cruel and bloodthirsty in the extreme, but you must remember that every one of those one hundred and thirty Hau Haus who were disposed of in this summary manner had borne a hand in the massacre of women and children, and that in a way too awful to write about; moreover we were fighting without gloves; and that it was war to the knife.

By the end of the second day the last of Rapata's men had returned, and the last prisoner had gone over the precipice; but the arch-devil,

Te Kooti, and some of his principal satellites, having escaped, were still at large.

I will now relate a short yarn which illustrates a phase of Maori customs, and how the astute Rapata got to windward of a Maori law.

One of the prisoners brought in was a man named Renata, who was a Ngatiporou Hau Hau of high birth, being not only closely related to Rapata himself but also connected to the highest chiefs of the tribe. Now this man Renata had been one of the original convicts sent to the Chatham Islands, but owing to his high connections he had, after a short detention there, been released and allowed to return home. He however showed but little gratitude for this indulgence, as he immediately joined Te Kooti on his landing. When his capture was reported to Rapata that gallant chief was somewhat nonplussed. Spare him he would not, and yet to order his immediate death might arouse the anger and draw the revenge of the great tribal chiefs against himself.

Anyhow Renata had to be killed, so Rapata sent word to his men that he did not want to see the prisoner. This was his death warrant, as no sooner had the captors received the message than they placed Renata with a batch of men who were philosophically waiting the volley and the long drop. Renata, however, was a *rangatera*, and would not submit to being put to death in such an offhand fashion, so that when he was formed up in the line of the unfortunates at the top of the precipice, and the firing party were capping their guns, he rushed at his captors, knocked down one, broke through the rest and fled into some scrub, but his plucky attempt was a failure, as he was followed by two men, who ran him down and shot him.

It now behoved Rapata to square the other chiefs, who were as yet ignorant of the execution, so, taking the bull by the horns, he called a meeting of the tribal notabilities, the agenda being. What was to be done with the delinquent? At this meeting Rapata made a most eloquent and diplomatic speech, pointing out how wrong they would be to spare such a man simply because he was a relation of their own. Again, what would the white men say if a man of good blood was allowed to go scathless while men of lower rank were shot by the dozen? In fact he so cornered them that they knew not what to say, until at last old Wikiriwhi, a chief of the greatest rank, who very probably was getting bored and quite possibly wanted his dinner, became so moved as to say: "We leave him to you."

"Then," rejoined Rapata, "he is a dead man"; and so he was and had been for twenty-four hours.

Of course a large number of Hau Haus had escaped with Te Kooti, and many of them, weakening on the job, returned in small batches to their homes, some having the temerity to show themselves in the white settlements, and these the weak-minded Government left unmolested, notwithstanding it was well known they were all more or less implicated in the various massacres. True there was not much evidence against them, as all their victims were dead, but this did not assuage the sorrow of relations nor mitigate their wrath, and on several occasions the white settlers very properly avenged themselves.

One case was as follows: A man named Benson, hearing the murderer of one of his relations had returned, bailed him up and shot him dead. On the following day Benson was warned by the town constable to attend as a juryman at the inquest of the defunct. This surprised him and he tried to point out to the representative of the law that for him to do so would be rather out of place as he himself was the shooter; but the sapient official refused to entertain the excuse and threatened him with all sorts of dreadful penalties should he not comply with the order. So Benson sat as juryman on his own trial, gave evidence against himself, and at the end of the inquiry was one of the twelve good men and true who brought in the following verdict:—"Shot by some person unknown, and serve him right."

One more case. The general killing was over when eight prisoners were brought in, and the Government representatives, who by that time were on the spot, thought they should receive a trial. This was equivalent to releasing them, as it is impossible to get a witness to bear evidence after he has been murdered. Anyhow these eight beauties were confined in a hut with a trooper on guard over them. Now it chanced that among the troopers was a man named Hunt, whose wife and family had been butchered by the gang these ruffians belonged to. He was a quiet, methodical man who said nothing, but awaited his opportunity; and it came. One day he was detailed as prison guard, which he mounted, having previously borrowed a second revolver from his mate. Hunt quietly took over the duty, entered the hut, made fast the door, drew his brace of revolvers and deliberately shot every one of the bounders, a plan so well conceived and carried out as to be worthy of the approval of both white men and Maoris.

Chapter 4

Back To the West Coast

Directly after the fall of Ngatapa, Colonel Whitmore returned to Wanganui, taking us with him, so as to play a return match against our old opponent, Titokowaru, and by the end of the month we were again on the bank of the Kai-iwi River, where Colonel Lyon had built a strong redoubt, and constructed a bridge of sorts. The little colonel was not a man to waste time, so decided to advance the following day by the track that ran inland. Although close to the camp this road passed through a very deep and densely bushed gorge, which, if held by an enemy, would cost a lot of lives to force. The colonel knew all about this, so during the evening he despatched Kepa with his Wanganuis to make a detour through the bush and occupy the other end, while shortly afterwards he sent me with four scouts to thoroughly examine the gorge itself, for which purpose he sent with us a white settler, who, owning the land there, of course knew that part of the country well.

Taking Pierre, George, Tim and a man named M'Kenzie with me, I left camp at dark, and worked quietly along one side of the ravine as far as I could get without running foul of Kepa's scouts; then I crossed it, and worked down the other side, but could neither see nor hear anything. I was, however, far from being satisfied, as the queer instinct a highly trained scout acquires warned me I was in the vicinity of great danger; moreover George, whom I had detached for a time to watch the greatest point of danger, told me, when he joined up, he fancied he had heard the sound of metal striking stone. I therefore determined to make a further examination.

We again proceeded up the side of the ravine, entered it high up and descended, guiding ourselves through the pitch darkness by feeling our way cautiously along the side of the track. This of course was running an awful risk, but I saw no other way of solving the problem. My men were all game; if we were cut off some firing must occur, the camp would be alarmed, and, if none of us reported, still the colonel would know the enemy were in occupation of the gorge.

Moving as quietly as death, and just as the dawn was lightening the sky, we reach the most dangerous point of the ravine, when M'Kenzie tripped in a rut and fell. Immediately a shot rang out, then two, and before you could say knife, both sides of the gully blazed with musketry. Hastily pulling Mac to his feet we all bolted, as, with the crashing of bush and yelling like fiends incarnate, a swarm of Hau Haus started in pursuit.

Lord, how we did run, M'Kenzie and the settler being in front, while myself and Tim, who would not leave me, brought up the rear. Fortunately we were close to the end of the defile, and as we came out into the open we somehow got separated, as each man took what he considered to be the best line for camp, which he knew must be alarmed by the firing. It was much lighter when we got into the open and tore through the stunted fern and *manuka* scrub, but, although you have no time for debate or argument when some two hundred howling savages, armed with *tomahawks*, are close up to you, still I glanced to my right and left, and as there was no cover to hide a running man I saw M'Kenzie and the settler some fifty yards away to my right, while Pierre and George were running somewhat closer on my left. It was a case of, "Go it, shirt tails, bowie knives is a-gaining on you," and you can bet your bottom dollar we did our level best. Nor was I hopeless, as I knew, with the little colonel in command, all the troopers would be saddled up, and the camp on the *qui vive* at least an hour before the glimmer of dawn.

The Hau Hau volley must have been heard, and the Maori did not exist who could catch the little colonel on the hop. I had no fear of being hit, as, although an occasional Maori would squib off his gun at us, still they could not stop to take aim or load, so we only had to keep ahead to win through, and each of us sprinted for what he was worth. Tim and myself had kept to the road, and had still plenty of run left in us, when I heard the hoof-thuds of galloping horses and saw the troopers come charging through the fern. But, alas! at the same moment I heard from my right the triumphant yell a Maori warrior lets go (which being interpreted means, "I have caught the first man").

In a moment Tim and myself halted and faced about; the party who had been actually in pursuit of us had also halted, taking cover;

and, looking in the direction from which the yell had come, I saw the settler staggering through the fern, closely pursued by a Maori, who just overhauled him, and was in the act of *tomahawking* him, as I fired; which took effect first, lead or steel, I knew not, but they both went down together.

In the first glance I had seen, a few yards in rear of this pair, another warrior, who, waving in the air a bloodstained *tomahawk*, yelled again the same triumphant cry, "I have caught the first man," and at the same moment I heard Tim's vengeful cuss: "Have ye, ye blaggard? Thin go to hell wid him." The two carbines rang out nearly simultaneously, and through the smoke I caught a momentary glimpse of the triumphant figure let fall his weapon and collapse.

Before either of us could speak a word a small party of horsemen reached us, while, in rear of them, advancing at the double, came two divisions of the Armed Constabulary, who, passing us with a cheer, swept forward and quickly drove the retreating Hau Haus back to the bush.

We now went up to where the settler and M'Kenzie were lying; the former we found alive, though badly wounded, but the latter, poor fellow, had lost the number of his mess; as for the two Maoris, they were past conversion.

It had been indeed a stroke of luck our flushing the Hau Haus as we did, although I could not take any credit to myself for the way I had engineered the contract, as we quickly discovered they had planned a most artful ambuscade in such a manner that, had the column entered the gorge in the ordinary way, it must have been cut to pieces. Poor M'Kenzie's tumble, however, had been too much for the nerves of some of the younger warriors, so they let rip, and thereby gave away the whole show.

The colonel, without losing a single moment, took advantage of the retreat of the Hau Haus, for troth! the little fiend, with all his faults, was a splendid soldier, always ready for a fight, so, without giving the enemy a single minute to gather together, he immediately rushed four divisions through the gorge, and took up a strong position some two miles on the other side of it. Here he remained for a couple of days, gathering together all his available forces, and then, on the 2nd of February, advanced to attack Titokowaru in his new stronghold of Tauranga-a-Hika, in which, he well knew, the main body of the rebel Hau Haus were massed.

It was late in the afternoon when we reached the place and saw we had a stiff job before us, for, although the natural difficulties were not nearly so hard to overcome as had been the case at Ngatapa, still it was a very strongly built *pah*, heavily palisaded, and extremely difficult to surround. It, however, had one defect, as in front of the *pah* and quite close up to it ran a long bank and ditch, which for some inscrutable reason the enemy had not cleared away, but which the colonel spotted at a glance, and ordered three divisions of the Armed Constabulary to immediately advance in skirmishing order and seize them. My division was one of those told off for this duty, so, without a pause, we extended from our centre and advanced. There was not much cover, but what there was we made use of, and although the Maoris kept up a tremendous fire, which we never paused to return, we doubled straight to our front and were soon inside the ditch and behind the bank without a man being hit.

Here we quickly opened fire so as to cover the advance of the other two divisions, who were equally fortunate, and on their arrival we poured a combined volley into the place, just to let the Hau Haus know the sort of music we expected them to dance to. I do not think we did much damage, as their works were so beautifully constructed that during the whole of the evening we never saw so much as a head to aim at. Still we kept on sending them an occasional volley, which they answered vigorously, and between these we collogued one another; as we were so mighty adjacent it was quite easy to carry on a conversation, and a conversation was kept up.

Chiefly, I regret to say, the dialogue was of a personal nature more pungent than polite, although now and again some old cannibal would call both sides to order and preach a homily on the etiquette that should be observed between hostile warriors when engaged in the serious pastime of war.

At last night fell, and we received orders to remain where we were, as it was the colonel's intention to surround the *pah* the following day, he quite rightly judging it to be far too dangerous a job to tackle during the dark. We had food in our haversacks, though water was scarce, and of course we could not sleep, especially as the Hau Haus every now and again fired a volley, so as to warn us they were awake.

One old buster was good enough to preach us an eloquent sermon, and tried hard to convert us to the Pai Marire faith. He had, previous to joining the Hau Haus, been a high-toned native Bible reader belonging to one of the Nonconformist fancy religions, and was loaded up to the muzzle with Bible texts, which he employed in the most laughable manner, interpreting them so as to suit his own arguments. Alas, poor old scallywag, not only was he wasting his breath in sowing his seed on barren land, but he also ran up against one of Kepa's men who was likewise an ex-Bible reader, and who proclaimed himself to be a devout Roman Catholic.

This sinner had the advantage, being not only better posted in controversy, but knowing more English, and through having been employed with the pack-mules had acquired a far greater number of Anglo-Saxon cuss words, therefore the elderly sinner was utterly routed and driven off the field, the Christian champion's peroration being as follows:—"You ruddy Hau Hau, you dance round pole all same as monkey monkey; you say prayers to Pai Marire, you make ruddy fool incantations, you say angel Gabriel stop bullets from kill you, you ruddy liar, you come out here, you ——, me show you damn quick you —— ——, angel Gabriel no have truck with such a —— —— as you, you black Debil's man, you go hell quick time, and burn for eber, you kiss my foot, you —— ——."

This is only a fraction of what our Christian hero said, and the apostle of Hau Hauism, handicapped as he was by the non-existence of cuss words in the Maori language, and having not yet acquired the promised gift of tongues, was reduced to silence and subsided.

After midnight the Hau Hau fire gradually died away, as did the religious arguments, till just before dawn not even the choicest abuse from our side could draw any response. Naturally this reticence on their part put us doubly on the *qui vive*, as we thought most likely the enemy were up to some devilry or another, a sudden sally or a flank attack, but neither of these we feared, as all our preparations were in order and we were ready for anything. Nor were we nervous about the main body, as we knew the impish little colonel, who could go a month without sleep himself, would not only be on the alert, but would jolly well have all his men awake and lively.

The dawn came at last, but brought no attack with it, complete silence resting on the *pah*, so one of our men, named Black, very pluckily jumped over the bank and walked quietly up to the place. As he heard nothing he climbed the fence and shouted out the *pah* was deserted.

We were soon inside it, and were astonished at its strength, all hands plainly seeing we should never have taken it without expending enormous labour in mining, or by reducing the defenders through starvation. It was evidently the latter Titokowaru feared, as it contained but little food or water, and he was fully aware of the fate of Ngatapa.

Without a moment's delay the pursuit began, the colonel with the main body making for Weraroa, while Kepa with a party of his own men followed up the spoor of the retreating Hau Haus. In a very short time he came up with their rear-guard, who turned, and in overpowering numbers attacked him, but he succeeded after a brisk hand-to-hand fight in getting clear of them, and turned the tables by hanging on their skirts until the firing brought up one of our divisions, when the Hau Haus were so roughly handled that they broke and fled and the pursuit went on.

Bivouacking that night on their line of retreat we advanced next day to Moturoa, where we had been defeated the previous year, and where we fully expected the enemy would make a determined stand. Strong as the place was, however, Titokowaru had not seen fit to hold it, but had passed on, so we took the opportunity of gathering together the remains of the poor fellows we had had to abandon on that unfortunate day, and cremated them.

Without going into nauseous particulars I may state there was ample evidence of how they had been desecrated by the enemy, which did not improve the temper of their comrades. Some sharp skirmishing ensued, in which we always got the best of it, but after a few days we had to fall back owing to the lack of food, it being impossible to furnish us, in the rough and broken country, even with the scantiest supply of rations.

As we retired the enemy followed us, and soon let us know they had done so, as a sergeant and nine men who had crossed the Waitotara River in a canoe, for the purpose of gathering peaches, were attacked by seventy Hau Haus. These sportsmen fired a volley at our men while they were picking the fruit, but hit no one.

The white men seized their rifles and made a bolt for the river, which they reached in safety, and where, had they made a stand under cover of the bank, they might have stood their pursuers off, as the already alarmed camp was in sight and quite close to, but instead of doing so they tried to escape in the canoe, and the Hau Haus lining the bank shot them down in a heap, killing seven and wounding one. The natives were immediately driven back, but not before they had dreadfully mutilated the dead men.

Just as we had recuperated and were about to again take the field we received the news of an outbreak at White Cliffs, north of Taranaki, which began by the cold-blooded murder of Lieutenant Gascoigne, his wife and three children, together with the Rev. Mr Whiteley. The latter was a man much respected by all classes of white men, for he was one of the very few missionaries who could deeply sympathise with the natives, and yet forbear to throw mud at his own countrymen.

This rising necessitated the colonel sending one hundred of his men to the White Cliffs, although he delayed not a moment, taking the field with the rest of us. News had filtered through that Titokowaru was at Putahi, and away we started, the enemy trying to cut off our food convoy by laying an ambuscade for us at the mouth of the Whenuakura River. It was a well-designed plan, but when it came to the scratch the Hau Haus fought half-heartedly and were easily beaten off by the ration escort.

I had been sent forward to scout, taking with me my usual companions, and after three days' arduous duty discovered that the Hau Haus were actually in great force at Otauto, a *kainga* on the left bank of the Patea River. Colonel Whitmore, on receipt of my report, immediately despatched Colonel St John up the right bank of the river to hold the drifts and cut off the enemy's retreat, while he moved up the left bank to rout them out.

It was a splendidly devised scheme and well carried out, but alas, it failed, for two reasons: first of all the enemy, growing nervous, had that night left the shelter of their *kainga* and camped outside it, taking up a position at least half-a-mile nearer than where we expected to find them. Again, just as we had deployed for the attack a dense fog came on and we of the advance-guard blundered right into the middle of the Hau Hau bivouac. We certainly completely surprised them, but owing to the dense mist, that without a moment's notice became as thick as one of London's very best, we were quite unable to do anything, in fact we could not see a foot beyond our noses, so there was nothing to do but lie down and wait.

The surprised Hau Haus, who were in almost as great a fix as ourselves, opened a tremendous fire, which, as they could no more see us than we could see them, did but little harm. Heavy firing was nevertheless kept up by both sides for nearly an hour, when, the fog suddenly rising, their camp was discovered close to, which we at once charged, the enemy rapidly retreating, followed by Kepa and his Wanganuis.

On the 16th of March Kepa, who was out bushwhacking, sent in word that he had located Titokowaru at Whakamura, and off we went, joining up to him on the evening of the 17th, when after another smart march our whole force lay in ambush within two hundred yards of the place.

During this interlude Colonel Lyon, who on that occasion was in command, ordered me to take the best scouts, creep up to the *pah*, and look for a weak spot. On doing so we scouts had a treat, as crawling right up to the place we could distinctly hear the speeches of old Titokowaru and his chiefs, who were holding a rather rowdy council meeting. They were evidently not a happy family, and their opinions greatly differed.

One old Johnny began his harangue by deploring their late losses, asserting that his special tribe had borne more than their share of the fighting, demanded that the retreat should be continued at once, asserted that either the angel Gabriel or a certain prophet was a humbug, that reiterating the word, "*Hau Hau*," and holding out the palms of their hands had, as far as his knowledge carried him up to date, saved no one from the bullet of the white man, that dancing round the Pai Marire pole had not as yet brought them the gift of tongues, otherwise their apostle would not have received such a defeat as he had done at Tauranga-a-Hika from the hands of a mere slave of a Roman Catholic.

Another then took the floor, and asserted that the late honourable member, who had wasted his breath, was quite wrong; that they had not abandoned Tauranga-a-Hika on account of their losses, but because they had no food or water, that the angel Gabriel only delayed helping them so that those weak in faith should be cut off; this being done he would come to their assistance with a legion of angels, and those white men who were not turned into stone would be driven into the sea.

The next speaker, I think, must have been Titokowaru himself or his representative, as he asserted that they would fight on that spot, that the white men could not reach them for three days, and wound up by assuring them he had received a revelation that they would gain a decisive victory.

The council then separated, and it required no great skill in the art of prophecy to foretell that should the coalition of the Hau Hau tribes get another good shake up they would fall asunder like a bundle of sticks when the cord binding it together is severed.

Creeping back I reported to the colonel, and re-joined the storming party to which I had been told off. The weary waiting was almost over, in another quarter of an hour the dawn of day would have given us the signal to charge, when a mounted native came out of the *pah* and rode towards us. Greatly surprised as we were, we lay as still as death, and he cantered right through our party without spotting one of us, only to come full butt against the main body. In a breath he slewed his horse round and galloped back, yelling as if he had the stomach-ache, and firing off a revolver. All our fine plans were knocked galley west; out rang the order to charge. We charged; crash went the fence, and head first, feet first, or landing in a sitting position, in we went, but it was too dark to see, much less to aim, and all we could hear was the yells of the astonished Hau Haus, who bolted hell for leather, without firing a single shot.

As soon as it was light enough to see, Kepa, with his Wanganuis, accompanied by a party of us white men, started in pursuit, but we found before we had proceeded far the Hau Haus had broken up and dispersed. We, however, succeeded in killing a few men, who had taken refuge up trees, and also captured three women, who, on being brought into camp, declared that Titokowaru had fled to Te Ngaihere, a historical stronghold that in ancient days had been looked upon as the last refuge of his tribe. By doing so he had lost the last remnant of his prestige, so that the haughty savage who had proclaimed only two months previously he was going to drive the white men into the sea was now a fugitive, abandoned by his allies, laughed at by his enemies, and with but few followers on whom he could rely.

But now the question arose: Where was this fabled Te Ngaihere? No one seemed to know its locality or what it was like. Everyone seemed to have heard traditions about it, but no one had ever set eyes on it. It was a place *tapu*, not to be talked about, much less to be visited, and whether it were a mountain, a bush, a lake or a cave, no one could give us a single pointer. However, if a place be worth finding it is worth prospecting for, so away went Kepa to scour the country one way, while myself with my usual followers took another direction. It was a big order, as I think you will allow, my gentle readers, to plunge into a trackless country and look for something not knowing what the deuce it was you were hunting for. Troth, for my own part, I consider that prospecting for the Holy Grail was a dry billet alongside the one I had shipped for.

Kepa was the lucky man to solve the problem, Te Ngaihere turning out to be a big island situated in the centre of a quaking swamp. In olden days this swamp had evidently been much deeper, but it still looked quite impassable for anything but a snipe, and both Kepa and

Whitmore deemed it to be so, the distance from the mainland to the island being quite four hundred yards.

The whole force, moved up by a night's march, camped close to the swamp and quite out of sight of the stronghold, and although in dense bush, not a fire was allowed to be lit during the whole time we were making our preparations for attack, though our scouts kept the island under observation day and night. It was now a case for all hands to off shirt, out *tomahawk* and work like beavers, constructing out of supple jacks, hurdles, fifteen feet long and four feet wide, in sufficient quantity to cross the quagmire. So well did we work and so well were we handled that in four days every preparation had been made, and at dark on the 24th we began to lay our frail bridge across the bog, this being finished at four a.m., when without a second's delay the column began to cross. The first lot of us got over dry shod, but then the bridge began to sink, so that the rear of the column had to struggle through slime and water, which took the rear-guard up to their middle.

Notwithstanding this drawback we were all safely across, then, leaving Colonel Lyon with a strong party to protect the bridge head, the little colonel moved on to the *kainga*, the inhabitants of which were in blissful ignorance of our proximity. With the scouts I crept right into the place and heard one old man lamenting to his wife that he feared the big evil man (Titokowaru) would soon bring the white men down on them.

It was now an extraordinary accident was about to happen that again saved Titokowaru and the remnant of his bloodthirsty tribe from our just resentment. The day broke clear, when the natives immediately discovered us. Their astonishment was most ludicrous, as they all thought we had dropped from the sky. Some ran away from us; some ran towards us, shouting out words of welcome; others, too overcome to move, could do nothing else but stand with goggle eyes and with palms stretched out, hoarsely muttering the mystic words "*Hau Hau,*" none making the slightest attempt to resist us.

The long-waited-for execution was just about to commence when the Wanganuis, usually so ready to begin killing, shouted out to us to be careful how we fired as two of their chiefs were mixed up with the now flying crowd. The colonel, not understanding the Maori tongue, fancied that because the Wanganuis had not fired we had in some miraculous manner fallen across an unknown friendly tribe, so ordered us not to fire. None of us did fire, and because we did not fire the

Wanganuis did not do so, so we simply stood and watched long lines of men, women and children wading through the swamp within a few yards of us, and it was only when the hindermost fugitives made very many indecent gestures at us, previous to disappearing into the bush, that the Colonel ascertained that the simple, frightened friendlies he had permitted to escape were Titokowaru and his own personal tribe, the most bloodstained fanatics in the whole of New Zealand.

Well, we sat down and looked at one another; and as each man thought over the forced labour of the past few days, of the long, dreary night marches, of the short rations, of the blistered hands and the torn feet which he had suffered and which, through that morning's miserable misunderstanding, he would have to suffer again, he forbore to swear, being unable to find in his repertoire any cuss words suitable to express his sentiments.

Notwithstanding his escape Titokowaru was beaten; he had lost his *mana* (luck); all the allies who had flocked to him in his prosperity deserted him like rats running from an unseaworthy ship, and after the retirement of the field force he was for a time hunted by small parties of local levies, together with a few of the Armed Constabulary belonging to the district, until he disappeared into the interior, where the Government let him rip.

The subjugation and disarmament of the tribes who had joined him being left to junior officers, Colonel Whitmore immediately started again for the east coast, taking all the available men of the West Coast Field Force with him.

We were therefore shipped on the steamers *Sturt* and *St Kilda*, on the 10th of April, reaching Onehunga on the eve of the following day. It was dark when we landed and got our baggage ashore, and we then started to march across the isthmus to Auckland, where fresh shipping awaited to take us down the east coast to Tauranga.

Auckland at that time was in its heyday of prosperity. The great Thames gold-digging was in full swing, and as our column of war-worn, bush-stained men marched through the brilliantly lighted and bustling Queen's Street the temptation for a spree was too much for some of our boys, many of whom had not been into a town or seen a white woman for three years, so they began to break ranks and slip away, determined to have one night's fling, no matter what it cost them. Consequently when we reached the wharf only about half of our men were present. There confusion became confounded, diggers, sailors, civilians and women of a certain class crowding in upon us, tendering the men bottles of liquor or tempting them from their duty. Waggons and drays loaded with camp equipage, ammunition, baggage and stores arrived, which all had to be transferred to the ship, and this was done chiefly by the officers, who then, as the ship was to sail at daylight, had to form themselves into a picket to collect their scattered and more than half-drunk men.

After a night of ceaseless work we managed to get all but sixty on board, the colonel remaining behind to gather together the stragglers; nor did he let slip the opportunity of venting his unjust spleen, as he reported to the Government that his men were all mutinous and his officers discontented.

This was not true, and caused intense bitterness right through the field force, as the men were not officers, they had slaved all night without a pause for food or rest until the ship sailed, which she did at the time ordered.

CHAPTER 5

The Uriwera Campaign

It was now high time to call on the Uriwera so as to punish them for past offences and teach them that, because they inhabited the very wildest and most rugged country in New Zealand, they could not with impunity murder white people and friendly natives.

The Uriwera are a queer tribe almost distinct from other Maoris, for although they belong to the same race, yet they have held but little inter-course with the other tribes, who look upon them as being somewhat uncanny, and perhaps stand slightly in awe of them. Their country at that time was absolutely unknown, no white man having ever entered it, and no Maori war party had ever possessed the temerity to attack them, so they lived among their inaccessible mountains and deep valleys, a people quite apart from any others. This strange people were, however, extremely war-like and ferocious, continually making raids on their neighbours. They had never had any cause to quarrel with the white settlers, yet they were one of the first tribes to join the king movement, and had fought desperately against Sir Duncan Cameron in the Waikato campaign; then they had joined the Hau Haus, and had committed many murders.

On Te Kooti's landing, without receiving any provocation whatsoever, they had joined him, and accompanied him in his raids on Poverty Bay, revelling in the brutal massacres that had taken place there, while, to make their cup of iniquity overflow, they had invited the arch-devil himself to come to their country, after we had routed him out of Ngatapa. Well, if they had invited Te Kooti, the little colonel invited himself, and he determined to twist their tails so as to teach them decorum.

As it was well known this was going to be a most arduous campaign, all hands, officers and men, had to undergo a rigorous medical examination, and even then only those were selected who were well known to possess determination and ability to put up with hardships without grousing, and of course every man was a past master in the art of bush fighting.

Colonel Whitmore's plans were very clever, though, when we came to carry them out, they were found to be too comprehensive, for although no man knew better than he did the great difficulty there is in carrying out combined movements in a rough country, still neither he nor anyone else knew what an infernal country we were going to soldier in, nor had even the most pessimistic man among us gauged the sufferings we were to undergo. The colonel, however, was far too good a soldier to leave anything to chance, so that each of the four columns about to enter this *terra incognita* at different points were strong enough to act alone, and give a good account of themselves should they even be attacked by the whole strength of the Uriwera plus Te Kooti's own men.

I should have gone in with the mounted column, which was to start from Napier and march up to Te Haroto, so as to block any fugitives from getting across into the Waikato country, but as I knew that the horsemen would have but little chance of fighting, I was very glad to hear that Colonel St John had applied for me to be attached to his column as boss scout. Tim, of course, I was allowed to take with me, while Pierre and George did not ask for permission, but came of their own accord, neither of these gentlemen being troubled with any qualms of conscience regarding discipline, orders or anything appertaining to red tape or respectability.

Colonel Whitmore's own column was to march from Te Matata, cross the Kaingaroa Plains and attack Te Harema Pah in the Ahikereru Valley; so far all plain sailing, no great natural obstacles to be overcome and fairly open country in which strings of pack-horses, though not drays, could be used. Here he would make a depot for stores. But then he was to strike into quite unknown pastures and try to meet Colonel St John at one of those mythical Maori strongholds, Ruatahuna, which, like Te Ngaihere, everyone had heard about but no one had ever seen.

Colonel St John was to move in from Whakatane, advancing up the river's bed, there being no tracks in that country, and to get to Ruatahuna as best he could, destroying everything *en route* in the way of *pahs*, *kaingas* or food he might come across; then, provided the two columns did meet at this mysterious trysting-place, they were to capture it, and then, combined, were to trust to Providence to find their way somehow or other across the Huiarau ranges, and join Colonel Herrick's column at the big lake Waikaremoana. The whole plan looked well on paper. It had required an indomitable man to conceive it, and would require indomitable men to carry it out, as, should any of the columns meet with a reverse, they could hope for no assistance from any of the others.

The heaviest fighting and the hardest work would fall to the lot of Colonel St John's column, as we not only had to fight our way right across the worst of the Uriwera country, but it was absolutely impossible for us to use a pack-animal of any sort, so that we must carry everything necessary on our own backs, or go without. Winter was also beginning, which that year promised to be a very cold one. It was quite impossible to defer the expeditions, indeed it was high time something should be done, as Te Kooti, just previous to our arrival on the coast, had made one of his lightning raids against the Mohaka Settlement, where (thanks to the—well, let us be charitable and call it discretion—of the militia officers, who, although amply supplied with men and horses, made no offer to resist him) he had brutally murdered over seventy white settlers and friendlies, so that we were all boiling to get after him.

Although everyone worked with a will, it was not before the 2nd of May sufficient stores and ammunition arrived to enable us to make a start, but at daylight the following morning the field force paraded in front of our camp at Oporiau, numbering, all told, two hundred and forty-five white men and one hundred and eighty friendly natives. That parade was a queer sight and one that would have made a stickler for military uniforms shudder. Our men, dressed in their blue jumpers with their shawls round their waists, and smasher hats, looked like disreputable Highlanders, while we were loaded up like pack-donkeys.

To give you some idea of our loads let me tell you what each man had to carry: a Schneider carbine with one hundred and sixty rounds of ammunition; a revolver with thirty rounds; and of course each man carried his tomahawk, sheath-knife and pannikin; then each four men had to carry, taking it in turns, an axe, shovel or pick; then every twelve men in like manner carried a case containing four hundred and eighty rounds of carbine ammunition; while each division had to carry five stretchers.

After these loads had been apportioned, each individual might hump as many blankets, as much clothing, rations and private property as he saw fit, but all officers under field rank had to take their turn at the extra ammunition, tools, etc., as well as to hump their own swag. True we were all picked men, tried and seasoned by many months of bush warfare, in robust health, and, with the exception of a couple of field officers, not a single man under the age of twenty-four or older than thirty.

Oh, my gentle tourist friend, you who buckle on a pretty, light knapsack, and tramp for a few hours on a summer's day along the shady lanes of Old England, and after a bounteous repast sleep in the lavender-scented sheets of some picturesque old-fashioned country inn, and fancy you have earned your repose, picture us, who had to hump our swags over what is perhaps the very roughest country in the world, perform our marches in torrents of cold rain or icy sleet, and sleep covered by a tattered blanket on the sodden ground, soon to be frozen hard by the bitter frosts of the New Zealand winter, for the months of May, June and July are the coldest in the year; and at the same time bear in mind we had to do all that living on foul, putrid bacon and mouldy lumps of what had at one time been the commonest of ship's biscuits.

I have previously stated I was delighted at having been told off to join Colonel St John's column, and that for more reasons than one, as he was universally loved and respected by every officer and man who had the honour and pleasure of serving under him. Colonel St John was at this time past middle age, tall and handsome, a gentleman to the tips of his fingers, and a thorough good sportsman. He had seen much service, had distinguished himself greatly both in the Crimea and in India, and although perhaps he lacked the great tactical skill possessed by Colonel Whitmore, still he could get more out of the men, as they loved the one and hated the other.

He was, moreover, just and considerate in his dealings with his junior officers, who regarded him more as a father than as a colonel. To me individually he was always most kind and friendly, and as he knew my father and family well I was only too pleased to serve under him.

It was on the morning of the 4th of May, Colonel St John's column commenced its march into the Uriwera country, the scouts having left the night before, my orders being to enter the Whakatane River, proceed up its bed, keep a bright lookout for ambuscades and fall back to the colonel every night.

The first day's march was a very bad one, as it necessitated the column crossing the river twenty-eight times during the twenty miles that brought the tired men to a deserted *kainga* called Tunanui, where we bivouacked with fair comfort, this being the jumping-off spot into the unknown.

The next day the same sort of thing had to be gone through again. The river-bed did not improve, while during the day heavy showers of sleet and rain soaked us through. Moreover, as we were now in the enemy's country we dare not light fires when we bivouacked, so that we had to get what rest we could during the bitter cold night, deprived of any warmth and without the pannikin of miserable tea we all so greedily looked forward to after a cold and fatiguing day.

The following morning at the first glimmer of dawn we scouts left the bivouac, and pushed on up the river-bed, but before we had progressed a couple of miles we came to a place where the river rushed through a deep, rocky gorge that prevented us making any further use of its bed as a thoroughfare. I therefore awaited the arrival of the colonel, who shortly joined me, and after a short discussion he determined the column should cross the stream and make its way up a steep, razor-backed ridge that sloped down to the water. We had considerable difficulty in crossing, as not only the current ran very fast, but the bed was composed of slippery boulders over which many of our men stumbled and fell.

At last they were all over, but long before the last man crossed we scouts had out *tomahawk* and were painfully chopping a path through the tangled fern, ground-vines and lawyers—the latter being scrub, bearing thorns shaped like fish hooks, and are as dangerous to come in contact with as their human namesakes—with which the steep slope was densely covered. On reaching the summit we found ourselves on a long serrated ridge running within a point or two of the direction we wanted to go, both sides of it being heavily bushed, but the ridge itself, thanks to its narrowness and the rocky nature of the soil, only carried stunted fern, through which we could march with comparative ease. We therefore thanked our stars for this slice of luck, and, after we had excavated the larger thorns, licked such scratches as we could get at to lick, and swallowing a handful of soaked mouldy biscuit, we scouts started, while the column was still painfully crawling up the slope.

Towards midday we came to where the ridge suddenly ended in a very nearly perpendicular drop into a deep valley, on the other side of which, situated on a *plateau* of the same altitude as that on which we stood, we saw a large *kainga*. The cover on our side was very good, so

I halted, sending back Tim and George a few hundred yards to await and report to the Colonel, while Pierre and I scouted to either flank, prospecting for the best place to descend. This I found, but when found it had not much in its favour to recommend it, as it simply bristled with huge boulders and trees, the ground in between which was, as per usual, a dense tangle of ground-vines, lawyers and tough fern. Still it was practicable, and the colonel on viewing it decided to make use of it to descend into the deep valley.

I also pointed out to him that across the valley ran up two steep spurs leading to the plateau upon which the *kainga* stood, and which perhaps, *faute de mieux*, could be used for attacking purposes. *Facilis decenstis Averni* may be true, but we found it by no means easy, much less pleasant, to descend that infernal hill, and it was only by lowering our loads, and even one another, down the worst places that at last, tattered and torn, we reached the foot, but fortunately, although many men were badly bruised, still no one had received sufficient injury to render him unfit for further exertions.

On reaching the valley the colonel, taking myself and scouts with him, moved forward to reconnoitre, while the main body rested, and as best they could repaired damages. We had, however, barely time to make certain that the aforementioned spurs were practicable when from the *kainga* on the plateau above out rang the report of a gun that, being multiplied by the echoes of the mountains and valleys, rumbled like thunder. Of course we thought we had been spotted, and cursing our bad luck we fell back to the main body as rapidly as we could. As there was nothing to be gained by delay the colonel determined to attack immediately, so throwing off our packs fifty of the most bruised men were rapidly told out to remain in charge of them, then, the remainder of the force being divided into two parties, we started off to force our way up the spurs.

Fortunately these, though steep and serrated, were not covered with thick scrub, so that the men relieved of their packs mounted rapidly, and as both parties were in sight of one another we could regulate our pace so as to arrive simultaneously at the top. Of course after we had heard the shot we had thought that it had been fired to give the alarm, and that the Maoris, resenting our intrusion, would do their best to obstruct our arrival; in fact we had made up our minds we should have to fight every yard of the way up the spurs. We however were agreeably disappointed, the shot not having been fired to give the alarm, but, as we were subsequently informed, it was fired to execute a mighty big pig.

The Uriwera were in blissful ignorance of our proximity. They had never fancied for a moment that white men would ever dare to enter their inaccessible country, and had therefore kept no lookout whatever, so that instead of meeting with a determined resistance, while mounting the narrow spurs, we reached the plateau, formed line, extended, and had advanced close to the *kainga* before they spotted us.

Whoop, then there was a deuce of a commotion, women and children running and screaming, men yelling, pigs grunting and singing hymns, while above all this turmoil out rang our bugles, which, together with our cheering, added to the din that was in a moment multiplied a thousandfold by the crash of firearms, while the echoes of all these noises combined were so extraordinary that anyone might have thought thousands of men were engaged, or that all the fiends in Hades were holding their annual beanfeast, and were all drunk at that.

Completely surprised as the Uriwera were, still they made a stout resistance, but they could not stand for long against our impetuous charge, for we swept through the village like a flooded reservoir bursting its dam, so that the surviving men, and there were not many of them, turned their backs and bolted for the bush. A number of men, however, unable to escape, took refuge in their huts, from which they still continued to fire. These were ordered to come out, and so as to expedite their movements their huts were set on fire. It was however only granting the inmates a polite choice of deaths, as those who came out were immediately shot, and those who remained in were quickly burned to death.

Our losses on that day were trivial, only amounting to one man killed and four wounded, while we captured fifteen women, a great many pigs and large stores of potatoes. The women, after being well questioned, we let go; the pigs were killed, and when each man had taken as much meat as he could eat and carry, the remainder, with the surplus potatoes, were destroyed. Truly it was a shocking waste of food, but absolutely necessary in savage warfare.

That night we fared sumptuously, those men not being on duty sleeping the sleep of the just, and next morning, as soon as it was light enough to see, we completed the destruction of the *kainga*, ate a big breakfast, and again made our way to the river above the gorge to proceed on our weary way.

It was now a case of looking out for squalls, as the news of our being in the country would have by this time been spread from one end to the other. The country itself was splendidly adapted for ambuscades. The Uriwera were past masters in the art of laying them, and now, being enraged by their late losses, would be burning to avenge them, there-fore it behoved us to keep all our senses on deck.

On reaching the bed of the river the colonel took every precaution, one of which being, instead of sending forward three or four scouts, who might be captured, he ordered a party of twelve men to precede the main body. These men were only to carry their own personal swags, so that they might be ready at a moment's notice to put up a fight. The loads the men of the main body had to carry on this day were very heavy. In the first place we had three wounded men, who, being unable to walk, had therefore to be borne on stretchers, and then every man had brought along with him as much pork and potatoes as he could stagger under. The bed of the river was also if possible worse than it had been before, as it was full of big slippery boulders over which the heavily laden men staggered and tripped as if drunk, many of them having very nasty falls indeed.

We had journeyed about two miles when the advance-guard halted, and at the colonel's request I accompanied him to the front, where we found the officer in command of them uncertain as to what course he should pursue. Our advance up the side of the stream we were on was blocked by a steep though not very high ridge that was covered as usual with densely tangled scrub, the end of it jutting out into the water, which was there too deep to allow the men to wade round it. Where we stood a rocky bar ran to the other side of the river, which appeared practicable, although the water rushed swiftly across it to the depth of perhaps four feet. The far bank of the river was low but heavily bushed, and behind the bush rose up a steep, razor-backed ridge, down the crest of which ran a narrow path broad enough in places for two men to climb it abreast.

After carefully studying the look of the country the colonel decided to cross the river and take to the path, so that when the main body had closed up the advance-guard began to wade over, the water in the centre of the stream, which there ran very fast, taking them half way up their chests.

That day they were being led by Lieutenant White, a very gallant fellow, much liked and respected by his brother officers and men. He had been wounded the evening before, but as he was able to march he insisted on taking his turn of duty at the point of danger.

Advance Guard ambuscaded: death of Lieutenant White

The advance-guard entered the ford and had crossed three-fourths of the way when from the dense brushwood on the far side, over which up till now the silence of death had reigned, came a tremendous volley, and down went poor White, shot dead, while four of his men, badly hurt, splashed the water like wounded wild-fowl. Immediately some of us dashed into the stream, recovered White's body, and dragged out the wounded men; at the same time one division opened a smart fire on the ambuscade, who, however, after a couple of volleys, ceased from returning it.

It was a nasty place; the ford was a very narrow one, the stream ran fast, and the colonel plainly saw that by hook or by crook the enemy's position must be turned, or, should he rely on a frontal attack, he would lose half his men. He therefore despatched one hundred men, with whom I went, to cut our way over the aforementioned ridge, ascend the river until we found a crossing, and then, descending the far bank, attack the flank of the enemy's position, he at the same time making a dash at the ford.

Away we went and tackled the job, having to put in two hours' hard chopping before we could get a crossing place, and then, when we had succeeded in crossing, we had to cut our way down the bank till at last we came close to the ford, when a toot on our bugle let the colonel know we were on the enemy's flank, there or thereabouts. Out rang his bugle, and with a cheer we tore and struggled through the remaining undergrowth, while a storm of whizzing bullets, which fortunately did us but little harm, tore the foliage to pieces over our heads. At the same time we charged we could hear close to us the shouts of the colonel's party as they dashed through the water, the sharp file-firing of his coverers and the volleys of the defending Hau Haus.

Bristling with wrath, we cut and forced our way through the last intervening scrub, fondly hoping that a good hand-to-hand scrap would recompense us for our past labour, but as both of our parties simultaneously broke through the curtains of greenery we found not one single Maori there to receive us.

Their lines of rifle pits had been beautifully constructed, and were admirably placed so as to both rake and enfilade the ford, so there could be no shadow of a doubt that had the colonel decided upon making only a frontal attack our butcher's bill must have been a very heavy one, or we might have been beaten back; as it was we had forced the ford with only the loss of Lieutenant White and some half-a-dozen men wounded.

A party of us at once rushed on up the ridge, exchanging a few shots with the enemy, who by some hidden path had gained a similar ridge some three hundred yards off, which they dared us to attack.

The colonel, however, was convinced that we were on the right footpath—else why had they taken the trouble to build such elaborate rifle pits to defend it?—and he was far too old a bird to be drawn away on a wild-goose chase. His plan was to push on to the famous Ruatahuna, of course attacking any *pahs* he came across, and not to lose time in running after Maoris, who, if he did so, would only retire in front of him.

As soon as poor White was buried, which was done as rapidly as possible, the only ceremonies being the volleys the Hau Haus fired at the burial-party, the whole force moved forward to attack the enemy, who had occupied another very strong position on the top of the ridge, from which they poured in a continuous fire at our party that was slowly mounting the steep and narrow track that ran up from the river. This track wound about so that both of our flanks were as often exposed as our front, so it soon became quite evident it would cause an awful loss of life to try and take their position with a frontal rush.

The colonel therefore again despatched a party to try and turn the Hau Haus' right flank, and again, after immense labour, the movement having been carried out, we made a combined rush, and charged, the rifle pits receiving two smashing volleys, and when we entered them we found nothing but three guns, which some of the Hau Haus must have dropped in their retreat. These rifle pits were also well constructed, and were well worthy of being better defended, but, by their having been vacated without a stouter resistance, we saw it was evidently the game of the Hau Haus to carry on a war of ambuscades and not risk a stand-up fight.

After a short halt we again moved forward, our advance-guard being fired into every few hundred yards, while sometimes, by way of a change, the enemy would tickle us up on the flanks; in fact it was a most sinful and cuss-wordy march, as the track, if you could call it such, was never broad enough to allow us to show a greater front than two men abreast, while the wounded men we had now to carry added considerably to the toil of our already overloaded men.

We had moved forward about three miles when we sighted on a spur, with a bush in rear of it, a *pah* which we afterwards learned was called Te Whenuanui. It was in a very strong position, but the works and fence were in a ruinous state, as the Uriwera had never dreamt of our entering their country, and of course had not had time since they had heard of our visit to put it into a proper state of defence.

The Hau Haus in the *pah* were evidently very upset and excited by our call, as they opened a heavy fire at us when we were quite eight hundred yards distant, which was of course harmless; and Colonel St John, splitting his command into three parties, gave orders for an immediate attack. The party I was with had been sent to the left, and as we had to get over some very rough country before we could charge, time was allowed us to get into position.

At last we were all ready; the bugle sounded the advance and charge, when we all rushed at the tumbledown works, to be met by the usual heavy but badly directed fire. There was nothing to make us pause; the rotten fences gave way before our rush, so with a cheer we burst into the place, just in time to see the tail end of the bolting Hau Haus disappearing into the bush, and to send a volley after them that hastened their departure. We did not pursue, as most likely they had planted a nice little ambuscade at the edge of the bush, and as a rule there is nothing to be gained by running your head against a stone wall or walking into a Maori trap, so we humped up our swags and the wounded men, whom we made as comfortable as possible, and occupied the *pah* ourselves for the night.

During the night we had one false alarm, caused by a patrol falling into a ditch, and various ill-bred Hau Haus prowled round us, telling us nasty things about ourselves. One of these lewd fellows kept it up till daylight, and so interfered with one man's rest that just at daydawn he took his carbine and went gunning after the disturber of his slumber. Good luck attended him, for just as it became light enough to see his foresight the retiring night prowler, all of a sudden calling to mind something very ribald that he had up to that moment forgotten to say, paused at the edge of the bush to unburden himself. Silly fellow, he had better have taken cover, for he had only made one in-decent gesture, and had only shouted a small portion of what he had to say, when something hit him, and, ceasing his oration, he took a header among the fern, where the last thing he ever heard in this world was the laughter of the men he had lost his life in trying to insult.

The Maoris had left us a bare larder in Te Whenuanui Pah, and our rations, bad as they had been when issued to us, were by now quite unfit for human food, and that day we ran completely out of even the offal we had carried, so we were not sorry when about midday we came across a *pah* called Tatahoata, which afterwards turned out to be the real Ruatahuna.

This *pah*, or rather fortification, was built on a flat, with a dense bush to its right front; the Whakatane River, with precipitous banks, on its left; a deep, rocky creek with high, scrub-covered sides defended its rear; while a small but thick bush commanded its right flank. It was indeed an ugly-looking place, but take it we must, or starve. After an hour spent in reconnoitring, the different divisions were told off for their several lines of attack, and, the advance being sounded, we all moved forward.

The Maoris were not only holding the *pah*, but they had detached parties in the bush who had to be driven back before we could rush the work itself. We had just about completed this portion of the game when, for some reason that has never been explained, the colonel's bugler, without receiving orders, sounded the cease fire, together with the retire twice over, and then fell, shot dead. The calls filled everyone with astonishment, nearly amounting to consternation, but of course the orders were obeyed, and before the O.C. and the few men he had with him could rush round with counter-orders the natives charged up to our retiring divisions and poured in a heavy fire, which killed and wounded a lot of men, among the former being Captain Trevor.

Orders or no orders, we were not going to stand that, so turning on our pursuers we flew at them like wild cats, and as just at that moment we received the new orders we pushed our charge so well home that we drove the Hau Haus before us like chaff, nor did they even make an effort to defend the *pah*, but bolted as hard as they could for the shelter of the bush and broken country, while we occupied the place, which we eagerly prospected for food.

It was not long, with two such sublime marauders as Pierre and George looking after my interests, before I had a good square meal stowed away under my waistbelt, and the colonel had just sent for me to settle about some scouting when we heard a distant bugle-call.

Our men started cheering, and shortly afterwards it was reported that Colonel Whitmore's column was in sight, while the little man himself, attended by a few men, came into the *pah* before sunset, his column camping some two miles away. That two columns should have been able to march through such rough country and meet at an appointed though unknown spot on the pre-arranged day, speaks well for the officer who planned the campaign, and also for the men who carried his plans out.

Chapter 6

The Taupo Campaign

The two columns having completed the first part of the programme by uniting at Ruatahuna it behoved our O.C. and the senior officers to turn to and stage the second act, but here Nature chipped in and bade them pause.

Our force was composed of picked men, admirably suitable for the work that lay before them, and, with the exception of the Arawa tribe, the only cowardly race in New Zealand, the whole outfit were full of fight and ready to go anywhere. Still it is a well-known fact that, no matter how good and willing men are, nevertheless they must eat sometimes, and we were, within twenty-four hours of our junction, absolutely without food The inclemency of the weather also greatly added to our sufferings, as we were never dry during the day, while the bitter frosts at night froze us hard. Moreover the enemy, though unable to face us in a stand-up fight, still lingered in our vicinity, and had even the cheek to commence fortifying a high hill overlooking the camp, a movement on their part that required a sharp skirmish to dissuade them from continuing.

Colonel Whitmore had brought some horses with him to Ahikereru; these now had to be killed, and the flesh served out in short rations, while parties were detached to try and locate the Maoris' hidden stores of potatoes. These *ruas* (potato pits), however, were so well concealed that we could find but few, and those we did find we had to skirmish for previous to looting, and even when we had gained them the supply did not equal the day's demand.

Nothing daunted, the little colonel still determined to carry out his original plans and make a push for Colonel Herrick's column, which by now should be on the Waikaremoana Lake, but here again he was thwarted, as the Arawas not only positively refused to accompany us, but also insisted on going home, and it was with considerable trouble they could be persuaded to carry to the coast our wounded and sick, who by now reached a considerable number. The indomitable little colonel had therefore no other option but to fall back, so he gave orders that the combined columns should start for Ahikereru, while the Arawas convoying the wounded should march straight for the coast by another route.

Previous to returning, however, he determined to attack and destroy a big *kainga* that my scouting-party had discovered while spud-hunting. This expedition, trivial though it might be, and of no importance, was yet a very popular one, all hands eagerly volunteering to take a part in it, not on account of any glory that might be reaped from its capture, but the men were all so hungry that they were only too anxious to undergo the extreme hardships of a long, bitterly cold night's march through rugged bush on the chance of being able to get a few mouthfuls of pork and potatoes; as for the chance of being knocked over or wounded, that was not taken into consideration at all.

I am only mentioning the above facts as during this insignificant affair an incident happened to myself that was the cause of making me the target for a lot of chaffy which though good-natured caused many a hearty laugh at my expense. It fell out in this way:

At dark a party of two hundred men, under the command of Colonel St John, and guided by myself and scouts, after the usual wretched march reached the doomed place some two hours before daybreak, and unable to surround it we lay down to freeze, starve and wait for the dawn. Lord, I was hungry, and being so close to the huts it came like balm to my soul, all of a sudden, to hear an old woman cry out: "It is time to prepare food let us arise and make ready the *hangis*" (ovens constructed of stones sunk into the ground; these being heated, the food is placed on them, water is then poured over it, when it is carefully covered up and the confined steam cooks the viands).

Presently there was a sound of women muttering and grumbling, then a fire was kindled, followed quickly by others, the combined flare from these lighting up the cooking places, while we, shrouded in the outer darkness, lay and licked our lean chaps as we heard the boss woman directing so many kits of potatoes and so much pork to be cooked in each *hangi*; verily I for one wanted no sherry and bitters to sharpen my appetite. Presently, the stones being hot enough, the fires are removed, and darkness again covers the scene as the food is placed in the ovens and covered up.

Again a weary wait, and just as we know breakfast ought to be ready the sky begins to lighten, and we can see the outline of the *kainga*. Surely in my impatience I may be forgiven for uttering the following prayer:—"O gods of war, ye who pass your days in fighting and your nights in feasting, listen to your humble votary. Hurry up Phoebus, the beggar's slack today. Grant us only light enough, and we vow to fight like bricks and eat like heroes. Let us but get at our enemies and to our victuals."

The light comes slowly. Will the colonel never give the word? His expectant bugler lies beside him, bugle to lip. The women inside the *kainga* call to the men: "Arise, the food is ready to be eaten," and we hear the yawns and grunts of the warriors as they wake up from their natural slumber, some of them soon to be put to sleep again in a speedier and more permanent manner. There goes the trumpet, endorsed by a cheer from our over-willing men as with a rush we dash into the village. Here takes place the usual turmoil: screaming women and children rush for the bush; men, resisting and fighting desperately, are shot down, while others are driven out of the place in headlong flight. We do not pursue, but, with mouths watering, instinctively gather round the *hangis*. The women had stated that the food was cooked; we required no expert evidence, off came the earth-covered mats, when the steam of the luscious pork and spuds rose to still further tantalise the famished men.

There was, however, no greedy scrambling. Starving we might be, but we were comrades in adversity and must fare and share alike. Squads of men fall in of their own accord, the food is rapidly distributed by the non-coms., and is more rapidly consumed by the hungry recipients. Then comes the turn of the officers, who, *noblesse oblige*, have had to wait, so as to make sure there was enough to feed the men before attending to their own wants.

There was, however, no fear on this occasion of anyone going short, as one oven remained still unopened, and around this we eagerly clustered. Pierre presents himself with his huge knife, the food is served out, juniors, taking precedence, receive their allotments first, and I had just received mine, consisting of a lump of pork about the size of my fist, together with a dozen or so of potatoes, all steaming and piping hot, served up on a fragment of a Maori mat, and with ravenous eyes was watching the succulent mess cool sufficiently to devour, when *bang, whizz, zip* comes a flight of bullets whistling over our heads.

"Damn," said the colonel. "Mr Burke, take thirty men and drive those blaggards back to perdition; it's like their infernal cheek to interfere with gentlemen while breakfasting," and the old fellow squared his shoulders and tucked in to his portion.

As I stumbled to my feet I did not say "damn," as it would not have been an appropriate expression on such an occasion, and I felt utterly unable to coin one suitable, so picking up my precious viands, which I carried in the mat on my left fore-arm pressed against my chest, where they raised blisters wherever they came in contact with my bare skin through my tattered shirt, in less than a minute I had the men extended, and charged at the bush, from the edge of which spurts of smoke told us that the Hau Haus, disgusted at the loss of their breakfast, were seeking *utu* by preventing us enjoying their forfeited repast. It was as we were advancing I discovered that, with the exception of my *tomahawk* and sheath-knife, I was unarmed.

This discovery somewhat flabbergasted me, but it at once flashed through my mind that I had been in the act of reloading four chambers of my M. L. revolver when I had received my share of the food, and that, in my greediness to eat, I had placed my still uncapped pistol on the ground beside me, and on receiving the unwelcome order, in my anxiety to carry off the food, I had forgotten the gun. No matter, thought I to myself, the men must do my shooting for me, so drawing my *tomahawk* I led them at the bush, where we quickly drove the enemy back for a few hundred yards, when they turned tail and made a clean bolt for it, while at the same time the recall was sounded from the main body.

After seeing that all my men were present and unwounded I gave the word to retire, and we started wending our way back to the *kainga*. I was now clearly entitled to break my long-sustained fast. True, I could not sit down to eat, but it is better for a hungry man to eat while walking rather than not to eat at all, so that as my men fell back at a brisk pace I opened my mat, and, grabbing a handful of the by now well-smashed and greasy potatoes, conveyed it to my mouth, instinctively slowing up my pace as I began to eat the precious food.

Lord, how good it was!—not tempting to look at, my gentle reader, nor was there any romantic refinement in the tableau of a gaunt, unshaven man, dressed in a tattered shirt and shawl, feeding himself with an unwashed, bloodstained hand while pushing his way through the tangles of a New Zealand bush.

Well, refinement or no refinement, 1 was thoroughly enjoying it; as I swallowed each grimy morsel 1 somehow, without noticing the fact, moved slower and slower, until my men had gained considerably on me, and I loitered perhaps fifty or sixty yards in rear of them. This of course was both foolish and wrong, and Nemesis the slut was on my spoor in a moment. I had swallowed some half-a-dozen handfuls of the smashed potatoes, and was thinking of tearing off with my teeth a mouthful of pork, when *fizz!* just past my ear whizzed a bullet. Disgusted, I turned round and saw a Maori lad, perhaps thirteen years old, with a revolver in his hand, running after me, who had evidently made up his mind to gain distinction by bagging a white man. His intentions, though highly commendable from his point of view, were deucedly unpleasant from mine, as the moment I stopped he fired again, making such a good shot that he put a bullet through my rags which seared my ribs like a red-hot iron.

Angry as I was there was only one thing for me to do, and that was to bolt, so, *infra dig.* as it might be, I bolted, and went tearing through the bush pursued by a native urchin who every now and again squibbed off a shot so as to keep me going. Of course I knew the report of the first shot would bring my men to the halt, and that I should be missed the moment they did so. This happened, as I had not run far when I spotted two men peering round tree-trunks and ready to fire. I ran between them, still closely followed by my youthful pursuer, who, being so set upon bagging me, did not spot the ambuscade until he was grabbed by the scruff of the neck and his pistol wrenched out of his hand.

He was a plucky little beggar, and his fortitude quite surprised us as he insisted upon being killed at once and not being made a prisoner, at the same time looking longingly at the provisions I still carried. He gently intimated he was sick with hunger. Angry as I was I still could not bring myself to kill the gallant youngster; and then again, the little beggar was hungry, which put us somehow in the same boat, so I gave him a half share of my rations, and, after gently admonishing him with my toe, bade him run after his people, which he did, while we continued to fall back on the main body, and I managed to finish my much disturbed and diminished breakfast.

The following day we marched to Ahikereru, and then it became evident, even to our little game-cock of an O.C, that we had shot our bolt, and that without a proper supply of food it would be an act of madness for us to try and surmount the tremendous Huiarau range of mountains, then quite unknown and deeply covered with snow. Even to stay where we were was an impossibility, as the distance to our base was so great that the supply of rations, never regular, must cease on account of the inclemency of the weather, so that much against his will he determined to continue the retreat, and take post from Fort Te Teko to Fort Galatea, along the Rangitaike River, as in these forts there were not only many provisions stored, but to which ran a good road along which both drays and pack-horses could easily bring supplies up from the coast.

My word, but we did enjoy ourselves when we reached our new cantonments!—plenty of good bread and meat to eat, plenty of tea, such as it was, to drink, and oh, only think of it, dry blankets and tents in which to sleep! We revelled in it, though the privations we had been through caused a terrible lot of sickness and we lost very many good men who could ill be spared. Somehow it has always seemed so rough to me that a good fellow who has run his risks, faced the music and done his duty through a hard campaign, should, after he has returned with a whole skin to comparative comfort, and maybe is eagerly looking forward to another go at the enemy, be rubbed out by some beastly sickness. The parsons say it is Providence; I maintain it is rotten bad luck.

We were, however, not allowed a long rest, as the colonel received information that Te Kooti intended to break through our lines, so as to get into the Taupo country, and perhaps from there into the Waikato, so that we were all kept very busy indeed. At Fort Galatea we mounted men had met our horses, therefore for a time I had done with the weary footslogging and was again in the pigskin, with all the huge Kaingaroa and Taupo plains to gallop over. This was indeed a change for the better, though the weather was awful, and the south-east blizzards which swept over the high inland plateau bit us to the very bone. It was not long before we mounted men located Te Kooti at a native village called Heruiwi, but he was in too great strength and far too well posted for us to attack with only a handful of cavalry, so that we had to fall back on Fort Galatea, purposing to guide up infantry to do the bush-whacking .

Te Kooti, however, was too old a bird to stay long on his perch after he knew he had been located. He therefore, breaking cover, crossed the Taupo plains making for Lake Taupo, but, so that we should remember him, he managed *en route* to ambuscade two despatch-riders. One of these succeeded in scraping clear and reached Galatea with the news that Te Kooti was on the move, but the other poor fellow was knocked off his horse and taken prisoner. Now I do not know whether in his Mission School days Te Kooti had ever read Byron's poems, though it is quite possible they had been a portion of the useless literature that mission folk hand over to youthful savages, but anyhow he treated the poor captured trooper in the same way as Mazeppa was treated, for, stripping him naked, he caused him to be tightly lashed on to his barebacked horse and then had the two of them cast adrift on to the Kaingaroa plains, where the poor chap perished miserably.

We were, however, quickly to receive further news of Te Kooti's activity. Colonel St John the day previous to the despatch-rider's escape had started to visit a semi-friendly chief at Tapuaeharuru, taking with him an escort of volunteer cavalry. On reaching a deserted *kainga*, called Opepe, as both the horses of his escort as well as the men were badly knocked up by the vile weather, he left them behind, there to recuperate, and rode on to his destination, accompanied by only four officers and an orderly, expecting to return to Opepe the following morning.

Of course both O.C. and escort were ignorant that Te Kooti, having broken camp, was on the move to Taupo, and none of them thought for a single moment there was any immediate fear of danger. Still the volunteers should have kept on the alert, or at the very least have taken the precaution of keeping their arms handy; but this they do not do, for, worn out and chilled to the bone, they simply enter the best of the huts, light fires, discard their arms and belts and strive to dry their dripping, sleet-soaked garments.

Presently two Maoris strolled up. "*Tena koutou*" (salutations to all of you), quoth they; "we are Arawas," and they stood among the troopers, warming themselves and expressing their delight at the chance of doing so.

In a few minutes three more turned up, with words of salutations on their lips and murder in their hearts; and this goes on until at last the infatuated volunteers grow suspicious and try to get hold of their arms; but it is too late. They are already outnumbered. A signal is given and the *tomahawk* does its work. Some two or three, however, escape, and reach Galatea, but nine of them lie butchered in cold blood. The colonel also had a most wonderful escape, as the Hau Haus, ignorant of his vicinity, moved off the ground immediately the slaughter was ended and continued their march towards the lake.

Of course directly we got the news at Galatea we were quickly on

Captured trooper's last ride

Te Kooti's spoor, but by the time we reached Opepe the Hau Haus had retired to the other end of the huge lake, where Te Kooti was immediately joined by the majority of the Taupo tribes. He was therefore again a leader of some six hundred desperate fanatics, and there was also every possibility of his being joined by the Upper Wanganui and the powerful tribe of Waikato.

Had the above coalition taken place it would have been a most disastrous affair for the colony, as Te Kooti would then have had nearly three thousand men at his disposal, but fortunately, just at the critical moment, his men chanced to murder an old and seemingly insignificant Maori, who nevertheless turned out to be a close blood relation of the most powerful chiefs of the Upper Wanganui tribes. These at once demanded *utu*, and became his bitterest enemies. Then with three hundred men he pays a visit of ceremony to the Waikatos, whom he insults, and whose country he is forced to leave, and so once more falls back to the Taupo country, where he locates himself south of the great lake and close to the volcanoes Tongariro and Ruapehu.

Of course at that time we knew but little of his movements, but it would have been bad policy on our part to have attacked him in the Taupo country immediately after the slaughter of the volunteers at Opepe. In the first place the country was quite unknown to us, while the scarcity of rations, the severity of the weather, the desertion of our allies, the Arawas, and the certainty that the smallest reverse we might receive would immediately bring to his banner all the wavering tribes, forced our O.C. to mark time till the weather improved and the big gaps in our ranks could be filled up by fresh men.

Colonel Whitmore took advantage of this pause to make a trip to Wellington to interview the Government, an interview that caused great changes in the plan of campaign, it being decided to mass every available man on the Taupo plateau, to build a chain of forts from Napier to Tauranga, so as to cut off all communications between the Uriwera and the Waikato, and at the same time to ensure safe storage for a sufficient supply of rations for what was evidently going to be a most arduous campaign.

Colonel Herrick's column was ordered from Waikaremoana to Napier, and started cutting a road for pack-horses up to Runanga, a high hill situated on the border of the Taupo plains, and here they built a strong stockade from which communications could easily be kept up with Opepe (now headquarters), a distance of twenty-two miles, and Ahikereru, a distance of eleven miles, while in between Runanga and

Napier were constructed three other forts.

Nor were we of the old field force idle. Winter or no winter, we kept hard at it, scouting and patrolling and learning the country thoroughly, so that when spring came on we should be ready to take the field again.

Our dear old O.C, Colonel St John, worn out with past hardships, had been invalided, but our regret at his departure was somewhat tempered by our hearing the news that Colonel McDonnell would take command in the ensuing campaign, which he shortly did, after making a splendidly plucky march across country from Wanganui to Taupo, a march that had the greatest moral effect on the natives, as they had up till then deemed the road impracticable for white men to negotiate even in summer.

CHAPTER 7

The Taupo Campaign—Continued

About this time I was despatched with the mounted division to Runanga, so as to reinforce Colonel Herrick, who on our arrival was able to take the field with two hundred white men and a strong native contingent, which he did on 8th September 1869, as on that day he despatched Henare Tomoana and Paora Hapi, friendly chiefs, in command of one hundred and forty natives as an advance-guard, the plan being to join hands with McDonnell, who was on his way from Patea, and we were to try and catch Te Kooti between two fires. These warriors, however, marched too fast, as they reached Tauranga Taupo twenty-four hours before they should have done, leaving the main body with the stores to come on as best they could.

Nevertheless they were there, and had occupied an old tumble-down *pah*, when they perceived Te Kooti and his Hau Haus marching down to attack them. Paora Hapi, who was a renowned fighting man, wanted to leave the defences, such as they were, and fight it out in the open, but Henare jibbed at the idea, so that our friendlies stood a siege of two days, and stood off the Hau Hau attacks very pluckily, though, through sticking to the *pah*, it gave Te Kooti the chance to capture and carry off one hundred and twenty of their horses.

True to time we arrived on the scene, but the Hau Haus, well served by their scouts, had received notice of our approach, and as a stand-up fight with mounted men in the open was the very last thing Te Kooti desired, he raised the siege and fell back rapidly into rough mountainous country. On the same day we received a rumour that Colonel McDonnell with the advance-guard of his force had reached Rotoaira, a small lake lying between Lake Taupo and the active volcano Tongariro, and I was ordered to ride through to him in order to open up communications.

This was rather a jumpy job, as every yard of the road ran through enemy's country, and it might well chance that *en route* I should tumble across Te Kooti's whole outfit; moreover, all the information I could get as to the whereabouts of the place was that it lay some ten, or possibly more, miles to the south, or perhaps south-east, or south-west, of where our camp was. However, I was well mounted, the country for New Zealand was fairly open, and I had had to chance it so often during the past four years that the dangers bothered me but little, so away I went and got through all right, although I was shot at and hunted quite enough to make it an exciting afternoon's ride.

Colonel McDonnell was very pleased to see me, as I was to meet him again, but I was more than surprised at the paucity of his force, which only consisted of seventy men. He, however, was expecting to be joined daily by his main body, and as nothing could keep him quiet he immediately started me off on the scout towards Tokanu. Here I found the enemy in force, and while trying to gauge their strength got spotted, and had to run farther and faster than I had ever run in my life, before or since, but fortunately managed to keep ahead until night came on, when I got back safely to camp, very nearly dead beat.

The colonel not being quite satisfied with my report determined to call on Te Kooti himself, so next morning we paid him a visit, when we found the bounder not only in a strong position but with fully six hundred men ready to receive us. These odds being a trifle too long even for fighting Mac, after an exchange of shots we fell back to Rotoaira, where we threw up a rough breastwork, and as we fully expected the Hau Haus to beat up our quarters we all kept a remarkably sharp lookout.

The night passed quietly and early the following morning the main body joined up. The colonel at once sent out scouts, who soon returned with the news that Te Kooti, having abandoned Tokanu, had fallen back towards Moerangi, hearing which the colonel, without loss of time, seized Tokanu, despatching me with orders to Colonel Herrick to join him there. This trip I got through without trouble, and, on the 16th of September, both columns joined hands at Tokanu, a very important strategical position, and one that we could not understand why Te Kooti should have abandoned without a desperate struggle.

The following morning Hare Tauteka, one of the friendly chiefs, turned up at the colonel's hut in a great state of mind, reporting that four of his scouts had been cut off, tortured and killed. This was decidedly unpleasant though, alas! by no means uncommon news. Scouts did at times get captured, and the Hau Haus, especially Te Kooti, had a nasty way of entertaining their captives. Still this news required verifying, as it was unusual for the whole of a patrol of scouts to be captured, one or more as a rule managing to scrape clear.

The colonel therefore asked Hare how he had received the information, whereupon he replied that his scouts should have joined up two days previously, and that no hope of their safety could be entertained for a single moment, as his pet prophetess had dreamed a dream that they had been captured, tortured and killed. The colonel demanded to see the lady, who with her son was trotted up, and two more loathsome objects could not be imagined.

The old dame was so hideous and unsightly that she would have afforded a gang of godly Puritans exquisite delight to torture and burn as a witch; while the son, who suffered from some horrible form of leprosy, appeared to be falling to pieces. Notwithstanding the old faggot's homeliness she was gifted with a most eloquent tongue, for no sooner had she appeared than she started in and prophesied a whole hurricane. Moreover, there was no Delphic ambiguity in her statements, as she stoutly asserted and maintained that the four scouts had been captured alive, tortured to death, and that their remains had then been thrown into a certain swamp, the name of which she mentioned.

Now of course we white men were inclined to laugh and ridicule the whole yarn, but refrained from doing so, as we should have deeply offended the superstitious Maoris, so, like the sailor's parrot, we thought profoundly, but said nothing.

The following day Captain McDonnell, with Kepa's advance-guard, joined up, and he reported that he had been informed by some semi-friendly natives that Te Kooti had captured four of our scouts, tortured them to death, and ordered their remains to be thrown into a certain swamp.

Upon hearing this news the colonel despatched a strong patrol of mounted men to search the place, and there, sure enough, we found the poor fellows' remains, which, from the treatment they had evidently been subjected to before death mercifully put an end to their sufferings, showed us plainly that the damned Hau Haus had spared no torment that devils could invent or fiends inflict.

The old Witch of Endor was now very cock-a-hoop, as her lucky dream sent up her scrip many points on the market, and her name resounded through the field force as being quite a first-class, high-toned, up-to-date and always to be relied upon dreamer of dreams and seer of visions, in fact a puka old-time witch that all respectable elderly Maori fighting men must needs give ear to.

Now prophets and cattle of that sort were rank poison to an O.C. of a column in which a large number of natives served, and our field force had many more of these critters on our strength than we were entitled to or desired, in fact they troubled us exceedingly, as, just when the colonel would want to make a move, some confounded old image, possibly suffering from a repletion of villainous ration bacon, would dream that the proposed expedition would be an unlucky one, and at once the whole of his congregation would plump themselves down and refuse to budge an inch.

This then was an opportunity that the colonel could not allow to slip, for, taking advantage of the old dame's stock being at so high a premium, he immediately subsidised her, and in future she dreamt dreams that concurred with his wishes, and, as our luck was in the ascendant, the natives were quite ready to do any work they might be called upon to perform. Truly there are more ways of killing a cat than drowning it in cream.

Subsequently we heard how these scouts had come to grief. They had been despatched to discover the route that Te Kooti would be likely to take should he attempt to break away round our right flank, and had put in four days' hard work. On the evening of the fourth day, having completed the duty, they were well on their way back to camp, and had cleared the acute danger zone. Of course they had had a very rough time of it, for, although the spring was now coming on, it was only by the date in the day's Order Book you were aware of the fact, as heavy sleet storms during the day and hard frosts at night had still to be endured. Well, as I said, they were fairly past the danger line, in fact a few more hours' tramping would have landed them safely in camp, when unfortunately they chanced upon an old potato clearing on which stood a few huts, while, worse luck still, one of them spotted a *rua* (potato pit) containing a lot of potatoes.

The temptation was too great for the worn-out, wet-through and starving men. Surely they might rest and eat; anyhow they would chance it. They did so; and entering the best hut they lit a fire, cooked potatoes, dried their dripping clothes and warmed themselves, then, overcome by the lassitude brought on by their full meal, and the unwonted heat, they fell asleep.

Of course they had played the fool, and had done what they well knew to be wrong, but yet I think St Nemesis might have closed her eyes on the *faux pas* of these poor scallywags, but she is not built that way, for she was on their spoor like a jumping wild cat before they had eaten a single *pratie*, and she punished their sin in a most cruel manner.

It happened this way: Although they were in blissful ignorance of the fact, they had been spotted by two separate parties of Hau Haus, each numbering forty men. These parties, posted on high ranges of hills, had not pursued them, as they deemed it impossible to overtake them, but when they saw them enter the hut they came down from their heights, and closely surrounded the place. One of them creeps up and peers through the chinks of the rickety door, and there he sees the four wretched scouts fast asleep, with their guns made fast to the hut-pole. In a moment the door of the hut is knocked into splinters, and before one of the inmates can move a finger they are overwhelmed by numbers, and securely tied hand and foot.

Next morning the captives are brought before the arch-devil, Te Kooti. They are all warriors of high repute and *rangateras* of the bluest blood, most valuable recruits if they can only be made to join the Hau Haus. Te Kooti knows this well, and for a long time does all in his power to persuade or intimidate them to join him, but to all his specious arguments and diabolical threats he only receives this one answer: "Do with us as you like; we are warriors of the Great White Queen, who fear not death, come it as it may."

As persuasion is of no avail the threats are put into practice, but I will not go into nauseating details. Frequently at intervals during the next twenty-four hours the torture is discontinued for a few minutes, and the offer of life renewed to the sufferers, but so long as speech remains the overtures are met by the same steadfast answer: "Do with us as you will; our honour is the honour of the Great White Queen; we fear not death, come it as it may." At last it came, and those four savage gentlemen yielded up their lives, but retained their honour.

If in the far future there should chance to be a *corps d'élite* among the legions of angels, I will wager my golden crown that those four Maori *rangateras* will swing their flaming *tomahawks* in its ranks.

Well, now let's get on with the main yarn. I have previously mentioned the infernal weather, which that year was the worst ever known in New Zealand, and as Taupo is always bleak and cold, we came in for more than our share of snow, sleet and frost; in fact, it being impossible for human flesh and blood to keep the field, the colonel occupied the two strong positions of Rotoaira and Tokanu, while Te Kooti remained quiet in his fastnesses, both sides having to sit tight for a bit, and wait till the clouds roll by.

While we are marking time for the clerk of the weather, I think I may take the opportunity of telling you about a wonderful occurrence that took place at Tokanu, which is situated among the hot springs and geysers close to the shores of Lake Taupo. Many of these are hot enough to cook in, the water boiling furiously, while many others are cool enough to bathe in, and there was one of the latter particularly favoured by all hands. Let me try to describe it.

On a flat of silica, quite smooth to the bare feet, are three huge basins, perfectly round, some seventy feet in diameter and all in a row, each separated at the surface by only a few feet of silica. Now the odd thing about these basins is, that the water in the two end ones rises and falls—that is to say, when the one nearest the lake is brimful the water in the farther one will sink out of sight, and vice versa. This takes place as regularly as clock-work, one being full and the other empty, while the middle one always remains brimful, and although the water in the two end ones is boiling hot, that in the centre basin is cool enough to bathe in.

This pool had been the favourite resort of the natives for untold generations, and had never been known to monkey—*i.e.* to blow up—so of course when we occupied the place we gladly made use of it; in fact it was full all day long, as in the inclement weather it was the custom of everyone not on duty to strip in his hut and rush off naked to the pool, into which he would plunge, and remain for hours in the hot water, thereby keeping himself warm and out of the icy sleet. Now we were entitled among other rations to a couple of half-tots of rum per day, but, like many of our other necessaries, we received them rarely, and when we did get one it was highly appreciated.

Well, one wretched afternoon all hands not on duty, perhaps one hundred and fifty of us or more, were in this bathing hole when, oh, joyful sound, the grog call rang out! Without a moment's pause every man in the water jumped out and ran as hard as he could to hustle on his rags and make the best of his way to the rum-bucket. We were just in time, for the last man had barely cleared the silica flat when, with a roar like ten thunder claps lashed together, up went the bathing hole, and what a minute before had been a placid pool of warm water became a roaring geyser, throwing up a huge fountain of boiling water at least two hundred feet into the air, while the screams of it were like ten thousand steam hooters blowing off at the same time.

Well, now that was a slice of luck, as had the bust up taken place one minute earlier the whole lot of us would have been blown to Kingdom Come in smithereens. Think of that, oh, my crazy, fanatical teetotalerising, red-nose wind-bag, only just think, one hundred and fifty lives saved by their smartness in answering the wicked grog call. Ponder over it, my brother, and lay this flattering unction to your soul, should you by chance have one, that bar the alarm it was the only call in the bugler's repertoire that would have been answered in such a unanimous and energetic style, but cheer up. Brother Stiggins, I will give you a tip. The next time you spout trash to your brother and sister fanatics, spin the above yarn, and if you only alter the grog call for the tea call, you will bring the house down. Surely you can't hesitate in telling such a tiny lie for so good a cause.

Just as the weather began to clear, a trooper riding despatch from Rotoaira to Tokanu returned at the gallop reporting that the road was blocked and that he had only scraped clear by the skin of his teeth.

The friendly natives refused to believe the yarn, so next morning the colonel, with a dozen of us mounted men, rode out to reconnoitre, and near Tokanu we found the Hau Haus had taken up a strong position on the spurs of a range overlooking the track.

They at once opened a heavy fire on us, but following the colonel's lead we galloped past them, and in a few minutes met a strong body of friendlies, led by Captain St George, who had come out of Tokanu to ascertain the cause of the firing. The colonel immediately dismounted, and led the natives on to the attack, while we mounted men cantered into action opening the ball.

The Hau Haus were in strong force, swarming on the top of the range across the spurs of which they had dug lines of shelter trenches, the first line of which, the colonel leading, we took with a rush, but the main body of the Hau Haus, undaunted, swept in masses down the spurs to drive us back. At the start we were far out-numbered, but were being reinforced every moment by fresh arrivals of friendlies from both camps, who, coming up at the run, threw themselves promiscuously into the fight.

The charge of the Hau Haus downhill at us was indeed a pretty sight, as they came on like mountain torrents, yelling like devils and waving their weapons in the air. McDonnell, however, had us well in hand, and shouted to us to restrain our fire, which we did until they were within ten yards of us, when at his word we all fired, and followed up the volley with a charge that effectually dammed their torrents of attack.

Faith, it was as swate a little fight as I have ever had the luck to take part in, for, although it took place upon the spurs of a range and we had to charge uphill, yet the battle-ground was free from bush till the summit was reached, so that we could see all the fun that was going on around us. Another factor greatly to our advantage was that, the scrap being quite unpremeditated on our part, none of our limbs of Satan (prophets) had been able to dream dreams, consequently our friendlies fought with all their native courage, which was in no wise handicapped by the lugubrious prognostications of some old humbug suffering from the mullygrubs.

A gay and festive hand-to-hand fight took place that lasted a few minutes, in which *tomahawk* clinked against *tomahawk*, and yell answered yell with all the reckless devilment of a good old-fashioned Irish faction fight, but at last the Hau Haus give ground, while we press them so closely, and drive them back so rapidly that they have to abandon their dead and wounded, who fall into our hands, the latter receiving the same amount of mercy as they would have bestowed upon us had the tables been turned.

Presently they give way and bolt, but we pursue just as fast as they fly, and reach the top rather breathless, but mighty adjacent to their shirt tails. Here they turn and try to make a stand, but without a pause we fly at them like a pack of wild dogs at a flock of sheep, and in less than five minutes they are driven across the summit of the ridge, and disperse on the far side, a broken, beaten, dispirited mob of fugitives, while we white men sit down and laugh, and our bould allies vent their superfluous energy in a blood-curdling war dance in which the heads of the defunct Hau Haus are passed from hand to hand like footballs.

This fight, Te Pononga, insignificant as it may appear, was yet of tremendous importance, although at the moment we were quite unaware of the fact, but we ascertained shortly afterwards that the celebrated Waikato war chief, Rewi, with six hundred warriors, had been spectators of the whole action. It seems that Rewi and his men had come to join Te Kooti, but had jibbed, as one of the lately tortured scouts had been a close blood relation to some of the most influential Waikato chiefs. This rift, however, had been nearly closed by Te Kooti's wonderful art of persuasion, who also braggingly prophesied that at his next fight he would utterly defeat the white man. Thereupon Rewi made the agreement that if he proved himself to be a true prophet then he, Rewi, would join forces with the Hau Haus and assist them in driving the white men to perdition.

Te Kooti therefore selected his ground (a great point in Maori warfare), went through all the Hau Hau ritual and uncanny incantations, danced the Pai Marire, wound his warriors up to their extreme height of fanaticism, and then sent a braggart message to Rewi ordering him to come and look on at his splendid victory. Rewi came, but when, instead of looking on at the victory, he saw the boasting prophet with his whole gang of scallywags driven off the chosen field in headlong flight he quietly packed his grip-sack, and without beat of drums returned to the Waikato, where he informed H.M. King Potatau that Te Kooti was a humbug as a prophet, and no great shakes as a fighting man, so Waikato sat tight and left white man and Hau Hau to fight it out alone, which was a deucedly lucky thing for us.

The following day, as we were ready to start in pursuit, the colonel received a message from Kepa asking him not to fight again until his arrival, as he was bringing with him seventy renowned warriors, and that he was most anxious to take part in the next action. This was indeed good news, as it would give us seventy trustworthy men in whom the colonel could place the most implicit reliance, and would also enable him to dispense with the services of some of the least warlike of the friendlies, who were now beginning to give a lot of trouble, especially the Napier Maoris under Renata Kawepo.

Kepa's advent was indeed a godsend, but more good luck was to follow, as on the very same day the splendid No. 2 Division of the Armed Constabulary marched into Tokanu, who, together with the Wanganuis, the Taupo friendlies and us mounted men, gave the O.C. a fighting field force sufficient to twist Te Kooti's tail without the assistance of the riff-raff who were always too ready to give ear to the romances of dreaming prophets.

While waiting for Kepa, McDonnell kept all hands, with the exception of the scouts, closely confined to the camps, as he was most anxious the Hau Haus should gain sufficient confidence to again collect in a body, which would enable him to deliver one more smashing blow, as in such a country it was quite useless trying to run down small parties of scattered fugitives.

His apparent supineness quickly bore fruit, as we scouts soon discovered that the broken Hau Haus were drawing together, and in a few days they had regained sufficient cheek to try and drive off horses and slaughter cattle grazing in the vicinity of the camps. Yes, slaughter cattle, my friends; for as regards meat rations we were now fairly well off, as, a pack-horse track having been cut through the bush to Runanga, droves of oxen could be sent up to the front, and as these beasts performed the journey on their own legs they required no transport. Other rations, however, were still very scarce, as we were only issued two days' groceries and biscuits for every eight days.

This had been all right up till now, as on our arrival in Taupo huge stores of potatoes had been captured, but alas, the succulent spuds had been eaten, so could not be issued again. It was therefore necessary to renew our stock, and we scouted hard to find any *ruas*, but although we found plenty of these underground storerooms, still they were invariably empty, the truth being that the Maoris of the district, having lost such large quantities to us, and also having had to feed Te Kooti and his hungry gang, were deucedly hard up for potatoes themselves, and it became evident to all that in the near future Te Kooti and his mob would have to hunt for new pastures on which to browse. This being the state of affairs, and no one being anxious to chase the bounder again across the island, we were all very hopeful, and most desirous of getting the chance to smash him once and for ever.

Kepa arrived, and his advent was the occasion of the most tremendous war dance I ever saw in my life, but it is quite impossible for me to describe it. Only one man has ever been able to picture with a pen an old-time Maori war dance, and as I can't pretend to in any way approach his gift of description, I won't try to do so. Anyhow it was a very wonderful sight, and was, I suppose, the last real war dance ever danced in New Zealand.

Of course a few years back, when our present king, (as at time of first publication), God bless him, visited Rotorua, the tame natives round about got up a burlesque *haka*, but although I was not present I will gamble it was not an old-time war-dance, as, had it been only a fraction of one, every white female and most of the white men then present would have fled off the ground overcome with horror and disgust.

While we looked on an officer said to me: "I wish to goodness, Dick, some of the infatuated idiots who for the past forty years have subscribed to the New Zealand mission funds could only see this ruddy lot of Christian natives dancing their war dance, for I 'ud bet my bottom dollar it would open their eyes and close their pockets." To these remarks I fully agreed.

We scouts had by now located Te Kooti, who at Pourere had built a strong redoubt after the European fashion, but without *kaponiers* or any other flanking defence. It stood fairly in the open, close to the foot of the burning mountain, Tongariro, while Papakai, the village of the great Taupo chief, Te Heuheu, was within two miles of it. Here Te Kooti, with the three hundred ruffians who had rejoined him, determined to make a desperate resistance, and as soon as McDonnell was aware of the fact he moved forward to deliver what he and the rest of us devoutly hoped was going to be the *coup de grâce* to the foul gang of murderers we had been so long in pursuit of.

The colonel's plan of attack was excellent, and I have no doubt we should have succeeded in surrounding and destroying the whole hive of vermin had it not been for the old image Renata, whose pet prophet chose to dream a dream just at the wrong time—i.e. the evening before the attack should have taken place, which said dream caused Renata and his three hundred Napier Maoris to squat down and refuse to budge.

The attack therefore was made anyhow, it culminating in a race between the Wanganuis, St George's natives and ourselves as to who should first get to hand-grips with the enemy. When old Renata found we were attacking without him he got into a terrible fluster, and with sixty of his men following him ran after us, screaming to us to wait for him, lamenting that he was disgraced forever, and cursing his pet prophet for all he was worth. His penitence, however, came too late, as a number of the Hau Haus had already got out of the place, breaking through the gap he and his men, through their confounded folly, had neglected to stop.

Pourere was rushed in a most orthodox style, as we surmounted the parapet, which was eight feet high, by climbing on to one another's shoulders and jumping on to the top of the defenders, whom we finished off with butt, tomahawk and revolver. It was quite a tidy little scrap, in which I came out the richer by receiving two tomahawk cuts and the poorer by having my shirt and shawl torn to pieces off me, a very serious loss, believe me, as until I got back to Tokanu every rag of clothing I possessed was my boots, a somewhat scanty well-worn Maori mat and bandages.

Pourere was a bad beating for Te Kooti, as, although we only found thirty-eight dead Hau Haus inside the work, yet during the pursuit very many were killed and wounded. We also captured thirty women and eighty horses. In this action Te Kooti himself was wounded, receiving a bullet through his hand, which, lacerating the thumb and forefinger, amputating the third finger, then passed through the fleshy part of his side.

Our loss as far as numbers went was trivial, four men only being killed and four wounded, but alas, we lost two men we could badly spare, one being the gallant and chivalrous Captain St George, shot through the head while leading his men to the charge, and the other, the best little fighting man I have ever known, Winiata Pakoro, whose name will resound as long as war is ever talked about by the Maoris.

He was killed in the following way:—The parapet of the work was eight feet from the ground line and four feet thick, being beautifully riveted with fern. When we rushed the place we advanced in extended order, and on the charge being sounded ran forward, stooping low and closing in as we ran. Now Te Kooti had asserted that the reason he built Pourere after the European style was that he acted under the direct instructions of the angel Gabriel, in which case his angelship showed very small knowledge of the art of fortification, as the line of loopholes was pierced six feet from the ground and straight through the parapet, not giving the bottom sills any downward slope, so that his men when firing could not depress the muzzles of their guns, consequently when they fired their volley at our charging ranks all their bullets went howling over our heads, not one single man being touched. In a moment we leaped into the ditch, and, as there were no flanking defences to enfilade it, we were quite safe, and all paused a moment, cheering and laughing, to recover breath.

Winiata, however, had no need of more breath, so forthwith scrambled up to the top of the parapet, and, discharging his rifle into the mob of defenders, called them all the naughty names he could think of, then throwing down to his comrades his empty gun he received from them another loaded one, which he also discharged in the same manner. He had done this three times, and was in the act of doing it the fourth when he tumbled backwards into the ditch with a bullet through his brains.

Her saintship Nemesis on this occasion made use of a rod she must have kept a long time in pickle for the back of that ancient sinner and believer in dreams, Renata Kawepo, the chief of the Napier tribe, and she served it out to him in this fashion.

Old Renata, who in no ways lacked pluck, at the last moment charged with about sixty of his men, but in the pursuit through the bush got separated from them. While alone he fell across a Hau Hau man and woman, the latter's husband having just been killed, and these two at once attacked him. It would have gone very hard with the poor old chap had not a trooper and an Arawa come to the rescue, who equalised matters by promptly killing the man, and then stood by and, acting as referees, watched a veritable hand-to-hand fight, no lethal weapons being allowed, between the infuriated Suffragette and Renata.

Now I regret to state it is impossible for me to report that the fight was fought in strict accordance with the Queensberry rules, or any other well-known code of laws drawn up for the guidance of pugilistic encounters, as after scrapping two rounds, during which both of them should have been frequently disqualified for foul fighting, in the third and last the vixen got the dog down, mauled him severely, tore the green-stone ornament out of his ear, taking the greater part of that organ with it, gouged out one of his eyes, which she promptly swallowed, and would have finished him off had not the Arawa, suddenly remembering that the Napier tribe would most probably demand *utu* from him for looking on at their chief being outed, put an end to the shindy by taking the Amazon prisoner.

The general verdict of the field force on this encounter was serve him right, and much more sympathy went to the woman than to Renata, as everyone was fed up with the pranks of the Napier tribe and bitterly blamed Renata for giving Te Kooti the chance of again escaping.

The Napier men, however, were furious, and, being high-toned Christians, demanded the woman should be given over to them so as to be tortured and killed. This modest request the colonel sternly refused, and promptly ordered all the women prisoners to be brought up to his own camp for safety. At the same time he solemnly warned the Napier scallywags that if they dared to play any monkey tricks he would let loose us mounted men to twist their tails, whereupon the disgusted Napier tribes said they would go home, and were promptly told to go to Hades, and they went not as far as they were recommended to go but to Napier, and this was only to be expected, for you see the beggars always hung back when ordered to march an unfrequented route or do anything of an arduous nature.

CHAPTER 8

Hide-and-Seek With Te Kooti

The Taupo Field Force now had to foot it in what the men called a devil's dance—*i.e.* marching and counter-marching all over the big inland plateau—for Te Kooti, having had sufficient fighting for the time being, simply refused to be brought to book. Ye gods! how we poor scouts were worked day and night, as on foot through the bush and across mountains, or on horseback, over the plains, we searched for the beggar high and low. Occasionally we would locate him, and, making for camp as hard as we could pelt, would report to the fretting O.C. we had him spotted. In a moment the column would start walking all day, or scrambling all night, till we surrounded the place, then rush it, only to find the still smouldering fires of his bivouac.

Back would march the disgusted column, and would scarcely have time to eat before fresh scouts tore in with the report, "We have got Te Kooti located." Away would go the swearing column, only to be sold again; and thus the dance went on. The fact of the matter was that the Hau Hau scouts were just as good as our own, and kept our camps under such strict observation that no party of men could leave them day or night without Te Kooti being at once warned of the movement, and so we could never depend on his remaining in the same place for more than a few hours at a stretch.

Eventually he disappeared altogether from our ken, and we were utterly nonplussed as to what had become of him. This was indeed a very grave and serious responsibility, as no one could surmise from which direction some horrible story of murder and rapine might be sprung upon us. Every officer and man, from the O.C. downwards, did his best to pick up the lost spoor, and despatch-riders were sent to ride day and night to inform the distant settlers and commandants of frontier districts that Te Kooti had been lost, and to earnestly warn them to keep on the lookout for one of his lightning raids, while the hearts of us poor scouts grew dark, as, although we had done all that human beings could do, yet somehow it seemed to ourselves that we were to blame for his miraculous disappearance.

At last it was discovered, after we had marched the boots off our feet, and our riding-breeches were more holey than a cold wet saddle demanded, that Te Kooti had retired into the King Country, where he again, in the most extraordinary way, raised another band of murderous ruffians.

There we could not meddle with him, for to have done so would have been to declare war against the powerful Waikato and Ngatimainapoto tribes, who at that time acknowledged no British rule. Moreover, starvation was again staring us in the face, as some rotter in the Government, having a large number of sheep to dispose of, and wool being at a very low price, suddenly discovered it would be cheaper to feed us on mutton than on beef, so flocks of sheep were despatched up to the front instead of herds of oxen. We should not have objected to the change, but alas, the sheep could not travel up the bush paths or swim rivers like oxen, and the few that did arrive were so long on the journey that we well-nigh starved before they reached us.

It was therefore absolutely necessary to reduce the strength of the field force, so as Kepa at this time received a message from Topia Turoa, the great chief of the Wanganuis, requesting his presence, as he, Topia, had received a letter from the Maori King, which he refused to open except in Kepa's presence, the Colonel sent home the splendid Wanganui warriors, and everyone was awfully keen to hear what news this wonderful letter contained.

In the meantime we starved, but never for a moment relaxed our vigilance or discontinued our scouting and patrols, as McDonnell knew full well that the least slackness on our part would encourage the wily Te Kooti to play us some dog's trick or another. At last we heard the purport of the king's letter to Topia, and as it throws light on some queer phases in old Maori etiquette I will tell you all about it.

The Maoris were the most hospitable people in the world, being bound to defend their guests, as their guests were bound to fight for their hosts. On this occasion, however, Te Kooti was, if not originally, an unwelcome guest, yet had misbehaved himself to such an extent that His Maori Majesty heartily wished to get rid of him, as he feared that he would attract such a following as to enable him, Te Kooti, to set up an opposition kingdom.

Nevertheless, although quite strong enough himself to eject the artful dodger from the Waikato, yet the laws of hospitality forbade him to act as his own chucker-out, and he therefore wrote to Topia stating that he, the king, withdrew his protection from Te Kooti and requested Topia to immediately assist Kepa in driving the murderers of women and children from the Waikato. This was nuts to Topia, as he sadly wanted *utu* for his old blood relation, Hona, the insignificant old man the Hau Haus had wilfully murdered shortly after they had played old gooseberry with the volunteer troopers at Opepe.

Accordingly on Kepa's arrival Topia sent out the fiery cross, and in two wags of a cat's tail had collected a *posse comitatus* of six hundred first-class up-to-date fighting men, whom he placed under Kepa's command as war chief, but he accompanied them himself so as to make sure that no monkey tricks would be played or that any of his men should suddenly fancy themselves to be prophets and start dreaming dreams, he, Topia, not believing in such necromancing when the serious business of war was on foot.

He likewise warned all hands he would interpret any dreams with his *tomahawk*, stated that Te Kooti's head was fit to be boiled (an awful cuss word for a Maori chief to use), and that he meant to have *utu* for the blood of his relative he had never seen. So with Topia, Kepa and six hundred fresh men on their track the Hau Haus did not draw dividends for their brutal murder of a poor old non-combatant whom they had deemed to be a mere nobody, and as such a fit object for their wanton cruelty.

Te Kooti however quickly tumbled to the fact that his game was up in the Waikato, as by one of his lightning marches he turned our right flank, and although he ran great danger in being caught between Topia's men and our column, when he would have been crushed like a nut in a pair of nutcrackers, yet thanks to a dense fog he scraped through between us and got clean away to our rear without our being aware of the fact, and it was only through my cutting his spoor the same evening that we knew of his desperate movement, and that he had made his way to Patatere in the country of the Ngaiterangi, a large portion of which tribe at once joined him.

Now this was one of the most extraordinary facts about this very extraordinary bounder. Here was a man possessed of no blue blood, yet Maoris regard high descent to be an essential in their leaders. Again Maoris have no faith in an unsuccessful general, and it was impossible to argue that he had been successful. True, he had succeeded in three or four raids, in which he had ruthlessly tortured and murdered women and children, yet whenever he had stood up to us in a fair fight, even although he had chosen the battlefield himself, he had been beaten and driven off the ground with a great loss of men. Moreover, he had set himself up as a prophet, and granted a lucky prophet had immense influence over the superstitious natives, yet on the other hand an unlucky prophet met with scant ceremony; in fact on more than one occasion Hau Haus relentlessly killed prophets who had misled them.

Now as a prophet Te Kooti was a distinct failure. He had over and over again declared himself to be invulnerable, yet he had been wounded twice, and on one occasion had had to be carried out of action on a woman's back. Moreover he had promised his followers time after time invulnerability, yet every tribe who joined him had lost heavily in killed and wounded.

Now this was sufficient to have damned a big chief even had he had a previous splendid record, and Te Kooti was no big chief, while his record previous to his, grantedly unjust, transportation was simply that of a rowdy chicken thief. Nevertheless, notwithstanding all his drawbacks and manifold short-comings, Te Kooti up to the end never visited a tribe that he could not either frighten or persuade numbers of that tribe to join his precarious fortunes, and this without doubt was a marvel, for the Maori is by nature a powerful reasoner and wonderfully clear-headed. Perhaps the most wonderful thing of all was that chiefs of bluest blood who would have pilled him like a shot, had he possessed the effrontery to put himself up for their club, still willingly submitted themselves to his rule and obeyed his commands.

On the 20th of January 1870 Topia's and our column met, and on the 24th our advance patrol surprised and rushed a *kainga*, in which we killed one Hau Hau and captured three others, who, after putting both themselves and us to a deal of trouble, owned up that they were Te Kooti's scouts, and that Te Kooti himself was camped a few miles away, this being the first authentic information we had received of his actual whereabouts.

Of course the colonel at once determined to go for him, and Kepa started off with two hundred of his men to get to the wily one's rear, it being arranged that we were to leave camp two hours before daybreak and make the frontal attack. The country we were in was a sinful one, and quite unknown to us. It was chiefly composed of deep pumicestone ravines with perpendicular sides, and there were so many of them that Tim's query, "Where the divil did the man who dug them hape up the stuff he excavated?" was quite justifiable.

The following morning, just as I was about to leave camp with the scouts, a dense fog came on, so thick that you could have cut chunks out of it with a knife, when of course it was a case of sit tight, as it would have been worse than madness for men ignorant of the locality to attempt to move. Time passed, the men fell in, and were ordered to lie down at their alarm posts—*i.e.* in square surrounding the camp—and wait quietly till it was possible to move.

Daylight came, but the fog was thicker than ever, the colonel got vexed, the men did not, as they had been vexed ever since they had rolled up their blankets, still although everyone had profound convictions as to the unsuitability of the weather, none expressed them, for to have done so would have only added to the sulphurous density of the atmosphere.

The sun must have been well up, although no one could see a foot in front of his nose, when to our intense surprise crash came a volley, and a storm of bullets swept over our recumbent force that plainly demonstrated to us that instead of our being the attackers the boot was on the other leg, and that Te Kooti was attacking us.

Now at first sight this move on his part might appear to have been a very considerate one, as it apparently was undertaken so as to save us the trouble of an early and unpleasant march, but the bounder had no such philanthropic motive, for it was in reality a very cute scheme.

Te Kooti had been warned the previous day of our presence, and judging we should start before daylight to beat up his quarters, he had, after dark, altered the position of his own bivouac, and then, by a detour, he had called on ours, expecting to find our camp protected only by a few men whom he hoped to spiffilicate, and then capture the reserve ammunition and anything else of value on which he could lay his dirty claws. It was a well-thought-out plan, but the fog coming on as it had done kept us at home, so that instead of his finding a weak camp guard, whom he could easily have destroyed, he found the whole outfit ready and only too willing to entertain him.

Well, rip came his first volley which was followed up by others, while we lay dogo, as what was the use of firing when we could not even see the flash of his men's rifles to aim at. For some time the above game went on, the Hau Haus occasionally firing a volley, ourselves lying quite silent, hoping that they would charge, and let us get to hand-grips, but this they evidently feared to do, as they were bothered by our silence.

At last the fog cleared, and we saw them, when the colonel ordered us to fire and charge, which we did, the enemy bolting like redshanks, pursued by Topia and his men, but the old chief, although a fine old duke, was not Kepa, so Te Kooti and his riff-raff, although dispersed, scraped clear with but small loss. They were, however, to suffer in another way by having the tables turned on them in a queer manner.

Kepa, as I before mentioned, had started the night previous to take up a position to the rear of the Hau Hau camp, but hampered by the fog he missed their old camping-ground, and stumbled by chance on to their new one, and, as the sound of the firing at our bivouac warned him what was going on there, he shrewdly guessed Te Kooti's game, and that the Hau Hau main body must be fully occupied. He at once took advantage of the situation by surrounding and rushing Te Kooti's camp, from which he easily drove out or killed the few men left in charge of it, thereby capturing eighty horses and an immense amount of loot. Thus the wily Te Kooti went out to shear, but, thanks to a fog, got shorn himself.

The loss of the horses and loot was a great blow to Te Kooti, who now disappeared again in his usual miraculous way. After days and nights of fatiguing scouting we eventually discovered him with two hundred men at Kuranui, where we at once attacked him. He, however, refusing to fight, broke his men into two parties, the trail of one leading towards Tauranga (Bay of Plenty), the other towards Tapapa. We captured some of his scouts the same day, who informed us that Te Kooti himself was with a party *en route* to Tauranga.

CHAPTER 9

The End of New Zealand Wars

The Taupo campaign had been a disastrous one for Te Kooti. At its commencement the larger portion of the Taupo and Tuhua tribes had joined him; the Waikato and Ngatimaniapoto were ready to do so; and the tribes of the Upper Wanganui, though neutral, were friendly towards him. Yet within five months he had been fairly beaten five times. The Upper Wanganuis under Topia had joined us, the Taupo and Tuhua tribes had lost heavily, and, becoming disgusted with him, had abandoned his fortunes, while the Waikatos not only laughed at him, but allowed Topia and Kepa to march through their country to attack him.

Te Kooti, therefore, was now a fugitive, with two thousand pounds' reward offered for his head, dead or alive, and although he did his best to make head against us yet he knew himself the game was up; although an occasional skirmish would take place no further action happened that could be called a battle. Yet our game was a difficult one to play, as we must keep the infernal ruffian on the move, or he would soon have gathered together another strong party, and all our work would have to be commenced afresh. Likewise there were other tribes who must be humbled and punished for having taken part in the numerous massacres. It was in one of these skirmishes that we lost an old comrade, who fell a victim to his predilection for other people's property, notwithstanding the fact that he was taking every precaution to guard himself from his fate.

I have previously pointed out that but little quarter was served out to Hau Hau prisoners, very many of whom preferred death to being made captives, especially if they could get the chance of killing an enemy before taking their own quietus, so that frequently when a Hau Hau found he could not get away he would sham death, and await the opportunity of shooting or *tomahawking* one of our men, and then resign himself to his death in such a philosophical way as to be "worthy of a better cause." Now a lot of these bounders carried a good deal of money, which they had looted from the white settlements, and therefore their pockets and pouches were well worth prospecting.

Among others who were not above replenishing their exchequers in this way were my two foreign scallywags, Pierre and George, both of whom regarded the looting of a defunct Hau Hau as a meritorious act. Now George, although a Greek, feared nothing, yet had a slight nervousness about being shot by a dead Hau Hau, so that he used to take considerable precautions, as when he approached a recumbent body he would do so crawling, and on arriving alongside the stiff 'un would gently insert between the ribs of the prostrate Hau Hau a huge knife, then, turning to his marauding comrade, would put his finger to the side of his nose, and with a Satanic grin murmur: "Dat makes all tings safe." These two beauties, being scouts, and having comparatively a free hand, had great advantages over the other men, as they would often be rabbitting among the slain before the action was over.

On the occasion of the catastrophe both Pierre and George dropped out of the firing line the moment the pursuit began, and started in to look after their own interests. They were both hard at work, and George, having just made "all tings safe" with one dead Maori, was in the act of going through his pockets when another seemingly defunct Hau Hau jumped up and blew a hole through him. Pierre, who was close by, shot the shamming Hau Hau, and then, being a thorough good business man, notwithstanding his intense sorrow at the loss of his mate, promptly went through his pockets as well as those of the two now very dead Hau Haus.

I was deeply sorry for poor George's untimely end, as although he was not quite the sort of man I should have cared to have introduced into society, and I was well aware he owed his neck over and over again to the hangman of various countries, still he had been a staunch comrade to me, and on scores of occasions had not only prevented me going hungry, but, by his marvellous instinct as a scout, had frequently saved me from losing the number of my mess, therefore both Tim and myself sorrowed exceedingly.

Te Kooti now left the Taupo country and made for Rotorua, where he attempted to persuade the natives to allow him to enter their *pah*, which, had they done so, Te Kooti would have murdered every soul it contained. The inhabitants, however, were saved from this act of folly by the arrival of Captain Mair, who immediately attacked him, and who, but for the bad conduct of his men (Arawas), who, although fighting in their own country and for the safety of their own families, acted in their usual cowardly manner, would have undoubtedly captured him.

Te Kooti, having been foiled at Rotorua, and knowing the net was closing round him, made a bolt for the Uriwera country, closely followed by Captain Mair. A sharp skirmish took place at Kaiteriria, in which, getting the worst of it in the beginning. Captain Mair eventually drove him off the field with the loss of his best fighting man, the infamous half-caste known by the name of Peka, who in reality was the son of a big white official, and also of his pet torturer, Timoti Te Kaka, the latter having been wounded and, caught alive, met a suitable death at the hands of the friendlies. Te Kooti, however, managed to escape, and with his Chatham Islanders fled to Uriwera.

It now very much looked as if we were in for another winter's campaign in that awful country, but our men were by this time fairly worn out, and as it had been too often conclusively proved that untrained, untried white men were worse than useless in the bush, and also that the Taupo line must be guarded by men who could be thoroughly depended upon, and not by new chums, the new Defence Minister determined on trying a novel plan, which was giving a contract to the friendly natives to run down Te Kooti and his broken ruffians, while we held the chain of forts along the Taupo line, and by continuous scouting and patrols kept the Hau Haus from again breaking through and disturbing other parts of the country.

Rapata and Kepa, with the Ngatiporou and the Wanganui tribes, gladly took up the contract, which amounted to this: they were only to be remunerated for work done—*i.e.* they received no daily pay, but were paid in the lump for the number of Hau Haus they killed and captured.

Another expedition was started, composed solely of friendlies, under their magistrate, Mr E. Hamlyn, who, starting in from Wairoa, were to thoroughly punish the natives of Waikaremoana.

It would take me far too long to describe the services rendered by these native columns and the bitter hardships they underwent following up, capturing or exterminating the remnant of Te Kooti's followers, nor did we pass our time reclining on beds of roses, for although we had the shelter of our forts and a sufficiency of food, such as it was, yet we were never for a moment idle, as we had always to keep on the alert, and over and over again had to head off and drive back small gangs of flying Hau Haus.

In this way the remainder of the year 1870 and the commencement of 1871 passed, during the whole of which period Te Kooti was hunted like a wild beast through the fastnesses of the Uriwera, while we guarded the line, and many volumes might be written about the wonderful escapes the scoundrel had. I myself know of no parallel case in history, where a man so hunted ever successfully evaded pursuit, but he eventually did so. After losing nearly all his men, either by bullet or capture, he at last succeeded in breaking through our line and escaping into the King Country, where the Waikatos, although they refused to give him up, effectually prevented him from causing any more trouble, and there he lived peacefully for twenty years, and died in the odour of sanctity.

Kereopa, the bloodstained apostle of Te Ua, remained with Te Kooti till the last, but, not being so lucky, was captured and hung, remarking at the time that he had always known he would have an unfortunate end, as when he swallowed the Rev. Mr Volkner's eyes one of them stuck in his throat.

And now my yarn is finished, as I think I have told you sufficient to give you some sort of an idea of what the colonial irregular forces went through while flattening out the North Island of New Zealand so as to render it safe for white settlers to occupy and dwell therein.

I must, however, ask you to understand that I have only told you of the small portion of fighting that I took part in myself, for the war raged in many places at the same time, so that I am clearly not to blame for being unable to give you a full account of all the fighting, as it was impossible for me to be in half-a-dozen localities at once.

So trusting to your charity that you will be to the few merits of his book ever kind, and to its manifold faults a little blind, Dick Burke bids you so-long.

Kiora tatau.

ALSO FROM LEONAUR
AVAILABLE IN SOFTCOVER OR HARDCOVER WITH DUST JACKET

THE RELUCTANT REBEL *by William G. Stevenson*—A young Kentuckian's experiences in the Confederate Infantry & Cavalry during the American Civil War..

BOOTS AND SADDLES *by Elizabeth B. Custer*—The experiences of General Custer's Wife on the Western Plains.

FANNIE BEERS' CIVIL WAR *by Fannie A. Beers*—A Confederate Lady's Experiences of Nursing During the Campaigns & Battles of the American Civil War.

LADY SALE'S AFGHANISTAN *by Florentia Sale*—An Indomitable Victorian Lady's Account of the Retreat from Kabul During the First Afghan War.

THE TWO WARS OF MRS DUBERLY *by Frances Isabella Duberly*—An Intrepid Victorian Lady's Experience of the Crimea and Indian Mutiny.

THE REBELLIOUS DUCHESS *by Paul F. S. Dermoncourt*—The Adventures of the Duchess of Berri and Her Attempt to Overthrow French Monarchy.

LADIES OF WATERLOO *by Charlotte A. Eaton, Magdalene de Lancey & Juana Smith*—The Experiences of Three Women During the Campaign of 1815: Waterloo Days by Charlotte A. Eaton, A Week at Waterloo by Magdalene de Lancey & Juana's Story by Juana Smith.

TWO YEARS BEFORE THE MAST *by Richard Henry Dana. Jr.*—The account of one young man's experiences serving on board a sailing brig—the Penelope—bound for California, between the years 1834-36.

A SAILOR OF KING GEORGE *by Frederick Hoffman*—From Midshipman to Captain—Recollections of War at Sea in the Napoleonic Age 1793-1815.

LORDS OF THE SEA *by A. T. Mahan*—Great Captains of the Royal Navy During the Age of Sail.

COGGESHALL'S VOYAGES: VOLUME 1 *by George Coggeshall*—The Recollections of an American Schooner Captain.

COGGESHALL'S VOYAGES: VOLUME 2 *by George Coggeshall*—The Recollections of an American Schooner Captain.

TWILIGHT OF EMPIRE *by Sir Thomas Ussher & Sir George Cockburn*—Two accounts of Napoleon's Journeys in Exile to Elba and St. Helena: Narrative of Events by Sir Thomas Ussher & Napoleon's Last Voyage: Extract of a diary by Sir George Cockburn.

AVAILABLE ONLINE AT **www.leonaur.com**
AND FROM ALL GOOD BOOK STORES

ALSO FROM LEONAUR
AVAILABLE IN SOFTCOVER OR HARDCOVER WITH DUST JACKET

IRON TIMES WITH THE GUARDS *by An O. E. (G. P. A. Fildes)*—The Experiences of an Officer of the Coldstream Guards on the Western Front During the First World War.

THE GREAT WAR IN THE MIDDLE EAST: 1 *by W. T. Massey*—The Desert Campaigns & How Jerusalem Was Won---two classic accounts in one volume.

THE GREAT WAR IN THE MIDDLE EAST: 2 *by W. T. Massey*—Allenby's Final Triumph.

SMITH-DORRIEN *by Horace Smith-Dorrien*—Isandlwhana to the Great War.

1914 *by Sir John French*—The Early Campaigns of the Great War by the British Commander.

GRENADIER *by E. R. M. Fryer*—The Recollections of an Officer of the Grenadier Guards throughout the Great War on the Western Front.

BATTLE, CAPTURE & ESCAPE *by George Pearson*—The Experiences of a Canadian Light Infantryman During the Great War.

DIGGERS AT WAR *by R. Hugh Knyvett & G. P. Cuttriss*—"Over There" With the Australians by R. Hugh Knyvett and Over the Top With the Third Australian Division by G. P. Cuttriss. Accounts of Australians During the Great War in the Middle East, at Gallipoli and on the Western Front.

HEAVY FIGHTING BEFORE US *by George Brenton Laurie*—The Letters of an Officer of the Royal Irish Rifles on the Western Front During the Great War.

THE CAMELIERS *by Oliver Hogue*—A Classic Account of the Australians of the Imperial Camel Corps During the First World War in the Middle East.

RED DUST *by Donald Black*—A Classic Account of Australian Light Horsemen in Palestine During the First World War.

THE LEAN, BROWN MEN *by Angus Buchanan*—Experiences in East Africa During the Great War with the 25th Royal Fusiliers—the Legion of Frontiersmen.

THE NIGERIAN REGIMENT IN EAST AFRICA *by W. D. Downes*—On Campaign During the Great War 1916-1918.

THE 'DIE-HARDS' IN SIBERIA *by John Ward*—With the Middlesex Regiment Against the Bolsheviks 1918-19.

AVAILABLE ONLINE AT www.leonaur.com
AND FROM ALL GOOD BOOK STORES

ALSO FROM LEONAUR
AVAILABLE IN SOFTCOVER OR HARDCOVER WITH DUST JACKET

THE ART OF WAR by Antoine Henri Jomini—Strategy & Tactics From the Age of Horse & Musket

THE MILITARY RELIGIOUS ORDERS OF THE MIDDLE AGES by F. C. Woodhouse—The Knights Templar, Hospitaller and Others.

THE BENGAL NATIVE ARMY by F. G. Cardew—An Invaluable Reference Resource.

THE 7TH (QUEEN'S OWN) HUSSARS: Volume 4—1688-1914 by C. R. B. Barrett—Uniforms, Equipment, Weapons, Traditions, the Services of Notable Officers and Men & the Appendices to All Volumes—Volume 4: 1688-1914.

THE SWORD OF THE CROWN by Eric W. Sheppard—A History of the British Army to 1914.

THE 7TH (QUEEN'S OWN) HUSSARS: Volume 3—1818-1914 by C. R. B. Barrett—On Campaign During the Canadian Rebellion, the Indian Mutiny, the Sudan, Matabeleland, Mashonaland and the Boer War Volume 3: 1818-1914.

THE CAMPAIGN OF WATERLOO by Antoine Henri Jomini—A Political & Military History from the French perspective.

THE AUXILIA OF THE ROMAN IMPERIAL ARMY by G. L. Cheeseman.

CAVALRY IN THE FRANCO-PRUSSIAN WAR by Jean Jacques Théophile Bonie & Otto August Johannes Kaehler—Actions of French Cavalry 1870 by Jean Jacques Théophile Bonie and Cavalry at Vionville & Mars-la-Tour by Otto August Johannes Kaehler.

NAPOLEON'S MEN AND METHODS by Alexander L. Kielland—The Rise and Fall of the Emperor and His Men Who Fought by His Side.

THE WOMAN IN BATTLE by Loreta Janeta Velazquez—Soldier, Spy and Secret Service Agent for the Confederancy During the American Civil War.

THE MILITARY SYSTEM OF THE ROMANS by Albert Harkness.

THE BATTLE OF ORISKANY 1777 by Ellis H. Roberts—The Conflict for the Mowhawk Valley During the American War of Independenc.

PERSONAL RECOLLECTIONS OF JOAN OF ARC by Mark Twain.

AVAILABLE ONLINE AT **www.leonaur.com**
AND FROM ALL GOOD BOOK STORES

www.ingramcontent.com/pod-product-compliance
Lightning Source LLC
Chambersburg PA
CBHW031623160426
43196CB00006B/258